CREATING CITIZENS

# CREATING CITIZENS
## HISTORY AND IDENTITY IN ALBERTA'S SCHOOLS, 1905–1980

AMY VON HEYKING

UNIVERSITY OF
CALGARY
PRESS

© 2006 Amy von Heyking

Published by the
University of Calgary Press
2500 University Drive NW
Calgary, Alberta, Canada T2N 1N4
www.uofcpress.com

No part of this publication may be reproduced, stored in a retrieval system or transmitted, in any form or by any means, without the prior written consent of the publisher or a licence from The Canadian Copyright Licensing Agency (Access Copyright). For an Access Copyright licence, visit www.accesscopyright.ca or call toll free to 1-800-893-5777.

LIBRARY AND ARCHIVES CANADA CATALOGUING IN PUBLICATION

Von Heyking, Amy J. (Amy Jeanette), 1965–
Creating citizens : history and identity in Alberta's schools, 1905–1980 / Amy von Heyking.

Includes bibliographical references and index.
ISBN 1-55238-144-7

1. Alberta – History – Study and teaching – History – 20th century.  2. Nationalism – Alberta – Study and teaching – History – 20th century.  3. Nationalism – Study and teaching – Alberta – History – 20th century.  I. Title.

FC3661.2.V65 2006    971.230071'07123    C2006-902845-1

We thank the Alberta Historical Resources Foundation for its support of this project. We acknowledge the financial support of the Government of Canada, through the Book Publishing Industry Development Program (BPIDP), and the Alberta Foundation for the Arts for our publishing activities. We acknowledge the support of the Canada Council for the Arts for our publishing program.

Cover design, Melina Cusano.
Internal design & typesetting, zijn digital.

**TABLE OF CONTENTS**

Acknowledgements vii
Introduction 1

1 Schooling for "Good Character," 1905 to 1920   7

2 An Education for "Group Living," 1920 to 1935   29

3 Nurturing Social Activists: The First Progressive Revision, 1935 to 1945   55

4 An Education for Utility: Defending Democracy in the Cold War Era, 1945 to 1970   91

5 Citizenship as Self-Actualization: Neoprogressivism in the 1970s   123

Conclusion   151

Appendix 1 / Curriculum Overview   155
Appendix 2 / Note on Sources   163
Notes   167
Bibliography   191
Index   203

# ACKNOWLEDGEMENTS

The research for this book took me to archives around the province and left me indebted to a number of helpful archivists. I would like to thank the Alberta Teachers' Association and the Calgary Roman Catholic Diocese for access to their collections. The superlative staff of the Edmonton Public School Board Archives provided invaluable assistance.

    Dr. D.C. Jones, Dr. B. Griffith, and Dr. R.D. Francis provided direction and support for the doctoral research that was the foundation for this book. I particularly appreciate the assistance of Walter Hildebrandt and the staff of the University of Calgary Press as they saw the project through publication. The two anonymous reviewers and John King and Windsor Viney of the University of Calgary Press improved my logic and my prose. Thank you very much.

    I would like to acknowledge the financial support of the Alberta Historical Resources Foundation and the Support for the Advancement of Scholarship Fund at the University of Alberta. I would also like to thank the Department of Elementary Education, University of Alberta for its support.

    Finally, I owe a particular debt to my parents for their love and support. I dedicate this book to my daughter Emily with my love.

# INTRODUCTION

> Nevertheless, the history courses I don't even remember must have had an impact because, as a result of what they taught me, I grew up with a whole set of misconceptions about the country which I have spent much of my adult life unlearning.[1]

In the 1990s, Canadian history, or at least the teaching of Canadian history, was a hot topic. University of Toronto historian Michael Bliss bemoaned the "sundering of Canadian history," and claimed that historians had become so specialized in their interests and so narrow in their focus, that they had essentially abdicated the responsibility of interpreting Canada's political past. The result, he claimed, was a Canadian population ignorant of their history, fragmented in their loyalties and apathetic about the country's future.[2] His assertions sparked a lively debate among Canadian historians about the nature of history and the purpose of history teaching. Citing the abysmal lack of historical knowledge among the Canadian public and the marginalization of history within school curriculum, Ontario educator Bob Davis wondered, "whatever happened to high school history?"[3] and historian Jack Granatstein demanded to know "who killed Canadian history?"[4]

The 1990s also saw public demands for more and better history instruction in schools. In the forums organized by the Spicer Task Force on National Unity, many "ordinary Canadians" claimed that inadequate history teaching was to blame for their lack of knowledge about the country's past and their lack of understanding of other Canadians. Keith Spicer, the chair of that Task Force, wrote quite incorrectly that, "astoundingly, and destructively, Canadian schools outside Quebec teach almost no Canadian history at all before late high school."[5] A national survey done by the Canadian Studies Association revealed that many Canadians supported more history instruction in schools.[6] The Dominion Institute, founded in 1997 largely in response to public interest in Canadian history, also polled Canadians and reported that many supported national standards of history teaching.[7]

By the late 1990s, several organizations had responded to the call for more information about Canada's past and more support for Canadian history teaching. The Dominion Institute created a number of educational projects and television documentaries to support the teaching of Canada's political, military and cultural history. Historica, a registered charity co-founded by Charles Bronfman, also aims to improve children's understanding and appreciation of Canadian history through resources such as the "Historica minutes," sixty-second movies dramatizing important events in Canada's past, and through school-based research programs such as the Historica Fairs.[8]

The popularity of Canadian history was also demonstrated by the public reception of the CBC's and Radio-Canada's *Canada: a People's History*: 2.9 million viewers watched the first episode of the television documentary series.[9] The series, out of which were also drawn books, video sets, a CD soundtrack and a multimedia website, tapped into Canadians' desire to know more about their past through well-researched and richly produced materials. Why the sudden interest in, and concern about, Canadian history?

Canadians' concern about history, and particularly about history teaching, was not a unique phenomenon. The 1990s also saw "history wars" fought in the United States over the development of national standards for history teaching,[10] and in Great Britain over the imposition of the national curriculum.[11] Russia and other former Soviet republics struggled with curriculum reforms in history that were the result of the fall of the communist regime and the end of its official version of history. History teaching in Germany was redrawn in order to cope with the challenges of reunification. A change in political regime also necessitated curriculum reform in South Africa. Japan continued to struggle with the legacy of World War II and faced accusations that its government and schools misrepresent that legacy to its young people. Even France, on the occasion of the bicentennial, found itself in the midst of a debate over the nature of its bloody revolution and the representations of that revolution in school texts.[12] In each of these cases, fierce debates about national history, and particularly about the way that history should be communicated to young people, reflected debates about national identity and values. They represented struggles of competing visions for the future, not simply interpretations of the past. As the American historians at the centre of the wars over national standards for history teaching in the United States discovered, "History is unceasingly controversial because it provides so much of the substance for the way a society defines itself and considers what it wants to be."[13]

Jack Granatstein explained his concern about the lack of history teaching in Canadian schools by stating, "If we have no past, then surely it must follow that we have no future."[14] More specifically, he criticized history teaching that emphasized the injustices in Canada's past, arguing that such negative messages about our history would only feed the apathy and despair that seem to dominate Canada's political culture, particularly in the wake of the failure of the Charlottetown Accord. Spicer too lamented the divisive nature of Canadian history teaching saying, "sadly, it shapes us mainly by its absence as a unifying force."[15] In seeing in history the need for a message of hope for the future, Granatstein and Spicer illustrate the argument made by historians and theorists of nationalism that nations are, in Benedict Anderson's phrase, "imagined communities."[16]

Anthony D. Smith acknowledges that individuals may negotiate many different identities based on different categories: gender, geographic region, socioeconomic class, ethnic origin, and religion, to name some. National identity, however, he sees as a particularly important kind of collective identity. It is multidimensional, drawing on many elements such as a common geographical location and a legal and political structure, but ultimately binding people together with common memories or myths.[17] As Canadian historian Brian Osborne asserts, in nation-states, "attention is directed to the nurturing of a sense of a common history and heritage that is shared by people who have never seen or heard of one another."[18]

In Canada, we have a long history of dialogue and debate about our national identity, largely because we have always recognized at least two Canadian "nations": French and English. This has made creating and sustaining common memories, a metanarrative acceptable to both linguistic communities, exceptionally challenging if not impossible. English-Canadian writers, historians and political commentators have been particularly challenged in their attempts to define a unique Canadian identity.[19] Most political commentators and philosophers tell us that we do not know who we are. There is no consensus about what it means to be Canadian; we have no sense of national purpose; we are, in fact, torn and divided by our conflicting definitions of ourselves as Canadian citizens and members of various linguistic, regional and ethnic groups.[20] Some commentators see this as a failure of Canadian nationhood; others see it as a healthy and defining characteristic of Canadian identity.[21]

The role of schools in creating and sustaining a sense of Canadian identity has also been debated since at least 1890, and generally schools have been criticized for their failure in this regard. Indeed, the failure to create a coherent sense of Canadian nationhood acceptable to French and English was often seen as the specific failure of history teaching in schools. Historian Ken Osborne identifies five eras over the course of one hundred years in which history teaching and the textbooks used in schools were attacked for their inability to excite and unite young Canadians.[22] Whether it was the Dominion Education Association sponsoring the creation of a common history textbook in the 1890s, or A.B. Hodgetts's 1968 national survey of history teaching across the country, critics of history teaching in the schools always stressed that a more peaceful and constructive future for the country would only come from a better understanding of its past. The argument essentially was that without a metanarrative, a mutually agreed-upon version of Canada's story, Canadians would remain divided and vulnerable. So if schools have not managed to communicate a coherent sense of nationhood, what have they taught?

In 1970, a special study commissioned by the Royal Commission on Bilingualism and Biculturalism concluded that history textbooks used in English- and French-Canadian schools essentially told different stories about the country's past and served to further distance the two linguistic (and cultural) communities from each other.[23] More recent studies have stressed the ethnocentrism of history textbooks. Studies done across Canada since the 1970s reveal the extent to which texts portrayed aboriginal people in negative terms. Other minority groups, defined by their ethnic origin, class or political leanings, were also portrayed in stereotypical terms or ignored.[24] Women's contributions to Canada were also trivialized according to historians who have analyzed school texts used in elementary and secondary classrooms across the country.[25] The images of other countries and cultures reflected in school curricula and texts are also now being studied and analyzed.[26] The often negative portrayal of minority groups, other nations and so on, reminds us of British historian Ian Grosvenor's contention that, "National identity is always contingent and relational and depends for its unity, coherence and security on the construction of boundaries which mark the difference between Self and Other."[27] Nations seem to need to construct their images and memories in contrast to "others" against whom the nation comes together.

An examination of history teaching in Alberta reveals that schools transmitted powerful messages to children about identity, their identity as Canadians and as westerners. The understanding of Canadian and regional identity that schools taught was selective, celebrating particular events, people and values and downplaying or vilifying others. These messages, embodied in curriculum and in teaching resources, were essential to creating and sustaining particular visions of the country and the region. The curriculum and teaching resources are an artifact of public thought, an expression of Albertans' understanding of themselves, their community and their aspirations. But as Michael Apple and Linda K. Christian-Smith remind us, school curriculum and textbooks are not embodiments of public thought in the sense that they represent some kind of public consensus about identity or citizenship. They are "conceived, designed, and authored by real people with real interests."[28] They are the reflection of dominant values of privileged groups who author them: teachers and university professors, educational bureaucrats. In this sense, curriculum, textbooks and other teaching resources are expressions of "official" ideologies regarding identity, community and citizenship. Apple and Christian-Smith stress, "Texts are really messages to and about the future.... They help set the canons of truthfulness and, as such, also help re-create a major reference point for what knowledge, culture, belief, and morality really are."[29] The ideas embodied in curriculum and texts reflect specific values, and by presenting the story of the past in certain ways, they are intended to prepare students for their future roles and responsibilities in society. Examining how this school content changed over time reveals that children in Alberta were inculcated with evolving understandings of who they ought to be.

This book examines how Albertans have interpreted themselves and their world through history and social studies curricula and texts from 1905 to 1980. These courses, more than others, addressed issues of identity by creating the country's and region's past and by preparing students for meaningful future citizenship. Tracing their evolution over the course of seventy-five years provides the opportunity to analyze the images of the nation, the region, and of "others" taught to generations of Alberta school children. It recognizes that teachers were not simply conduits for these messages, nor were children passive recipients. Official messages embodied in school content may have been imposed on teachers and students, but they could also challenge or undermine them.

This study, therefore, attempts to illustrate the curriculum building and implementation process in addition to outlining the content of that curriculum. It illustrates the impact of socio-economic and political pressures on schools and school content. It examines the people responsible for curriculum revisions, their beliefs about children and the nature and purpose of schooling with regard to the creation of a national identity. It recognizes the complex process by which official curriculum is created. It explores the extent to which the vision of the curriculum builders was reflected in, or refuted by, public discourses about history, identity and citizenship. It illuminates the challenges associated with curriculum implementation and the extent to which classroom teachers supported, negotiated or undermined official visions of schooling, identity and citizenship.

Why is a study of Alberta school curriculum significant? First, Alberta has a unique political culture in that conservative governments have fostered very progressive educational revisions. Whether it was William Aberhart's Social

Credit government's implementation of progressive education reforms in the 1930s, or Peter Lougheed's Conservative government's approval of a social studies program grounded in the relativistic "values clarification" approach, examining Alberta's experience with school curriculum provides interesting insights into curriculum policy development and implementation, and the relationship between the political and bureaucratic masters of provincial education systems with regard to school content. Second, some historians have suggested that Canadian schools failed to foster a Canadian identity because provinces have jurisdiction over education.[30] In other words, provincial ministries were local or regional in their vision and perhaps were able to undermine national initiatives and downplay the importance of creating a national spirit. Given Alberta's strong history of regional grievance and regional identity, it provides an interesting case study of the extent to which provincial ministries supported or undermined messages about national identity. Finally, developments in Alberta reflected developments in other parts of Canada, the United States, and Great Britain. A local study like this one, of Alberta schools and school curriculum, can lead to insights of general significance applicable to other jurisdictions. The history of our schools and what they taught has much to tell us about the complex process of shaping identity, of helping children find out what it means to belong.

# 1

## SCHOOLING FOR "GOOD CHARACTER," 1905 TO 1920

The North West Territories experienced a boom after 1896. Farmland and an effective immigration campaign attracted many settlers to what would soon become the province of Alberta. Between 1901 and 1911 Alberta's population increased from 73,000 to 374,000.[1] The tremendous population growth and settlement activity created important challenges for a fledgling school system.

The province of Alberta was officially established on 1 September 1905. Alberta's first premier and minister of education, the Hon. A.C. Rutherford, inherited a legislative framework for public schooling organized in the School Ordinance of 1901. The 1901 Ordinance created a Department of Education to set curriculum, choose texts and employ school inspectors. Local school trustees were elected and allowed to collect a school tax that would supplement the grants per teacher and per pupil paid by the provincial government. In 1905 there were 562 schools, 1,210 teachers and 34,000 pupils in Alberta. By 1920 there were 135,750 students in Alberta schools.

There are some sources that indicate what Albertans expected of these schools. Newspaper accounts of school construction and infrequent editorials on educational policy give glimpses into public discussion about education. The newspapers generally covered the remarks of regional boosters who saw effective schooling as an intrinsic part of the drive for economic progress. For example, in the *Edmonton Bulletin* on 28 January 1909, a school trustee from Innisfail explained the connection between education and economic development to delegates from the Alberta School Trustees' Association:

8 CREATING CITIZENS

If the fertility of our land is to be maintained at its natural high standard or improved, while at the same time made to contribute to personal and national wealth, if our mines are to be developed, if our forest wealth is to be exploited ... if our educational institutions are maintained and perfected and our commercial advantages pushed to their limit, then we must see to it that our children receive the proper equipment, because the children of the present are to be the farmers, artizans [sic], engineers, scientists, teachers and law makers of the future. Great natural resources and consequent great industrial and commercial advantages will never make a great nation. The most valuable asset of any country is an educated citizenship.

Editorial writers argued that this progress could best be realized by providing Alberta students with a practical education, one that would prepare them for their role and work in this new society. On 13 July 1906 an editorial in the *Lethbridge News* criticized the traditional academic focus for high school education. He stressed that school work "should be carried on with a view to directly preparing the pupils for their life in the world, rather than to preparing them for a university course or for some other further course of study." On 23 December 1909 the editorialist in the *Lethbridge Daily Herald* insisted that schools must educate for culture and utility, and that in recent years the former had been overemphasized at the expense of the latter. The editorial congratulated the federal government for heeding the calls for more practical education and appointing a royal commission to investigate the possibility of providing better technical education throughout the Dominion.

The Royal Commission on Industrial Training and Technical Education was chaired by J.W. Robertson, a former federal Commissioner of Agriculture and principal of Macdonald College of McGill University. The Commission toured the country and visited technical schools in the United States and Europe. It received 1650 submissions, and in the assessment of historian George Tomkins, it "stimulated a nation-wide debate over issues that became central to the formulation of Canadian curriculum policy over the next generation."[2] The Report of the Commission was a statement of principles of the "New Education," the child-centred and vocationally oriented education reform movement of the late nineteenth century. It recommended that schools across the country offer courses in manual training, school gardening, nature study and domestic science.[3]

The Report summarized the state of technical education in Alberta before World War I. Included in its survey was agricultural education, a chronic concern for Alberta educators. Nature study was included in the course of study for the junior grades, and agriculture was offered for optional study at the secondary school level. Chief Inspector of Schools, Dr. John T. Ross, reported to the Commission that there was little interest in nature study in rural schools, where it was usually restricted to the creation of a school garden.[4] In city schools, industrial education was limited to manual training for boys and domestic science for girls. There was no prescribed course in manual training and the Department of Education provided no funding for such courses; city school boards responded to public demand by creating these courses and offering them on their own initiative. In 1914, manual training and domestic science were only available to students in Calgary, Edmonton, Lethbridge and Medicine Hat.[5] Despite the recommendations of the Committee, few schools were ever able to offer the range of vocational courses the Commission suggested.

While some Albertans saw the need for technical education that would give students vocational skills to build the province's economy, schooling in this period was largely academic. It was intended to have "elevating" as well as practical results. According to some accounts, settlers in the province desired a school curriculum that would acquaint their children with the best of the English tradition, rather than a program that would be local and practical in its focus. Paul Voisey, in his history of the community of Vulcan in southern Alberta, asserts: "the settlers did not want sweeping changes; for them the schools still remained an important link to a heritage that needed to be preserved on the frontier and passed on to new generations."[6]

**PRESERVING THE CULTURAL HERITAGE**

The original course of study for Alberta was inherited from Ontario in 1902. The only adaptations made for the young territory were an increase in the amount of English required of students and some flexibility in the choice of courses required for a high school diploma.[7] Until 1911, the school system was divided into Standards: Standards I to V were elementary years, Standards VI to VIII were secondary schooling. Pupils at the secondary level represented from two to four per cent of the total enrollment. The proportion remained the same through 1912 and 1913, when the grade system was introduced with Grades I to VIII representing elementary education and Grades IX to XII the secondary level.

The curriculum in elementary schools was set by the Department of Education. While the early years were dominated by instruction in reading, writing and arithmetic, more subjects were added as the students prepared for the high school entrance examinations that would determine their future educational course. In order to continue to the secondary level, students in Standard V (later Grade VIII) wrote departmental examinations in literature, composition, grammar, spelling, geography, arithmetic, geometry, British and Canadian history, drawing, and nature study.

At the secondary level, students wrote departmental examinations every year. In order to receive a high school diploma, students had to pass Standard VIII (later Grade XII) examinations in Literature, English Language and Rhetoric, Essays, Constitutional and Industrial History, Physics, Chemistry, Algebra, Geometry, Trigonometry, and two languages other than English. Options included Latin, French and German.

The first serious attempt to write a made-in-Alberta course of study came in 1910. Dr. Henry M. Tory, president of the University of Alberta, was appointed to chair a committee to rewrite the curriculum. Also appointed were four school inspectors, the superintendents of the major urban school systems, twelve teachers and a professor from the University of Alberta. The actual writing of the curriculum, however, was done in subcommittees chaired by subject specialists from the university and staffed by others selected by Dr. Tory or heads of committees. Fred McNally, later Deputy Minister of Education, was working as a school inspector when he was asked to serve on the English subcommittee by its chairman, Dr. E.K. Broadus. McNally had taken graduate courses in English with Dr. Broadus in 1909 and 1910; he acknowledged that the English course was written by Dr. Broadus.[8]

The new course of study introduced in 1912 reflected the influence of University of Alberta faculty. Reading, which had been taught separately, was incorporated into the literature course; new textbooks were introduced in arithmetic, geometry and Latin; Greek was added to the course of study. The revision, rather than recognizing the need of most Alberta students for practical, technical or vocational education, clearly articulated the connection between high schools and the University of Alberta.

It also clarified the purpose of history teaching. The Report of the Revision Committee specifically directed elementary school teachers to introduce children to history through stories about historical heroes, biblical passages, fables and tales of ancient times. The committee reminded teachers that the aim of instruction should not be to memorize facts, but "to leave in the minds of the pupils general impressions of the results of right and wrong actions, to arouse an intelligent interest in people, places and events, and to develop a genuine taste for the subject." More formal history teaching began in Grade V. In the higher grades, students were expected to study the causes and effects of historical events. The purpose of this study was clearly defined: "The state should ultimately emerge as the highest of human institutions and loyalty to the state as the first virtue in the citizen." In case there was any doubt as to what was meant by loyalty to the state, by Grade VIII students were expected to appreciate "the greatness of the British Empire of to-day and our privileges as Citizens of that Empire." History was the most important subject in citizenship training; it was through the study of history that students would identify themselves as Canadians and as members of the British Empire.[9]

In addition to writing the programs of study, the academic elite in universities had an impact on education through the textbooks they prepared for use in schools. History instruction, for example, usually consisted of reading from the authorized textbooks that were written by university professors or acknowledged subject-area experts. Philip Myers, author of the high school text *General History*, was a professor of history and political economy at the University of Cincinnati. R.B. Mowat, author of the British history text used in Grade X, was a Fellow of Corpus Christi College, University of Oxford. The British history text used in Grades VII and VIII for almost twenty years was written by an English university professor but adapted for use in Canadian schools by University of Toronto historian George M. Wrong. J.G. Bourinot's *How Canada is Governed* was used in Alberta schools from the 1890s to 1924; Bourinot was chief clerk in the House of Commons and was recognized as a leading expert on Canadian government and history. In this period, scholars with expertise in specific subject areas were recognized as educational experts and in the best position to present material for use in public schools.

### HOW TEACHERS TAUGHT

It must be acknowledged, however, that it cannot be assumed that Alberta teachers delivered the program as defined by the curriculum documents; nor can it be assumed that students learned the "official" curriculum. Reminiscences and local histories detail some of the considerable barriers that faced teachers in delivering the required programs and that faced students in learning anything in substandard schools. After outlining the challenges faced by residents of the Vulcan community in building and maintaining their schools, in recruiting and paying competent teachers, and in providing adequate teaching supplies, Paul Voisey concludes:

Frontier schools hardly represented a perfect replication of an imported cultural institution when untrained and inexperienced teachers knew little of the heritage they supposedly implanted, or if they ignored some important aspects of it, or if they slept instead of presenting it, or if they spent most of their time maintaining order, or staying warm, or dividing their attention among children of many different ages and levels, or if the recipients often missed school for a variety of valid reasons, or if a few books and materials aided the process, or if lack of funds, teachers, or students forced temporary school closures, or if the messages conveyed held little meaning for children of the prairie frontier.[10]

Reports of the period indicate that, in the hands of under-educated and overburdened young teachers, the school curriculum was often poorly taught. According to the school inspectors who observed Alberta teachers, when it was actually done, history instruction was particularly boring. It was characterized by the memorization of dates and names, reliance on the textbook, lack of knowledge on the part of the teacher, and few attempts to connect the events of the past with current events in the news. In 1907, Inspector Ross wrote that while teachers were generally teaching the required historical material, "many of our instructors neglect to discuss current events of interest with the pupils. Therefore many pupils are capable of discussing conditions in England at the time of Alfred, who know nothing of what is happening in the world to-day."[11] In 1915, Inspector Boyce reported that "History still remains the most abused subject in the course of studies. The old method of giving notes and loading the pupils' memories with bald facts is still with us. In few instances is it made an interesting lesson and the matter treated as a real and vital subject."[12]

Students' recollections tell the same story. M.I. McKenzie, who attended a one-room school near Innisfail, remembered learning through "drill and still more drill," and while literature often provided an exciting escape, "History consisted of kings, queens, dry-as-dust dates of battles, and terms of acts and treaties to be remembered till the exams were over."[13] Historian George Stanley recalled that instruction at his Calgary high school consisted of copying the notes the teacher wrote on the blackboard and then repeating them verbatim on the examination.[14]

But if teachers relied on textbooks and memorization, much of the blame rested with the provincial examiners who set essay questions that were clearly drawn from the required texts. The 1907 examination in General History in Standard VII (Grade XI) asked students to "Sketch briefly the Punic wars and indicate the effect of this struggle upon (a) the Carthaginians, (b) the Romans, (c) the progress of civilization." The answer could be found in Chapter Twenty-Nine of Myers' *General History*. In 1908 students were asked to "Sketch the struggle between Plebeians and Patricians" as outlined in Chapter Twenty-Seven of the same text. In 1911, students in Standard VIII had to "Explain Ricardo's Theory of Rent" and "Distinguish extensive and intensive farming, subsistence and capitalistic farming." The answers were found in Chapter Eight of Cunningham's *Outlines of English Industrial History*.[15]

Many educators defended the emphasis on the memorization of historical facts. The author of one teaching methods text used in Normal Schools stressed that "So much is said to-day about the uselessness of teaching facts that it is well to remind teachers that there can be no lessons drawn from history without a knowledge of the facts upon which these are based ... for beginners history must necessarily be largely a study of facts."[16] Educators stressed that history developed imagination and taught critical judgment but it must first be grounded in the memory. Others argued that a familiarity with historical facts was simply essential for anyone who claimed to be educated. There was, in this period, a sense that education could be a path to success and a symbol of success for the self-made man. The signs of respectability for such men included manners, appearance, correct language and schooling. Educators assumed that a familiarity with the "leading facts" of Canada's and the world's history were as much a characteristic of this kind of respectability and cultivation as a knowledge of the poems of Tennyson and the plays of Shakespeare. As a teaching methods text explained, children need to know the basic facts of history because "public speakers frequently cite historic incidents to substantiate an argument or illustrate a point; newspapers and periodicals are constantly using historical facts, and unless the reader is acquainted with history he does not understand these allusions."[17] Historical literacy, familiarity with the basic facts of history, was important for the citizen of "good character."

**THE CURRICULUM OF "GOOD CHARACTER"**

The belief that Alberta should be shaped by citizens of "good character" was embedded in the school curriculum and textbooks of this period. The curriculum and texts transmitted a powerful image of Canada to Alberta students and told them very explicitly what their responsibilities were in this young, prairie society. They portrayed Canadian society as harmonious and orderly. They embodied a Whiggish belief in material and spiritual progress. They emphasized Canada's role within the British Empire. These themes came together in the attempt by schools to create virtuous students who would serve their community.

Teachers in this period knew that classrooms had to be orderly. Their Normal School texts told them that teachers should cultivate students' intellectual and moral discipline. This discipline could only be transmitted by appropriate management that "should have for its aim the maintenance of order and diligent application to work, the development of right habits, and the formation of character."[18] Clear illustrations of the well-managed classroom were often included for clarification:

School children in Standard, 1917–18. Glenbow Archives, NA-3969-24.

Proper signals for movements are useful in securing prompt obedience. A single stroke of the bell may be used to call attention; a slight downward movement of the hand may be given as a signal to take seats; a slight upward movement may be used as a signal to rise. The numbers one, two, etc., may be used for taking books and slate, or placing them in the desk. Signal words should be spoken in a low decided tone, with falling inflection. A second signal should not be given, until the movement required by the first has been executed.[19]

Educational leaders also reminded teachers of the importance of order and good discipline. The 1912 Curriculum Revision Committee said that "All school work should convince the child of the advantage of order and government.... Class organization brings the community sense and the administration of the school develops regard for authority."[20] In 1909, James McCaig, the Superintendent of Edmonton Public Schools, reported that the "educational services of the city are fundamental to the whole question of intelligence, social efficiency, public order and a right standard of life and conduct."[21] There is every indication that teachers took their responsibility for inculcating order and self-discipline seriously.

Miss D. Garrison, who taught at Edison school, saw that order was maintained during meal times: "the pupils had to eat decently and leave the desks neat and clean, and also stay at the 'table' for a set time – no slopping around the room or throwing food."[22] Maisie Clark, who taught in several one-room schools, strove to apply the advice she was given by a Normal School instructor: "We may not be able to keep the dirt out, but we could improve the appearance of the room if everything was kept tidy. It would be good training for the pupils in neatness and order."[23]

Classroom order was often kept through strict discipline. George Stanley remembered his Grade II teacher covering his mouth with adhesive tape to stop his whistling. While he said discipline problems were rare in high school, he did recall one male high school teacher pulling a disrespectful student from his desk and shaking him until his teeth rattled.[24] Inez Hosie, who attended school near Rimbey, said a teacher who strapped the students "kept good discipline."[25] Hugh Teskey, who attended a small rural school in Claresholm, was terrified of his Grade III teacher, who "was obsessed by the idea that children are fundamentally bad, a condition that could be corrected only by liberal use of the rod."[26] Charles H. McKenzie, whose first teaching position was in a one-room school near High River, recalled receiving a very poor teaching report from Inspector Russell because he failed to exercise adequate leadership in his classroom. The following year, he bullied his students and beat them for minor infractions; his teaching reports were much more positive.[27] But whether life in all Alberta classrooms was so harsh or not, the curriculum and textbooks stressed the importance of harmony and order.

The *Alexandra Readers* were the required texts for reading instruction in elementary schools. These early readers featured stories that embody a romantic view of nature. Children are described playing in the snow, collecting flowers, walking in the woods and learning about life on a farm. Nature is depicted as kind, beautiful and a powerful moral force. Life is bucolic; all live in harmony with nature. Illustrations show cherubic children cuddling kittens.[28]

The stories in the readers depicted characters that are rewarded for their obedience to authority. For example, in "The Sentinel's Pouch," Frederick the Great of Prussia promotes a private who insists on obeying orders despite being tempted to disobedience by the disguised monarch.[29] Other characters in the selections learn to curb their ambitions and appreciate their humble homes. The restless boy in "The Quest," "traveled here and there, / But never content was he, / Though he saw in lands most fair / The costliest homes there be."[30] He, like the boy in "The Golden Window" and the "Country Mouse," changed his perspective and was happy with his lot in life after discovering that his adventures only brought disillusionment.[31] Along with the poet John Howard Payne, they concluded that "No more from that cottage again will I roam / Be it ever so humble, there's no place like home."[32]

While the moral of some selections might have been to exercise prudence, they could easily have been interpreted to mean that children should simply give up unseemly ambitions and be content with a humble place in society. The young boy in Oliver Goldsmith's "Moses Goes to the Fair" is deceived by a con artist at the market. When he returns home and his treasures are revealed as worthless, his father concludes, "Our family had now made several vain attempts to be fine. 'You see, my children,' said I, 'how little is to be got by attempts to impose upon the world. Those that are poor and will associate with none but the rich are hated by those they avoid, and despised by those they follow.'"[33] The *Primer* included "The Mouse's Troubles" in which a mother mouse scares her hungry child with tales of fierce cats so that the young mouse concludes, "I want the cheese, but I am afraid of the cat. I think I shall stay at home to-day."[34]

The readers contained powerful messages about order and self-discipline. Children were told to appreciate rules and the appropriateness of the social order. Alberta school children heard the moral of "The Three Bears" often: "Silverlocks never forgot the fright that the sight of the three bears had given her, and ever afterwards she was very careful to keep away from places where she had no right to go, and not to meddle with things that did not belong to her."[35]

History curriculum and textbooks also emphasized harmony and order. They downplayed divisions of class, ethnic origin and religion. Christianity was characterized as a social force that united the classes and races of Canada and of Great Britain. For example, Symes and Wrong in their *English History*, used in Grades VII and VIII for almost twenty years, emphasized the cultivating and unifying impulses Christianity brought to England at the time of its conversion:

Among the English the new faith wrought many and great changes. They became less brutal. Gradually slavery died out, and personal goodness came to be admired no less than the personal valour so glorified by the fierce English.... Music, architecture, and poetry, all were used in the service of the new religion, and each played its part in the improvement of the English race. Something, too, to break down the barriers between the different kingdoms the new faith did.[36]

History texts treated those who rebelled against the natural order harshly. Americans, for example, were condemned for their disloyalty to the British Crown. Textbook authors argued that self-governance for the American colonies would have come without violence had the colonists been more reasonable in their approach to disputes about taxation. They exposed the "lawless" nature of America through vivid descriptions of the trials suffered by the United Empire Loyalists. One author, whose textbook won a dominion competition and was used across the country, accused the rebellious colonists of "an utter absence of generosity to their vanquished opponents."[37] The rebellious colonists were vilified as "farmers and mechanics"[38] in contrast to the Loyalists who were celebrated as "the best material out of which to build a nation."[39]

Textbook authors either dismissed the supporters of the 1837 Upper Canadian rebellion as a fringe element or claimed they had been duped by the unstable William Lyon Mackenzie: "Only the extreme members of the party were misled by the impulsive Scotsman, who allowed his admiration for a republican form of government to overcome his loyalty to his country."[40] The rebels of 1870 and 1885 were also dismissed as treasonous. Buckley and Robertson in the *High School History of England and Canada*, stressed the fact that Louis Riel had captured men loyal to Canada, including "Thomas Scott, a brave, outspoken, loyal subject. For some reason or other Riel had taken a strong personal dislike to Scott, and, after giving the form of a trial, had him sentenced to be shot. The sentence was carried out under circumstances of great brutality."[41] Historians described the 1885 Rebellion in detail and after colourful descriptions of battles and the courage of the government forces, concluded that "it only remained to punish the rebel leaders who had defied the authority of the Canadian government. Riel was tried at Regina, and, though ably defended, was found guilty of treason."[42]

Educators in this period stressed that order and harmony were necessary in order to ensure political and material progress. History textbooks are particularly good examples of the extent to which those who dominated educational decision-making and those who created teaching materials believed in material and political progress. History, as taught in Alberta schools, was Whig history. The past was venerated because it was the story of progress, leading to the success of the present. Few textbooks stated this Whiggish view as clearly as William Swinton's *Outlines of the World's History*, used early in the twentieth century. He described his approach to the writing of history as answering the following questions: "What have been the great steps in human progress, – the discoveries, social and political changes, advances in thought and skills, that have carried forward civilization and the 'betterment of man's estate' (Bacon); and what is the series of events that has brought the world up to its present standard of enlightenment and knowledge?"[43]

D.M. Duncan's *Story of the Canadian People* featured several chapters called simply "Progress," in which he discussed improvements in education, transportation and industry. Significantly, passages detailing material progress only appear in those chapters covering Canada under British rule. Buckley and Robertson argued that the history of Canada since 1814 "has been the history of growth in wealth, in population, and in enterprises for opening up the country to settlement, and for utilizing her natural resources."[44] Symes and Wrong demonstrated their belief in progress by concluding their textbook with chapters celebrating a number of nineteenth-century accomplishments: "The Great War" (the Napoleonic Wars); the "Great Inventions" (the Industrial Revolution); and, the "Great Reforms" (an outline of reform measures passed by the British Parliament from 1832 to 1837).

Political progress, particularly the movement toward democracy, was the common theme for world history textbooks used in Alberta. Myers celebrated the great moments in history, like the Battle of Marathon, in his *General History*: "The battle decided that no longer the despotism of the East, with its repression of all individual action, but the freedom of the West, with all its incentives to personal effort, should mark the future centuries of history. The tradition of the fight forms the prelude to the story of human freedom and progress."[45]

Canadian historians also took up the story of freedom, but their central theme was the growth of self-government. Duncan's story was one "of French failure through the folly of absolutism, monopoly and feudalism; of British success through the wisdom of self-government, freedom, and equality."[46]

Herbert Butterfield argued in *The Whig Interpretation of History* that Whig historians divided the people of the past into "the friends and enemies of progress" and so stood in judgment of men and ages.[47] The history taught in Alberta schools certainly displayed this tendency. Not simply individuals, but even races were judged according to their level of "civilized" accomplishment. Myers provided a racial hierarchy in the introduction to his world history in which he stated that the Black races "since time immemorial ... have been 'hewers of wood and drawers of water' for their more favoured brethren."[48] He described the Teutonic element of European civilization as the most important because "they had personal worth. It was because of this, because of their free independent spirit, of their unbounded capacity for growth, for culture, for accomplishment, that the future time became theirs."[49]

The Standard VII General History examination in 1907 asked pupils to "account for the unprogressive character of Chinese civilization." Those with good memories would have repeated Myers' explanation: "The Chinese in strictly obeying the injunction to walk in the old ways, to conform to the customs of the ancient, have failed to mark out any new footpaths for themselves; hence one cause of the unprogressive character of Chinese civilization."[50]

Predictably, native groups in Canada were harshly judged by Whiggish standards of progress. W.H.P. Clement said:

To the early Europeans the Indian was not an attractive figure. They describe him as of unclean habits and without morals. Master of woodcraft, he was seen at his best when hunting. Upon the war-path he was cruel, tomahawking, scalping and torturing with fiendish ingenuity. A stoic fortitude when himself tortured was about his only heroic quality.[51]

Edith Marsh, in a history of western Canada used in elementary schools, explained the need for external controls on the immoral behaviour of natives:

Now, Indians who would come and shake hands in the friendliest way with the lonely settler in his shack were just as likely, when drunk, to murder him and burn his little house to the ground. To save the Indian from ruin, and protect the white man in that country, laws were made prohibiting the sale of liquor to the Indians.[52]

Duncan, in his *Story of the Canadian People*, provided gruesome accounts of the persecution Jesuit missionaries endured at the hands of natives. The death of Brebeuf was described this way: "Fire, hot irons, boiling water, all failed to make the hero flinch. 'His death,' we are told, 'was the astonishment of his murderers.' In a throng they pressed forward to drink his blood, in the hope of winning bravery, while one chief tore out and devoured his heart."[53] His stories were accompanied by detailed engravings.

In these Canadian histories, the enemies of progress included the French colonial administration. Clement said of Jean Talon that "His rule in New France was a fatherly despotism, well meaning indeed, but most destructive of all self-reliance on the part of the colonists."[54] Duncan identified the corruption of colonial officials as one of the key reasons for the British victory. The Conquest came as a relief to the people of New France, according to these historians. Duncan insisted that French-Canadians "won by the fairness and leniency of British rule, gradually became reconciled to the change which had taken place."[55] Clement celebrated the magnanimity and foresight of the British in passing the Quebec Act: "By taking this course Great Britain, as we shall see, gained the hearty support of the most intelligent and influential of the French-Canadians in her struggle with the older American colonies, then on the point of revolt."[56]

On the other hand, authors celebrated the friends of progress. The years of the Roman Empire and the period of enlightened despots provided plenty of opportunities for hyperbolic description and celebration. Myers referred to Julius Caesar as "the greatest man their [the Romans'] race had yet produced or was destined ever to produce."⁵⁷ Peter the Great had "almost superhuman strength and energy," and was "a man of miracles."⁵⁸ Frederick the Great was "one of the few kings of whom it can be said that they were kings by right of genius as well as by right of birth."⁵⁹

There was also no shortage of heroes in Canadian history. Authors recounted the exploits of famous explorers, martyred missionaries, glorious warriors and gifted statesmen. Alberta school children were introduced to these heroes in the *Alexandra Readers*. The *Third Book* included the story of Pierre de la Vérendrye who gained neither fame nor fortune through his travels but persevered in his exploration of the Canadian West:

> His men had often mutinied and deserted him. Winter had overtaken him when supplies were low, and in these times of famine he and his men had lived on roots and bark, coarse parchment, and often on the flesh of the sleigh dogs. His eldest son, Jean, had been cruelly murdered by the Indians, while he was journeying to one of the eastern forts for supplies. Still the brave explorer's courage did not fail, and he pressed on hoping to find some sign, or hear some word that would tell him his quest had not been in vain.⁶⁰

The story of Laura Secord was also included in the reader. She too was described in heroic terms, stoically enduring pain and injury in order to complete her appointed task.⁶¹

The *Fourth Book* introduced children to Madeleine de Verchères, explorers Leif Ericsson, Alexander Henry and Alexander Mackenzie, and to the struggles of the Red River settlers. Isaac Brock and Jacques Cartier were celebrated in poetry, the latter by Thomas D'Arcy McGee. In McGee's poem, the people of St. Malo anxiously await Cartier's return from the New World. When he returns, amidst much rejoicing, he regales them with tales of the wild land he has discovered and the blessings he brought to it:

> He told them of the Algonquin braves – the hunters of the wild,
> Of how the Indian mother in the forest rocks her child,
> Of how, poor souls! they fancy, in every living thing
> A spirit good or evil, that claims their worshipping;
> Of how they brought their sick and maimed for him to breathe upon,
> And of the wonders wrought for them through the Gospel of St. John.⁶²

History texts for older students also celebrated heroes of progress. Duncan offered a typical assessment of Champlain: "A romantic spirit of adventure, coupled with a fervent zeal for the saving of souls, made light of treacherous rapids, the lurking dangers of pathless forests, and the haunting terrors of Iroquois vengeance."⁶³

The most glowing tributes, however, were saved for politicians who worked toward self-government in Canada. Lengthy descriptions of the Fathers of Confederation were included in every textbook. Even John A. Macdonald, whose personal faults were occasionally acknowledged, was portrayed as a loveable – if slightly flawed – visionary.

But if the textbook authors celebrated the politicians who sought self-government, they also made it abundantly clear that Canada should be thankful for, indeed should be defined by, its relationship with the British Empire.⁶⁴ They stressed that it was in this historic connection that Canadians would find the key to unity and prosperity in the future. The entire classroom culture of Alberta schools in this period supported this assertion.

The extent to which the Canadian viewpoint was in fact a British imperial viewpoint was demonstrated powerfully through pictures and symbols. The *Alexandra Readers* had pictures of the Queen or the Prince of Wales inside the front cover and the Union Jack was clearly displayed in the first pages. Maps of the world – with the British Empire in pink – were included in textbooks and in the schoolroom. On 28 January 1909 a school trustee described his district school to the *Edmonton Bulletin*:

On the end, facing the door, is a picture of the King and Queen, with neat little Union Jacks and Canadian Flags, surmounting each to teach loyalty by association.... On one side are life-sized pictures of Shakespeare and Milton to inspire admiration and appreciation of our literary inheritance.... We also have good pictures of Lord and Lady Aberdeen, for whom our district was named, as we are mostly Scotch. These pictures are large in size and all nicely framed.

The symbols of the Empire became even more important during World War I. In 1915 the Edmonton Public School Board ordered large (18" x 36") Union Jacks for city classrooms as a visual reminder of the struggle.⁶⁵ Many holidays or special events with imperial connections were celebrated in schools. Special exercises and the flying of the flag marked days such as Trafalgar Day and Empire Day.

The songs and stories central to the elementary school curriculum were largely British in origin. George Stanley remembered singing songs such as "Scots Wha' hae Wi' Wallace Bled," and "Men of Harlech," the words to which were included in the *Alexandra Readers*.⁶⁶ The content of the readers was almost exclusively drawn from the best of British literature: Dickens, Scott, Tennyson, Wordsworth, Bunyan, Eliot, Goldsmith, Browning and

Ruskin, to name a few. Stories about the Knights of the Round Table, the Battle of Blenheim and selections from "Tom Brown's Schooldays" ensured that Alberta children would be familiar with English culture. Even the nature stories in the early readers had an overwhelmingly British tone. One can only speculate what prairie children imagined as they read about primroses, bluebells, foxglove, gentian and violets, about burbling brooks and days at the seashore with nursie. The British ethos of the readers was unmistakable and reinforced even by Canadian poets such as Frederick George Scott whose poem, "The British Empire" was typical of the selections in the *Fourth Book*:

> Not by the Power of Commerce, Art or Pen,
> Shall our great Empire stand, nor has it stood,
> But by the noble deeds of noble men –
> Heroic lives and heroes' outpoured blood.[67]

High school literature classes consisted entirely of British content. The made-in-Alberta curriculum created by Dr. Broadus of the University of Alberta required that high school students memorize the poetry of Scott, Shakespeare, Wordsworth, Tennyson, Coleridge, Gray, Shelley and Milton, to name a few. Prose selections studied included works from Eliot, Macaulay, Goldsmith and Burke.

Civics and history instruction stressed that Canada's identity was defined by its relationship with Britain. As R.S. Jenkins, author of the text *Canadian Civics*, said, "The word 'colony' we do not like, and we usually speak of ourselves as a 'nation.' Some object to the name 'nation,' because it ordinarily means an 'independent nation' or 'sovereign state,' and we do not claim to be that, but desire to be part of the Empire."[68]

Departmental examinations ensured that students could identify the benefits of British-style parliamentary democracy. In 1908, the Standard VIII history examination included the following questions:

"The principal characteristics of the English constitution are inapplicable in countries where the materials for monarchy or an aristocracy do not exist." Explain this and point out the strong features of a monarchy.

"The merit of the British constitution consists in the close union and fusion of the legislative and executive authorities." Explain and compare with Presidential Government in this respect.

Though civics education for elementary school children consisted mostly of stories about important individuals, the stories were usually about British figures or Canadians of British background. The course of study recommended that teachers include instruction about King Arthur, Alfred, Canute, William I, Queen Elizabeth, Oliver Cromwell, Lord Nelson and Queen Victoria, as well as General Wolfe, Sir Guy Carleton, Alexander Mackenzie and Sir John A. Macdonald. Formal history instruction, which was required from grades five through twelve, always included Canadian and British history. The interpretation of that history presented in textbooks is illuminating.

For example, students learned that the agents of the British Crown and of the Hudson Bay Company treated Indians compassionately. Edith Marsh, in her elementary school text, *Where the Buffalo Roamed*, said that "the Indians looked up to the 'White Chief' for the same reason that they did to the flag and the Company's traders. It was because the great Company always dealt fairly with them. The traders did not take advantage of their ignorance of the value of goods and were always ready to help them. No Indian was ever turned away empty-handed and hungry."[69]

D.M. Duncan stressed the virtues of Britain when he explained her success in building the colonies in British North America: "Where sons of France had failed, sons of Britain were to succeed, under the more favourable conditions of toleration, freedom, and equality."[70] Even when he acknowledged the harshness of some British policies, he implied that they were carried out with sympathy for the victims. In describing the deportation of the Acadians, he said, "the unfortunate Acadians were placed on board, care being taken to keep families together, and even members of the same village."[71] W.H. Clement also acknowledged the weaknesses of some officials, but always ascribed the highest motives to them. For example, he criticized the Family Compact's treatment of critics and its use of patronage, but he concluded that "while we must strongly condemn the system, we must not forget that even among the officials there were many able and upright men, to whom we owe much for the material progress of the country."[72] Indeed he argued that their misuse of power was the direct result of their fear of separation from Britain, an understandable concern.

In their study of world history, students were clearly intended to learn that the motives of the British Empire, in extending its territories or in increasing its wealth, were pure. While other Europeans were motivated by greed or glory in founding an overseas empire, the British operated under principles of strict necessity. The *Highroads of History* series reviewed the nineteenth-century war against Napoleon and concluded:

So Britain emerged victorious from her hundred years' struggle with France. The fight had been for foreign empire and the command of the sea, and both of these were now won. As we have seen, it was on our part a fight for existence. Britain needed an overseas empire and a safe passage for trading-ships if she was to become anything more than a small European state. France needed neither of these things, for she is so placed and endowed by nature that she is quite capable of supporting a large population by her own natural resources.[73]

The content of history textbooks and readers provided students with a common language, a common mythology, about the history of Britain and Canada. Every textbook included the famous and inspiring words of important historical figures. Queen Elizabeth was quoted as saying, "I know I have the body of a weak and feeble woman, but I have the heart and stomach of a king, and a king of England too."[74] King George's comment about General Wolfe was proudly recounted: "Mad is he? Then I hope he will bite some of my other generals."[75] The final words of Sir Humphrey Gilbert could have been repeated by generations of Alberta school children: "Courage my lads! Heaven is as near by sea as by land."[76] William H. Swift, later deputy minister of education in Alberta, recalled his participation in the local cadet corps during World War I. As a young boy, he opened a recruitment meeting in Tofield by signalling Admiral Nelson's famous words, "England expects every man will do his duty."[77] The students of this period were encouraged to think of these great men and women as human beings who once lived, breathed and ruled. They were people who lived lives of epic proportion. They were intended to be examples of virtue and strength to pupils who could take pride in their accomplishments. Children learned they should live up to the models they provided. Textbook author Edith Marsh told children, "If they would be worthy successors to such men as the early explorers, they must put the welfare of their country before their own interests. Only so long as her people are loyal to the good old Union Jack, and true to the highest aims of life, will the Canadian West be a great and glorious part of the Empire that girdles the globe."[78]

Of course this pride was ethnocentric: students who were unable to trace their ethnic or racial ancestry to British roots were left with few doubts about the inadequacy of their heritage. The *Primer* in the Alexandra series included descriptions of an Indian Boy, a Japanese Girl and a Little Arab. The selection "The Little Turk" conveys the tone of these selections:

I am a little Turkish boy. I go to school every day. I sit on the floor with my legs crossed. We all study aloud at our school. I wear a red fez at home, at school, and when I go for a walk. My sisters do not go to school. They cannot read nor write. They do just what their brothers tell them. Many sisters are afraid of their brothers. My sisters are not afraid of me. I like to play with them.[79]

In history lessons, students were often asked to judge the characters of races of people with the expectation that the virtues of Anglo-Saxons would be stressed. The 1911 Standard VII history examination directed students to "Point out the excellences and defects of the Greek character. Contrast with the national character of the Hebrews, Romans and Anglo-Saxons." While groups farthest removed from the British generally came in for the harshest treatment, even other Europeans were occasionally unable to measure up. For example, Symes and Wrong described King George I as "an ugly little man, coarse in his tastes, slow-witted and quite ignorant of English. In habits and ideas he was entirely German."[80]

Students learned that historically, groups who invaded the British Isles had the good sense to become Britons: "The Normans could not overcome Robin Hood, nor could they overcome the English people. They beat them and robbed them, and put many of them to death; but the English people would not give in. As the years went by the Normans became English, and were proud to call themselves Englishmen."[81] Authors expressed the hope that contemporary difficulties would be solved in a similar fashion. After outlining the unfortunate series of events of the Boer War, the authors of the *Highroads of History* concluded, "[L]et us hope that as the years go by Britons and Boers will become the best of friends. It will be a happy day when the Boers are glad to call themselves Britons and are proud of the British flag."[82]

Educators associated British background with a specific set of personal virtues they sought to inculcate in children. They were transmitting what they understood as an education for "good character." Good character was defined by personal virtue and right conduct. An interesting description of these virtues was included in the Edmonton Public School Board's Bylaws and Rules of Order:

All teachers shall use their best endeavours to impress on the minds of pupils regard for justice and truth; to indicate a respect for the property of others; to induce respect for seniors and superiors, as well as regard for the weak, the young, and the very old; to encourage kindness to animals and to develop feelings of humanity, patriotism, and universal benevolence; to stimulate industry and frugality and plain living; and to generally assist pupils in acquiring the virtues and habits that adorn the good citizen.[83]

Educators believed that historical and fictional stories containing strong moral messages were powerful examples of virtue for students. Normal school texts of the period defended this teaching approach. *Public School Methods* explained that "Through the study of history the pupil lives in imagination with the good and great of the past. He learns by what qualities they succeeded, how they extolled virtue and condemned vice, and that because of their heroic struggles for truth and liberty we enjoy the privileges under which we live. Consciously or unconsciously, he is influenced by the lives of these men, and thereby his character is strengthened."[84] J.J. Tilley stressed, "History abounds in examples of courage, patriotism, devotion to duty, nobility of character, in short of all the higher qualities which ennoble mankind. When these are properly considered, with the many painful contrasts found on the pages of history, the mind is led to form judgments thereon, which will have a reflex influence on the character of the person forming them."[85]

And so readers featured stories about historical characters along with Bible stories about the Three Wise Men, the Good Samaritan, and Christ's resurrection. Grimms' fairytales, Aesop's fables, and the stories of Hans Christian Andersen and Jean de la Fontaine all embodied explicit moral lessons. Through these stories and others, children were encouraged to be persistent in trying to achieve, obedient to their elders, truthful, thoughtful, kind, gentle with animals, and generous to others.[86]

Children were reminded of the virtues of self-reliance and initiative by role models such as Dick Whittington, the poor boy who traveled to London to seek his fortune and became Lord Mayor. Not only did Whittington find his reward in wealth, he remembered his humble origins and was always kind and generous to the poor. Robert Clive was celebrated as a man who overcame youthful idleness and found redemption in his efforts to bring India into the Empire. In "The Page and King," Frederick the Great anonymously rewards his page with a large amount of money when he discovers a letter that "contained the thanks of a mother to her son for sending her so much of his wages to support her, and also her prayer that God would bless him and help him to do his duty well."[87]

In addition to the stories, the readers contained "gems of wisdom," brief aphorisms that reminded students of the importance of a virtuous life. The *Second Book* included gems such as:

> Who says "I will" to what is right,
> "I won't" to what is wrong,
> Although a tender little child,
> Is truly great and strong.
>
> Be good, sweet maid, and let who can be clever,
> Do lovely things, not dream them, all day long,

And so make Life and Death and that For Ever
One grand sweet song.

Life's field will yield as we make it,
A harvest of thorns or of flowers.

Try! Try! and try again;
The boys who keep on trying
Have made the world's best men.

Kind words are little sunbeams,
That sparkle as they fall.

The message that children should be kind to others was embedded in other texts as well. Jenkins' civics text suggested that the solution to cruelty in the world was as simple as exercising personal kindness toward others:

When we read the history of early times, we are overpowered at the amount of suffering that seems to have been caused needlessly. In the ordinary pursuit of business and pleasure horrible and unnatural things were done. Probably some time in the future a similar charge will be brought against our own age. It would be well, if every day every one of us would think of the cruel things that we have seen done or that we ourselves have done, and then try to discover how much of the suffering thus caused might have been prevented. There is hardly any doubt that, if such a course were consistently followed, we should soon have a bright and happy world.[88]

This education for good character was not intended to be specifically religious education. On 9 March 1909, James McCaig, Edmonton school superintendent, told the *Toronto Globe* that if a westerner "were to be told of the clerical ideal which was charged primarily with fitting men for heaven he would take no stock of it because its results were uncertain or unknown." On the other hand, when it came to defining the ultimate aim of education, he insisted that "the service ideal would be just the thing." In this he had the support of Alberta politicians such as Louise McKinney, who told the 1919 National Conference on Character Education that "The purpose of life is citizenship. What is citizenship? Citizenship is service to the world in which we live."[89] Alberta students learned that good citizens serve others.

The course of study clearly stated that "the study of civics should develop public spirit and inspire to useful public service through the example of public men whose work is brought within the understanding and appreciation of the pupil." The readers, more than anything else, stressed the duty to serve others. Stories celebrated military heroes who demonstrated courage in battle, did their duty and died a good and noble death. Poems praised the selflessness of men like St. Christopher: "The lesson of Saint Christopher, / Who spent his strength for others, / And saved his soul by working hard / To help and save his brothers!"[90]

Lessons in service were intended even for the youngest readers. The *Primer* included "The Tired Shoes," which said: "When grandma wanted flowers, Willie ran for them. When mamma wanted eggs Willie went to bring them. When papa wanted the paper Willie ran to get it. No wonder the shoes are tired."[91] The teacher's handbook for the series directed teachers to discuss with their students how they could have helping hands and helping feet at home.[92] Alberta school children were taught that they could build a better world by serving others.

Alberta schools in the period before World War I transmitted powerful messages about the nature of citizenship and the English-Canadian identity. The education for "good character" that marked this era emphasized the need for social order and harmony in order to ensure political and material progress. That the virtues the schools were cultivating were specifically associated with British gentlemanly conduct was assumed. School materials, particularly those used in history and civics, transmitted the message that individuals have the power to determine their own future and that through hard work and service to others, Alberta would become a prosperous society. But rapid modernization and the desire for social regeneration brought on by World War I suggested to educators that individuals were caught in complex forces of social and economic change. They began to doubt that educating children in virtue or good character was an adequate response to the task of social improvement. Instead, they argued that children should be prepared for citizenship in a modern society that would require specific skills of cooperation and a more complex understanding of the nature and responsibilities of citizenship.

# 2

## AN EDUCATION FOR "GROUP LIVING," 1920 TO 1935

From 1920 to 1935, Alberta underwent considerable economic hardship. The political and social landscape of the province was also transformed. Politicians and the Department of Education were pressured to offer more varied programs and courses with more vocational relevance for students. As a result, opportunities for secondary school education were expanded and a curriculum revision was undertaken. An emerging group of professional "educationalists" in the Department and in the Normal Schools tried to apply the principles of the New Education, as they understood them, in this revision. The language of the revision indicated a move toward a more "scientific" approach to schooling, but little changed in academic courses such as history and citizenship. Teachers continued to rely heavily on textbooks to guide their teaching and the texts were still written by the academic elite of the universities. That said, new ideas about the nature of good citizenship and the Canadian national identity were introduced through English, history, and citizenship courses.

The 1920s represented, in large measure, the attempt of the citizens of Alberta to deal with the economic, political and social repercussions of World War I. The economic climate in this period was unstable. The return of the veterans resulted in serious labour disputes, such as the strikes in the coal mines of the Drumheller valley in 1919 and 1925. The oil industry around Calgary grew in importance, but the mainstay of the province's economy continued to be agriculture, and farmers became the victims of the Great Depression, brought to an end only by the advent of World War II.

The economic hardships of these years resulted in new demands being placed on the public schools. The total number of students enrolled in the school system grew dramatically until the 1930s. The proportion of students registered at the secondary level steadily increased, largely because older students had fewer employment opportunities. From 1930 to 1935, registrations in Grades IX to XII increased from 21,280 to 30,253.[1] As enrollment increased, there were public calls for the expansion of secondary education in areas of the province where it had not been available. Groups such as the Women's Institutes encouraged the government to set up scholarships that would allow rural students to pursue secondary education. They argued only two per cent of rural students finished high school, and if this trend were allowed to continue, the need for more scientific farmers would never be met.[2]

The increased enrollment in secondary school programs was accompanied by a new emphasis on the relationship between education and business success. In the tough economic times of the interwar period, the uneducated and unskilled were particularly affected by unemployment. At the beginning of the 1922–23 school year, the *Calgary Herald* editorialist penned a special plea to students to remain in school and emphasized the material rewards of an education by arguing that businessmen "are demanding a higher standard of education both for boys and girls entering business life for two reasons: they know that the better-educated one is the better the service that can be rendered to the employer, and they know also that a good education more fully equips one for larger later earnings and makes one's life richer and fuller."[3]

Changing economic circumstances also seemed to increase demands for more vocationally oriented education in rural areas. Rural communities demanded courses they saw as more appropriate and more useful for children in rural areas than the traditional academic high school curriculum. In 1925, the Educational Committee of the United Farmers of Alberta told the premier that teachers in rural areas should stress home economics for girls and manual training for boys and curtail the time given over to Algebra and Latin because "we fail to see why rural students should injure their health or eyesight in acquiring mastery over material which there is about one chance in a dozen that they will use in after life."[4]

The changing political landscape of the province also had an impact on classrooms. In 1921, Albertans elected representatives to the legislature untested in the political arena and eager to experiment in governance in ways unheard of in British parliamentary democracy. The U.F.A. called for reforms that challenged the foundational principles of parliamentary democracy: direct legislation and an end to cabinet solidarity and secrecy. The election of the U.F.A. marked a shift in the power base of the province, from the north of the province to the central and southern parts of the province, and from the relatively powerful urban lobbies to the rural areas. For education, this meant that the deplorable conditions of rural schools came to public attention.

The 1920s were also a time of considerable social change. The women's movement had won its fight for suffrage. While prohibition was repealed, the organizations such as the W.C.T.U. and I.O.D.E. that had played such an important role in these debates continued their community activities. Men's business and philanthropic associations, such as Rotary, flourished. Clubs and community associations were active and provided adults and children in many Alberta communities with many opportunities for organized leisure activities.

Improvements in communication and transportation decreased the isolation of many rural communities in the province. People could drive on newly improved roads to take advantage of the amusements found in larger centres. More settled farming patterns afforded people more leisure time. New technology in the form of movies and the radio brought an increase in American-style pleasures. The changing youth culture of the province and its obvious fascination with these new opportunities for entertainment caused considerable concern among educators. In 1926, J.A. Smith, Inspector of High Schools, reported that "the attraction of the motor-car, motion pictures, and public places for social activities are removing the student from the disciplinary influences formerly exerted by the home."[5]

The behaviour of youth was a topic sure to generate interest in the Letters to the Editor column of every newspaper. One father's letter to the *Calgary Herald* expressing disapproval of the fashions of young girls, their manner of dancing, and the fact that they were frequenting men's bowling alleys caused two months of discussion on the editorial page. Girls defended their behaviour and their clothing; mothers argued that there were new moral dangers for boys, too, in the form of new billiards halls. The editor finally called a halt to the debate by putting the new freedom for girls into perspective: "notwithstanding the recent extreme styles of dress – fashions, by the way, not created by today's young girls – the young girls of today have as high an average of common sense, of the substantial qualities that will have to go later into home-making, as ever had the girls of any preceding generation."[6]

Parents in the 1920s found no shortage of advice on raising their children to cope with the new challenges. The *Herald* published a series of articles in 1922 entitled, "How Parents Fail." Popular magazines like *Maclean's* published articles in the "women's" section that reminded parents to discipline their children consistently and introduced them to "scientific" ideas about child rearing, such as the significance of I.Q. measurement.

Schools began to establish organizations and to offer programs that would partner with parents in helping children navigate the treacherous waters of adolescence. By 1922, there were seventeen parent–teacher organizations in Calgary alone. The national Home and School Association was founded in 1927. A survey of the programs of the early organizations in Calgary indicates that most parent–teacher associations were more interested in helping parents understand their responsibilities than in encouraging them to become involved in educational matters. For example, the parents of Crescent Heights high school students learned about general hygiene, dress for the high school girl, and "The Responsibility of Parents in the Moral Education of the Teen Age Boy and Girl."[7]

High schools broadened their academic focus and took on some responsibility for the appropriate social development of their students by introducing a wide array of extra-curricular activities. In 1924, Rachel Horner, valedictorian for the graduating class of South Calgary High School, outlined a typical time-table for students in her school: "Monday and Thursday, basketball practice; Tuesday, Literary Executive meeting; Wednesday, Glee Club."[8] Charles McKenzie taught in Red Deer in 1922–23. He recalled that his extra-curricular teaching duties included leading cadet training, coaching girls' basketball, and practicing hockey with his male students on Saturday mornings.[9] Educators saw these supervised activities as crucial to the proper socialization of Alberta's young people.

In the 1920s, Alberta's Department of Education also recognized the importance of revising the formal school curriculum to respond to the economic, political and social challenges facing the province. The department undertook an extensive survey of public opinion regarding elementary education in 1921. Questionnaires were sent to groups such as the U.F.A. and U.W.F.A. locals, women's institutes, the teachers' alliance, school boards, boards of trade and social clubs. The responses were summarized and sent to a curriculum revision committee composed of representatives from various groups around the province and chaired by the Supervisor of Schools, G. Fred McNally. The U.F.A. government, impressed with this wide representation, created a similar committee for the revision of the high school program. It is significant that while the revision committees consisted of representatives from many different public organizations (with the notable exception of the University of Alberta), the new curriculum was actually written by school inspectors, administrators and teachers chosen by Dr. McNally. These educationalists sought to legitimize their positions as educational "experts" through further education, professional association and through their curriculum-building activities.

## THE EDUCATIONALISTS MAKE THEIR MARK

Fred McNally was part of the first generation of educational policy-makers in Alberta to receive graduate training in the field of education. In January 1914, he was already serving as a school inspector when the Department of

Education offered to send him on salary to Teachers' College in New York in preparation for assuming the principalship of Camrose Normal School. While in New York, he took courses from the foremost thinkers in American education: E.P. Cubberley, G.D. Strayer, E.L. Thorndike and William H. Kilpatrick.[10] He was among the first of a long list of Alberta educators to receive graduate training at American universities. M.E. LaZerte, who later became the first Dean of Education at the University of Alberta, also served as a school inspector before World War 1. After serving in the war, he enrolled in graduate studies at the University of Chicago.[11] Other prominent educationalists involved in curriculum building included Dr. A.M. Scott, Superintendent of Calgary schools, and W.G. Carpenter, Superintendent of Edmonton schools.

In an effort to distinguish themselves from classroom teachers, these educationalists established discussion groups in Calgary and Edmonton in 1927: the Educational Progress Club in Calgary and the Education Society of Edmonton. These groups were clubs to which potential members were invited and admitted only with the approval of other members. At a time when the young Teachers' Alliance was concerned with salary issues and the question of job security, these clubs were set up to provide leaders in the educational field with an opportunity to discuss issues and engage in research, to assert their professionalism. By 1939, the membership rosters of these clubs included many administrators in the Department of Education and in school boards, and instructors at the Normal Schools, but very few classroom teachers.

The curriculum revision initiated in 1921 was the first serious attempt by these educationalists to model a curriculum on the principles of the "New Education." Australian scholar R.J.W. Selleck distinguishes six different schools of thought within the confused and often contradictory reforms identified by this label. Describing late nineteenth- and early twentieth-century British educational reforms, Selleck includes: those who wanted practical courses such as manual training included in a curriculum that would be relevant and useful for all children; social reformers who saw physical education and health reform measures within schools as key to the fight for social justice; naturalists who, following the ideas of Johann Pestalozzi and Friedrich Froebel, argued for teaching methods that would nurture the natural strengths of children and be suited to their interests and capacities; Herbartians, who sought to demonstrate the effectiveness of German educator Johann Herbart's coherent five-step instructional plan, which seemed to provide technical assistance to teachers seeking practical guidance; the scientific educationalists, who were united in their attempt to reform education on the basis of empirical, psychological studies but drew questionable conclusions from the often unsophisticated mental testing experiments of British researchers such as Francis Galton and Cyril Burt, and Americans such as G. Stanley Hall and E.L Thorndike; and finally, the moral educationalists, who saw moral education grounded not in religious or denominational schooling but in practical ethics as fundamental to the task of uniting the public in a commitment to community service, social improvement and nation building.[12]

All of these ideas were taken up by Canadian educators in the latter decades of the nineteenth and early decades of the twentieth centuries in the name of the New Education.[13] By the time Alberta educationalists undertook this first detailed and public re-examination of their curriculum, reforms such as manual training and domestic science, school gardens and agricultural education, public health initiatives within schools, child-centred kindergartens, and streaming students on the basis of IQ scores, had already been in place in other areas of Canada, in some cases for decades. Indeed, it could be argued that Alberta educationalists sought, in their curriculum revisions of the 1920s, to introduce reforms that were already twenty years out of date. For example, in the new Citizenship course for elementary schools, educationalists drew heavily on the ideas and publications of American Dr. Felix Adler, founder of the Ethical Culture movement, and on the work of the English Moral Instruction League, a group historian Selleck describes as in decline in Britain by 1908.[14]

Alberta educationalists did not display a particularly sophisticated understanding of any of the theories of the "New Education" in their curriculum reforms in the 1920s. From their reading and graduate education, they essentially understood that education should be approached more "scientifically." There was little consensus, however, about what that meant. For the Normal Schools, it meant that for the first time, teacher training would vary according to the age level the future teacher would be teaching. Courses in adolescent psychology and effective high school teaching methods were introduced. An attempt to categorize and teach Camrose Normal School students on the basis of their results on an intelligence test was mercifully short-lived, as was a directive to assign them "effort quotients" as well as traditional grades.[15]

The consequences of the "scientific" approach to curriculum for the school system included the introduction of six separate streams or high school diploma programs: Normal entrance, matriculation, agricultural, commercial, technical and general. Alberta educationalists at this point did not generally see the school as an agency of reform; they insisted that the school should equip students to meet modern demands of adult work life. Alberta educationalists reflected this understanding of the purpose of schooling when they explained in the new curriculum that the school "shall prepare the individual to do better those things which he is likely to have to do anyway."[16] Happily, this philosophical justification for differentiated vocational education complemented increasing parental demands for more practical education for their children.

With this revision, the Department of Education wrote programs of study and provided funding for subjects urban school boards had introduced several years earlier: manual training, domestic science, health, and physical training. Now these subjects would be available to all Alberta students, including those in rural areas. Changes were also made to the traditional academic subjects. The high school history program continued to include classical, medieval, British and Canadian history, but now downplayed political history in favour of social and industrial history. The new course of studies explicitly rejected the mental discipline theory of learning by stressing that history instruction should not emphasize the training of the memory, but rather should give students the opportunity to practice "scientific" skills such as searching for data, categorizing information and drawing conclusions.

The language of the advocates of moral education within the "New Education" movement was evident in the new elementary program. Formal history instruction was delayed until Grade VII. Instead, students took a course called Citizenship that would include, among other things, opportunities to practice the specific virtues of citizenship, defined as helpfulness, sympathy, loyalty, tolerance, justice, fair play, reverence, sacrifice.[17] While the old curriculum guides identified required passages in textbooks, the new curriculum for Citizenship included course objectives and suggested teaching activities such as class excursions and the telling of history stories that would allow students to meet those objectives. Teachers were told to emphasize direct experiential learning with their students rather than indirect learning through textbooks.

In Grades I and II, the objective of the Citizenship course was to develop group-consciousness. It was the responsibility of teachers "to provide suitable work life activities in classroom and school, as a medium through which the citizenship experience obtained by children naturally in family and play-group will take form and meaning in accordance with what is implied in living as an adult member of present-day organized communities, social and political." Specific direction was provided for teachers in the suggestion that lessons that reminded young children of the importance of caring for school supplies and readers could be broadened and applied to the larger community through community beautification projects. In Grades III and IV, at which point formal history talks were introduced, students were introduced to the responsibilities and restrictions on individual behaviour that were the natural consequence of living in social groups. The history talks for Grade IV students were intended to introduce them to the "romantic" life of the western Indian.

In Grades V and VI, students were "to cultivate experience in organization" by participating in "pupil-group" discussions, debates and competitions and organizing the schools' Junior Red Cross or Junior Civic League activities. History talks for Grade V students, which drew their content from the fur-trading era in western Canadian history, were intended to emphasize the sacrifices made by explorers, traders and missionaries in building trade relationships and communities in the new land. In Grade VI, students heard and read stories about life in medieval England. For students in Grades VII and VIII, teachers were directed to "use the children's experience in organization to reveal the nature and the value of institutions of political communities." Groups such as Indian warrior bands, modern families, classrooms and more formal community organizations such as rural districts and towns were to be studied as examples of the benefits of group organization. History lessons, formally scheduled in these grades, were drawn from centuries of British and Canadian history. Teachers were specifically directed to avoid the memorization of content. Rather, students were simply to appreciate the gradual evolution of social and industrial life and the material progress of Britain and Canada under British rule.[18]

Teachers reacted swiftly to the new program in Citizenship and History. Reports of local committees from Calgary and Edmonton to the Teachers' Alliance argued that the objectives of the citizenship course were too vague and the programs of study impossible to understand.[19] Despite the demand that the Department write the programs so that "reasonably intelligent" people (presumably people such as themselves) could understand them, the Department made no attempt to address the concerns of teachers and better specify the required content of citizenship courses. It is an ironic consequence of the attempt of educationalists to use more scientific jargon to "professionalize" teaching that it served instead to further separate the educational leadership from the teaching force.

### TEACHING WITH THE TEXT

As a result of this new approach to curriculum-writing, teachers were often unsure how to translate the course of studies into classroom lessons. The *A.T.A. Magazine* came to the aid of many teachers by providing "Teacher Helps" and articles on specific courses. Usually the articles consisted of notes that could be given directly to students. In 1924, Mrs. Jordan, a teacher from Medicine Hat, outlined her approach to the Citizenship courses in Grades VI, VII, and VIII. The article consisted entirely of a summary of early English and imperial history.[20] The "Teacher Helps" columns often consisted of questions teachers could assign their students for review or use on examinations. Teacher Earl Buxton remembered purchasing little manuals from the Institute of Applied Arts that summarized the history students in Grades V to VIII were supposed to learn. He said that while the course of study provided general themes, such as "The Canadian Pacific Railway," it did not provide specific information he could communicate to students.[21]

Many teachers apparently found these aids useful because school inspectors soon began to discourage their use. In 1931, Inspector Fife insisted that too many teachers depend on the "Teacher Helps" for the organization and presentation of history lessons and "the effect is deadening to the teacher's initiative and resourcefulness."[22] His colleague Inspector Liggett in Olds agreed, saying that the use of "pre-masticated material in the form of printed notes ... is a great pity, especially in history, a subject that offers so many opportunities for interesting and profitable class discussion."[23] In the 1934 *Annual Report*, Inspector Crispo noted that "history is penned into the scope provided by concentrated, synoptic pamphlets." He recognized that "the materials in use are not in themselves objectionable; but the cramped manner in which they are used by teachers who reduce the teaching of these subjects to a checking process, very similar to a correspondence course, is not real teaching."[24] The *Report* criticized teachers for the overemphasis on the teaching of facts in elementary Citizenship classes and reminded teachers that "the use of printed materials lowers the vitality of the teaching."[25]

The student scribblers that survive in archives demonstrate the dominance of the teaching through text approach.[26] They include short compositions on Sir Francis Drake, Admiral Peary or the Founding of Rome. Students answered questions that could have appeared on history examinations twenty years earlier: "Give a brief estimate of the character of Henry VIII." Some student exercise books include notes taken from the blackboard; others include outlines or themes provided by the teacher and the corresponding page numbers from the required texts. Teacher Earl Buxton recalled that as a high school student in Lougheed in the 1920s, his teacher left him with the text, Mowat's *History of England and Canada* and the direction to: "read and find out what you can about Walpole for next day." In the next class, Buxton would be directed to write down everything he remembered from his reading. In his assessment, "I think that kind of experience was good."[27] History lessons at Camrose Normal School in 1928–29 consisted entirely of copying blackboards full of notes on British history, the content of Grades VI and VII history, according to Buxton.[28] It is hardly surprising that text reading and note-taking also became Buxton's favoured teaching method in the 1930s.

The extent to which history instruction was equated with textbook reading is apparent from the remarks of educators. W.H. Swift insisted that as a teacher in the 1920s, "teaching consisted of using the textbook and following the outline in the Department of Education Manual so that everybody throughout the province was teaching the same thing."[29] This view of teaching did not change with the revision of the course of study in the 1920s. Inspectors' and teachers' assessments of the new courses were in fact opinions of the required textbooks. In 1924, Inspector Smith praised the new British history text for Grade X: "Its clear and full explanation of the essentials of British History makes it the most valuable text that is placed in the hands of our Grade X students. Its biographies are very inspirational and its handling of European politics appeals strongly to the average student."[30] In 1925, however, he blamed the high failure rate on the Grade IX history examinations on the fact that few students could read the required text, *A Short History of Early Peoples*.[31] Elementary school teachers complained from the introduction of the new program that they did not have suitable texts or reference material to turn to for their "story telling" lessons in civics and history.[32] They criticized the Canadian history text required for Grades VII and VIII, Grant's *History of Canada*, because it was organized thematically rather than chronologically and neglected essential factual content.[33] Inspectors who supported the new program seemed frustrated by the inability of teachers to move beyond a factual chronology of Canada's past. In 1925, Inspector Aylesworth lamented, "strange to say, too many teachers still teach by pages in the History, rather than by topics."[34]

The resolutions submitted to the Alberta Teachers' Alliance Annual General Meetings indicate the extent to which teachers felt bound by the required texts. The 1925 AGM passed a resolution calling for the removal of one hundred pages from the Grade X history text.[35] Clearly, teachers felt incapable of simply skipping the pages they didn't want to teach. At the 1927 AGM, a resolution was proposed which called for the Grade VII and VIII history courses to be modified in order to more closely follow the required texts. After some discussion, the resolution was reworded to call for a modification of the texts to better suit the requirements of the courses.[36]

It is clear, therefore, that teachers in the period 1920 to 1935 continued to teach history in the traditional way: by requiring that students read the textbooks. Revisions to the course of study and new textbooks were not sufficient to change what American historians David Tyack and Larry Cuban call "the grammar of schooling."[37] Evidence suggests that young teachers continued to teach the way they were taught, regardless of what policy-makers intended. Given the fact that teacher lectures and text readings were also the favoured teaching methods of Normal School instructors, teachers really were not provided with any helpful models to implement change. It was clear that if serious reforms were going to be implemented in Alberta classrooms, more specific direction and assistance was going to have to be provided to teachers.

Moreover, even though the new group of educationalists had written the curriculum documents, a glance over the authorized textbooks in history and citizenship demonstrates the extent to which those subjects continued to provide traditional messages about Canada's identity and the nature of citizenship. This is not surprising, since many of the textbooks were again written by the academic elite of the universities. Authors included W.L. Grant, principal of Upper Canada College; W. Stewart Wallace, librarian of the University of Toronto and first editor of the *Canadian Historical Review*; R.B. Mowat, a Fellow of Corpus Christi College, Oxford; Mack Eastman, a professor of history at the University of British Columbia; and A.L. Burt, a former professor of history at the University of Alberta. Some professional educationalists prepared texts for younger students. In 1925, for example, the Department of Education authorized a series of history readers for use in the elementary grades, written by Donalda Dickie, who was an instructor at all three Alberta Normal Schools. But the preponderance of academics suggests that while the curriculum revision signalled a shift in educational rhetoric, it did little to change the content of school knowledge and made only limited changes to the understanding of citizenship to which Alberta students were acculturated.

## THE TRADITION CONTINUES

Despite the rhetoric of the New Education and the attempt of educationalists to bring a "scientific" attitude to the curriculum, the traditional messages about good citizenship prevailed in readers and in the history and citizenship program. The good citizen, for example, should recognize the progress made in the human condition over centuries and celebrate the individuals who made that progress possible. Despite the experience of warfare and the economic problems of the 1920s, educationalists and textbook authors continued to imply that a study of history would reveal an inevitable improvement in the human condition. The 1922 course of studies in high school History stressed that all future citizens need an understanding of the progress of the past in order to ensure a healthy future: "The story of man, the unremitting labor, the exhaustless patience, the marvelous ingenuity, the searching thought, the growing spirit of co-operation and self-sacrifice, which have achieved the things of civilization and made them precious – this story is the birthright of every boy and girl."[38]

Authorized textbooks reflected this understanding of material, political and moral progress. W.L. Grant's *History of Canada* demonstrated the extent to which history was still identified with a chronicle of material progress when he described the years 1713 to 1750 as years of slow growth, so that during those years, "Canada had little history."[39] The history talks incorporated into Citizenship lessons in elementary schools were intended to celebrate the accomplishments of great men in history so that students would appreciate the ability of men to transform and improve society. The new *Canadian Readers* included stories about heroes such as Edith Cavell and Lord Kitchener, and about courageous explorers such as Sir Humphrey Gilbert and Jacques Cartier. The heroic men of the Mounted Police made their first appearance in school poetry in "The Riders of the Plains":

> The thunderstorm sweeps o'er our way,
>   But onward still we go
> We scale the rugged mountain range,
>   Descend the valley low;
> We face the dread Saskatchewan,
>   Brimmed high with heavy rains
> With all his might he cannot check
>   The Riders of the Plains
> Our mission is to plant the rule
>   Of Britain's freedom here,
> Restrain the lawless savage, and
>   Protect the pioneer;
> And 'tis a proud and daring trust
>   To hold these vast domains,
> With but three hundred mounted men,
>   The Riders of the Plains.[40]

Historians have often pointed to the influence of a considerable number of American settlers to explain Alberta's political radicalism, particularly the success of the U.F.A. But despite sympathy for American ideas of democracy, the prevailing ethos of the school curriculum of the 1920s and early 1930s remained largely British. The curriculum and the texts continued to emphasize British virtues and the importance of the British connection for Canadian nationhood. The good citizen exercised these virtues and appreciated this connection.

Calls for a uniquely Canadian perspective in the school curriculum emerged during World War I. School inspectors criticized a curriculum that introduced students to far-flung parts of the Empire but did little to acquaint them with their own country or region of the country. Inspector Torrie from High River reported, "Pupils are found who can glibly name the rivers of Asia flowing north or east or south, who cannot tell you whither the stream flowing by their own school leads."[41] In 1919 the Chief Inspector of Schools in Alberta, G.W. Gorman, insisted that the most glaring defect of the school system was its inability to produce "Canadianized scholars."[42] In 1920, Inspector Mackenzie expressed alarm at the reluctance with which many immigrants adopted a "Canadian" way of thinking and called on the schools to step up their efforts in teaching patriotism:

The instinctive aversion to naturalization evinced by a number of our cosmopolitan immigrants, the tardy acceptance of others who are prompted ultimately by purely business motives, the non-appeal of Canadianism to the rising generation who still cherish the traditions and sympathies of their parents, and the anticipated increased immigration of 1921 challenge the schools which are the fountainhead of all national ideals to recognize the need for an increased and immediate vigorous effort to inculcate a real and positive affection in these people for the land of their adoption.[43]

In this call for a heightened sense of Canadian patriotism in schools, Alberta educators were not alone. According to historian Neil Sutherland, "in 1921 persons 'having both parents alien born' formed 34 per cent of the total population of Canadian birth under ten years in Manitoba, 42 per cent in Saskatchewan an, and 41 in Alberta."[44] Evidence suggests that immigrants were interested in education for their children, and before World War 1 in Alberta, Ukrainians pressed for bilingual education.[45] But as the war got underway and in the years following, educational leaders in the western provinces advocated assimilationist policies and programs for schools.[46] The National Conference on Character Education in Relation to Canadian Citizenship, held in Winnipeg in 1919, was an excellent reflection of the "ideology of Anglo-conformity, assimilation, service, social stability, and hostility towards radical change" that informed Canadian educators' understanding of citizenship in this period.[47]

There was, however, also a new emphasis on the creation of a uniquely Canadian identity in this period.[48] This was reflected in an increase in Canadian content in elementary school readers and in history courses across the country. School readers were still dominated by selections from British authors, but the new *Canadian Readers* also featured Canadian authors such as L.M. Montgomery, Ralph Connor, Duncan Campbell Scott and Pauline Johnson. Heroic and inspiring tales from English history still figured prominently, but Canadian students now also read about the exploits of explorers, voyageurs and fur traders, and the valour of Victory Cross winners such as Alan McLeod. John McCrae's *In Flanders Fields* was included in all senior readers. Authorized history textbooks too featured sections about the growth of Canadian art and literature emphasizing the country's maturity and increasing cultural uniqueness.[49]

Publishers of this period provided teachers and students with important sources of information about the country. The Ryerson Press and J.M. Dent both produced series of Canadian history readers that were used extensively in Alberta and throughout Canada.[50] Dent also published a series of Canadian Geography Readers that were intended to introduce children to the landscape, resources and industries of every region of the country.[51] History textbook authors tried to bring the thrilling narrative of British history to their treatment of Canadian history. Edmonton school teacher M.H. Long's *Knights Errant of the Wilderness*, a book about the explorers who discovered and mapped Canada, is an excellent example of this.[52]

The most emphatic celebration of Canadian accomplishments came in descriptions of the Great War. Textbook authors described Canada's achievements during the war as the height of its development as a nation. They stressed that Canada joined the war at the outset partly out of a sense of loyalty to the mother country but also because of a sense of her own national interest. Lengthy descriptions were provided of the battles in which Canadian troops were involved: the Somme, Arras, Ypres, Vimy, Passchendaele and the Second Amiens. Textbook authors celebrated the accomplishments of Sir Arthur Currie. They emphasized that Canada signed the Treaty of Versailles in her own right, not simply as a colony of Great Britain. Indeed, they even acknowledged that Canadian and British delegates to the Paris Peace Conference occasionally disagreed about the best plan for peace.

But there was no doubt that the idea of Canadian citizenship and identity Alberta schools fostered still reflected considerable pride in the accomplishments of the British Empire and the English people. When pressed by critics who identified American inroads into Alberta schools, the U.F.A. government always defended the British character of Alberta schools. It supported the scholarships the I.O.D.E. provided for students with the highest scores on the departmental examinations in British history, Canadian history and English literature. The government also appreciated the efforts of the I.O.D.E. to provide Empire Day medals and book prizes for inspectorates with large numbers of foreign students and supply funds for the purchase of historical pictures for schoolrooms.[53]

The province's teachers supported the pro-British views of the government and of the I.O.D.E. In 1925, the A.T.A.'s Annual General Meeting passed a resolution that demonstrated its understanding of patriotism: "Whereas, in Alberta there has been a display of unpatriotic sentiment by a number of men not allowing their children to pay respect to the British Flag, or sing 'O Canada'; and whereas, this Association is pledged to inculcate loyalty in the British Empire; therefore be it resolved that we register our strong disapproval of these actions."[54]

The content of history courses continued to emphasize British history and reflect a pro-English sentiment. The curriculum revision of 1922 insisted, "Our laws and institutions are for the most part fundamentally British in their origin and genius and therefore the proper foundation to their study is a knowledge of the history of the Mother Land." The new course still required Alberta students to appreciate the strength of British parliamentary democracy and unique British virtues: "Students should be taught to take a just pride in their citizenship in the British Commonwealth ... it should be founded rather on the fact that, on the whole, the British people have stood throughout their long history for freedom and justice in the world and that they have made great and enduring contributions to its civilization."[55]

It is possible that the U.F.A. government was particularly sensitive to charges of imposing its "American" ideas on Alberta's children in schools. After all, schools were not generally seen as political institutions; the content of schooling was understood to be a matter of cultural improvement, not of political indoctrination. When *Maclean's* magazine exposed the extent to which American texts had "penetrated" the Canadian school system, it set off a national debate that had an impact on Alberta as well.

In its July 1, 1929 edition, *Maclean's* featured an article which argued that Canadian youth were being inundated with American popular culture and with American interpretations of recent history in their classrooms. It argued specifically that American texts, "are not suitable for use in Canadian schools if our children are to be educated from the Canadian and British viewpoint."[56] The article condemned two textbooks: West's *Modern Progress* and Myers' *General History* for their lack of recognition of the efforts of Canadian troops in the war. The article caused a flurry of responses and resulted in formal and informal inquiries in many provinces to examine the influence of American textbooks in schools.

The U.F.A. government was quick to point out that the textbooks featured in the article had not been authorized for use in Alberta since 1923. Nonetheless, the Edmonton Chamber of Commerce struck a special committee to examine the issue of the Americanization of textbooks in Alberta schools. In 1930, Premier Brownlee received the report of the Committee. The Committee discovered that all textbooks used in public, i.e., elementary, schools in Alberta were edited and published in Canada. They identified only three American textbooks used in high schools in the province. They admitted that none of the texts included material derogatory toward Canada, but advised that a special pamphlet should be prepared and distributed to schools covering Canada's contribution to the war effort in more detail.

While the Chamber Committee seemed to be assured that the U.F.A. government had not introduced an American bias into history classes, they were troubled by the information about pools and other cooperative institutions contained in the required text for the Agriculture course:

With respect to the other text books on the Alberta curriculum your Committee finds that in the text book on Agriculture, used in the high schools, certain statements have been made on the subject of co-operative marketing that in the opinion of the Committee criticizes too harshly the methods of the grain trade, and are of a class of statement that should not be made against any section of the business community unless founded on incontrovertible truth, after which it is then a matter of grave and doubtful propriety whether a school text book is the place to raise such an issue.[57]

The displeasure of the Chamber of Commerce demonstrates the difficulty the U.F.A. government faced in any attempt to introduce their new ideas about political or economic systems into schools. The U.F.A. locals annually sent resolutions to the Premier and the Department of Education requesting that more information about cooperation in the industrial system be included in the school curriculum. The government responded by including information about cooperatives and pools – particularly the Alberta Wheat Pool – in textbooks for courses in Citizenship, Agriculture and Economics. In the early 1930s, however, U.F.A. locals demanded that special courses on cooperation be introduced into schools and that high school teachers be given "a better understanding of the principles underlying our experiment in democratic government, with a view to gaining a more sympathetic attitude on the part of these teachers toward this effort."[58] The government assured the locals that some effort was being made to prepare suitable materials for students and teachers, but there is no indication that anything of this nature was ever distributed to schools in the province.

While specific information about cooperatives was not included in the new history and citizenship courses, they did emphasize the need for social harmony within Canada and cooperation among all people globally. After the experience of World War I and the political and economic challenges of the post-war period like the Winnipeg General Strike, even the most optimistic educationalists or textbook authors could not fail to recognize that harmony

A PLEASANT HOME SCENE

From McCaig's *Studies in Citizenship*

must be learned and fostered. There was considerable public pressure to use schools not to convince students of the existing harmony of society, but to give students the skills and the sentiment that would result in social stability at home and peace among nations. If the hallmark of the earlier curriculum had been harmony, in the period following World War I, it was cooperation.

Citizenship classes asserted that social cooperation must begin at home. The texts celebrated the harmony of the home and family and stressed domestic tranquility:

The happiest homes are those in which all the members of the family work together and have their interests in common. In the evening, they sit around the table together and tell of the strange or amusing things that have happened during the day. They brighten the remainder of the evening with songs, games, telling stories, or reading interesting books. They picnic together, they go to the country together, if they live in the town, or to the town together, if they live in the country. The entire family is united in close bonds of sympathy and affection.[59]

The elementary school Citizenship program specifically directed teachers to use these examples of domestic affection and cooperation as a basis for developing skills that students would then transfer to the larger community. For example, Grade III teachers were expected to use the analogy of game playing in school and home to clarify the nature of group cooperation in the work life of adults involved in house construction or farming.[60]

The history curriculum emphasized that the hard lesson learned through the conflict of World War I was that countries must cooperate in order to maintain world peace. The course of studies for high schools stated that after the "catastrophe of 1914," students need to learn about the history of all nations and education must "play its part in raising young Canadian citizens from the ideas of narrow nationalism, or even imperialism, to a higher plane of internationalism, where they will be swayed by no prejudice of race, creed, or tongue."[61] The League of Nations Society had particular success distributing its materials in Alberta schools and even convinced Fred McNally, Deputy Minister of Education, to require Grade XI history students to write an examination on a special pamphlet about the League prepared by University of Alberta professor A.L. Burt.[62]

The history curriculum, however, was not just concerned about international cooperation. Perhaps in response to national concerns about the division between English and French exposed by the war, the new curriculum required teachers to deal more kindly with the French and the French regime in Canada: "Our history should be so taught as to give English-speaking Canadians a clear and sympathetic understanding of French-Canadians and *vice versa*. On such a mutual understanding, and on the tolerance and cooperation which spring from it, depend the unity and prosperity of our common country."[63] Was this new emphasis on cooperation and tolerance evident in the content of the texts?

Despite requests from organizations that stories glorifying war be removed from texts, the new *Canadian Readers* included Tennyson poems such as "Charge of the Light Brigade" and "Rule Britannia," stories celebrating the courage of Lord Nelson, and the story of Alan McLeod, who won the Victoria Cross during World War I. There were no stories about French Canada.

W.L. Grant's text, used in Alberta schools from 1924 until 1938, did treat aboriginal groups and the French more sympathetically than texts from a previous generation. While earlier historians had denigrated aboriginal Canadians for their cowardice and savagery, Grant praised their love of freedom, which was after all, one of the defining characteristics of the modern age: "Freedom marked the life of the Indian from his earliest days. Children were rarely punished and never whipped. Women were held in higher honour than is usually the case with savages."[64] Grant even suggested that blame might be more equitably distributed for the 1885 rebellion. He insisted that though Riel was rash and vain, he was also sincerely religious. He credited him for voicing the legitimate grievances of the Métis. "But though our Canadian soldiers fought well, and though Riel deserved his fate, we must not forget that it was the deafness of the Government to the claims of the half-breeds, and not any real disloyalty to Canada on their part, which brought on all the bloodshed and expense,"[65] insisted Grant.

Grant was also unusually sympathetic toward the French. He praised them for their resiliency and persistence in the era of exploration and discovery. He emphasized the unique nature of the society of New France. While earlier historians had assumed that the despotic nature of the French regime was transplanted into New France, Grant stressed that there was unusual fellowship and cooperation between the habitants and seigneurs and that the feudal obligations in New France were not so onerous as they were in the Old World.

Authors like Grant and A.L. Burt maintained that the cooperation displayed by French and English Canadians over the years could serve as a lesson for the rest of the world. Canada's tolerance of dual nationalities seemed to model the supranationalism demanded by the League of Nations. The texts by Grant and Burt which traced the development of self-government in Canada, emphasized the role played by French Canadian politicians in the struggle for responsible government. They saw Canada's ability to balance its own interests and those of the whole British Commonwealth as an illustration of the limits on national autonomy that could be reasonably imposed upon governments.

The idea of citizenship embodied in the history and citizenship courses of the period after World War I stressed the importance of skills of cooperation. Indeed the constant references to cooperation and the community are striking in contrast to earlier programs that stressed individual virtue and character. In this period, the good citizen was expected to recognize the cooperative nature of society and the need for the individual to behave suitably, to conform. The Citizenship course recognized the challenge of developing the individual talents and abilities of students while at the same time preparing them for a social life that demanded common ideals and standards. It also, however, was clear as to which imperative should prevail in cases where they seemed to conflict: "At every moment of his active life the child faces situations in which society demands that certain traditions and conventions in the way of speech, action and bearing be respected.... Training is emphasized in the first three grades and specific practice demanded that approved reactions may become habitual." The purpose of schooling was to equip children for the expectations of social life, and these expectations should be respected because they are the product of historical experience: "While the conventions and standards of a civilized community may be very rigid in their requirements, they are nevertheless the product of years of experimentation in community living."⁶⁶ Simply put, the good citizen, in the period following World War I, played by the rules.

The emphasis on "getting along" and "playing by the rules" led naturally to the use of the metaphor of sportsmanlike behaviour in the descriptions of good citizenship. The principal of South Calgary High School, T.E.A. Stanley, told his students that "Life is a game, and we shall have taken a long step in advance when our citizens are true sportsmen. Give every man a chance and let the best man win."⁶⁷ There was considerable literature in this period that equated good citizenship with good sportsmanship and claimed that appropriate training in games and organized sport encouraged the skills and sentiments necessary for good citizenship. Appropriately, the 1922 curriculum revision modified the physical training program, which had consisted entirely of military drill. The new course for boys and girls consisted of formal gymnastics, marching, athletics and games, apparatus work and rhythmic work. It directed teachers to spend considerable time on organized games because these develop important physical, moral and social skills. The new program was intended "to develop certain moral and social qualities, or at least to provide situations which will provide a basis for such development, e.g. self control, self reliance, ability to cooperate."⁶⁸

Textbooks assigned in Normal Schools emphasized the importance of organized games and supervised play in the normal development of children, particularly in the development of social skills necessary for good citizenship. W.A. McIntyre explained that through play students "are learning to be attentive, patient and self-controlled, and more important still, they are learning to co-operate with their companions in a friendly manner."⁶⁹ Henry S. Curtis in the Normal School text, *Education Through Play*, described the playground as the most perfect democracy: "on the playground there is no rich or poor, high or low. You have 'to deliver the goods' if you stay on the baseball team, though your father is a millionaire. There is always an almost complete equality between those who play together."⁷⁰ The call for supervised, healthy play was taken up by Alberta's school inspectors. In 1920, Inspector Russell in Camrose was disappointed with the failure of local teachers to properly guide and supervise playground games: "It is very remarkable that so few teachers are alive to the great opportunities that are afforded them on the school grounds for the inculcation of a becoming school spirit and for the laying of the foundation for the fundamental principles of good citizenship. Why there should be this lack of inclination or this indifference towards this very vital part of the school work, I am unable to conceive."⁷¹

Some teachers understood the importance of physical games and sports in developing the habits of good citizenship in their students. They concurred with the idea that the lessons of the schoolyard and organized sport would be transferred to the greater lessons of doing one's duty for society. Teacher Herbert T. "Pete" Coutts, later the Dean of Education at the University of Alberta, was so involved with coaching sports that his teams at Claresholm High School were called the "Petes." He recalled in his memoirs that he recited the poem "The Torch of Life," by Sir Henry Newbolt to his classes at the beginning and end of every year in the 1930s:

> There's a breathless hush in the close tonight –
> Ten to make and a match to win –
> A bumping pitch and a blinding light,
> An hour to play and the last man in.
> And it's not for the sake of a ribboned coat,
> Nor the selfish hope of a season's fame,
> But his captain's hand on his shoulder smote:
> "Play up! Play up! And play the game!"
>
> The sand of the desert is sodden red, –
> Red with the wreck of a square that broke, –
> The Gatling jammed and the Colonel dead,
> And the regiment blind with dust and smoke.
> The river of death has brimmed his banks,
> And England's far, and Honor a name,
> But the voice of a schoolboy rallies the ranks:
> "Play up! Play up! And play the game!"
>
> This is the word that year by year
> While in her place the school is set,
> Every one of her sons must hear,
> And none that hears it dare forget.
> This they all with a joyful mind
> Bear through life like a torch in flame,
> And falling fling to the host behind:
> "Play up! Play up! And play the game!"[72]

Clearly some teachers continued to transmit the messages about personal virtue and sacrifice that they had imbibed in a previous generation.

Many teachers supported a concept of citizenship that had much in common with the understanding of Christian service so much a part of the social gospel. W.B. Poaps reminded colleagues that they cared for children's souls and stressed that "the school should be a society with interests common to all and it should promote, as no other agency can do, those altruistic virtues which are characteristic of a righteous people." He identified specifically virtues such as obedience, courtesy, forbearance and justice.[73] W.E. Hay, in a 1927 article, defined the unique qualities Alberta schools should foster: resourcefulness, initiative, conscientiousness, diligence, reliability, clean living, respectability, high thinking, and a spirit of tolerance.[74] A group of Grade II teachers from Calgary recommended to the curriculum revision committee that the best way to teach students good citizenship was for the teacher to be a good citizen: "courteous, sympathetic, honest, tolerant, careful in speech and manner and eternally vigilant."[75]

The committee in charge of the revision took this advice to heart. In its final report, it emphasized "the urgent need of vigorous stressing of principles of morality, citizenship and manners among the children of Alberta." Despite the committee's large and diverse membership, "all agreed that every effort should be made to strengthen the school as a great agent for the development of virtuous self-reliant citizenship with right habits and right ideals." The development of character was the ultimate purpose of schooling and the committee recommended "using the material of the courses in History and Literature for this purpose."[76]

Accordingly, textbooks used in literature, citizenship and history classrooms continued to emphasize the virtues associated with good character and effective citizenship. The *Canadian Readers* included the stories of the Good Samaritan, Florence Nightingale and Edith Cavell. Selections for very young readers included a story about a fishermen and his wife who paid the consequences of their greed, and the story of a young girl whose pet bird was eaten by a cat because she failed to obey her parents' request that she close a window.[77]

The virtues of good citizenship were also taught to very young children through stories included in *The Garden of Childhood*, a collection commissioned by Britain's Moral Instruction League and recommended for use in Alberta's elementary school citizenship classes. The stories were not specifically religious, nor were they drawn from scripture. Instead, they featured fairies or other magical figures teaching young children lessons in traditional virtues such as neatness, obedience, honesty and courage. The children in the stories correct themselves and resolve to exercise these virtues because they do not want to risk the disapproval or disappointment of parents or peers. For example, in "The Land Where There Are No Punishments," Geoffrey pays the price for refusing to wash properly. The Queen of the Land makes the lesson clear:

"I see you are cured of your wish to be dirty," said the Queen very kindly, "but before you go you must listen to what I have to say. When boys and girls do not like being clean they get into the bad habit of not washing themselves enough. Then they get very tired, and that makes them careless and thoughtless. They don't take the trouble to please mother and make her happy. Do you like to see mother unhappy?"[78]

The assigned citizenship textbook for Grades VII and VIII also illustrates the extent to which traditional notions of citizenship as good character prevailed. Author James McCaig stressed the responsibility of the family in providing the character training that was, in essence, citizenship education: "They [children] are trained in habits of self-control, truthfulness, honesty, consideration for others, and proper respect for the feeble and the weak ... All these qualities are the marks of the good citizen."[79]

The continuing importance of good character as a hallmark of good citizenship is also demonstrated by the continuing emphasis on the heroes and villains of history. Like the history courses before the war, school history in the 1920s and early 1930s was taught in order to demonstrate the superiority of certain values. In the lives of the great men and women of history were examples of virtues such as courage, loyalty, patience and justice. History demonstrated that the good would be rewarded and the wicked punished. Clearly, students were supposed to learn about the importance of living a life guided by a sense of right and wrong. They were supposed to be inspired to honour the legacy of those who came before and continue their struggle to improve society. McCaig reminded students that "It is our duty, then, to find out how we should act from day to day, so that the people about us and those who follow after us will be the better because we have lived."[80]

Historian Ken Osborne has pointed out the essentially passive view of citizenship these ideas embodied. He argues "citizenship education in these years was often seen in prophylactic terms, as a way of preventing the spread of political radicalism."[81] By emphasizing character building, educators depoliticized citizenship and de-emphasized active participation in the political process. Increasingly, however, the call to serve others, by recalling the virtues of the past, was seen as an inadequate response to the demands of citizenship in a modern society.

As the economic crisis of the 1930s worsened, calls for significant educational reform increased. In 1934 the provincial Home and School Federation condemned the revised high school curriculum; members argued that university preparation still dominated the high school program and therefore denied most students adequate vocational preparation.[82] Other organizations criticized schools for supporting outdated and ineffective economic and political institutions. The Educational Committee of the U.F.A. said the roots of the economic crisis of the 1930s could be found in the educational system of years past.[83]

But if schools were to blame for the current crisis, then presumably they could also lead the way to its solution. By 1930, writers in A.T.A. *Magazine* displayed remarkable optimism in the ability of schools to teach all children, and to contribute to the attempt to restructure society in the same way that scientists contribute their efforts toward technological improvement: "That there may be serious practical difficulties to be overcome is not denied. But the end to be achieved is worth the effort, and the accomplishment of that end will be a feat of educational engineering, comparable in social importance to those great feats of mechanical engineering of which the present age is justly so proud."[84]

The assumption that schools could restructure society by reforming school curriculum had important implications for citizenship education and the teaching of history. Citizenship and History courses were singled out not just as ineffective in preparing Alberta children for citizenship, but as potentially destructive. These courses had simply inculcated students with an uncritical loyalty to the state and fostered militarism, so critics argued. They had taught students to venerate the past and turn away from the urgency of current problems. One writer in the A.T.A. *Magazine* argued that history teaching had resulted in a "cult of ancestor worship" among young people and an exaggerated respect for the accomplishments of the upper classes.[85] Another writer asked, "What earthly difference does it make whether the child learns that King John was a very wicked man or not? If she ever gets any real education, she will have to start all over again, and learn that 'wicked' is only a tag we put on people and names ... history lifts to the skies many men just as selfish as John, and calls them great."[86]

The traditional approach had implied that students could be prepared for the present by learning the values of the past; these writers argued that only an emancipation from the past could solve the problems of the present and prepare for the future. Of what possible use could the study of history be to such an endeavour? As one teacher pointed out, "Industry has been disturbed for three years by the clouds of depression, and so far, no historian has supplied one practical suggestion for the alleviation of unemployment, or one single thought to dispel the aura of despair."[87]

What kind of history teaching could dispel despair and suggest solutions for economic and social crises? No history teaching could, strictly speaking, address the future. Rather, the solution was to replace the teaching of history with the social sciences. In 1934, the Annual Convention of the U.F.A. called for sweeping changes in citizenship education so that schools would spread "the idea of the advance of society towards a new form of social organization in which the principle of a struggle for private profit shall be displaced by the principles of equity, justice, mutual aid and social well being."[88] In the same year, the A.T.A. requested that the social sciences be included in the curriculum.[89]

In the end, however, the abandonment of history courses and the introduction of social studies did not come at the insistence of the U.F.A. or the A.T.A. It was the new cadre of educationalists, who were serving as inspectors and in the Department of Education, who had imbibed progressive ideas about education in American graduate programs, who tried to transform Alberta's school system. They created the programs and introduced reforms intended to equip the schools to restructure society and address the problems facing Alberta.

**3**

## NURTURING SOCIAL ACTIVISTS: THE FIRST PROGRESSIVE REVISION, 1935 TO 1945

The Great Depression had an enormous impact on Alberta. The collapse of the agricultural industry brought on by depression, protectionist economic policies and drought affected all sectors of the province's economy. The agricultural crisis decimated the economy: per capita income fell from $548 in 1928–29 to $212 in 1933.[1] Less income meant less spending and so employees in all sectors of the economy were thrown out of work. Farmers in the southern and eastern parts of the province left; the unemployed went to the cities hoping for work or at least better access to relief.

Albertans saw the U.F.A. government, in power since 1921, as incapable of addressing the severe economic crisis. The provincial administration was extremely cautious in dealing with the crisis, cutting costs and rejecting radical solutions such as the monetary theories espoused by British engineer Major C.H. Douglas. The U.F.A. organization, on the other hand, became more sympathetic to leftist proposals for dealing and it found support among the federal Ginger Group. In 1932, leading members of the U.F.A., such as William Irvine, were instrumental in creating the Cooperative Commonwealth Federation. The rift between the socialist C.C.F. and the more conservative provincial U.F.A. made it difficult for the government to present an effective platform in the 1935 provincial election. The U.F.A.'s problems were further exacerbated by the allegations of sexual misconduct that surrounded Premier Brownlee and his minister of public works in early 1934. Brownlee resigned his premiership before he was found guilty of the charges, but the combination of political ineffectiveness and moral disgrace finished the U.F.A. government.

The 1935 election brought the Social Credit Party to power in Alberta. The Social Credit movement was based on the monetary theory developed by Major Douglas. According to Douglas, the Depression resulted from inefficiencies in the capitalist economy: total wages paid to employees could never equal the cost of production, so consumers would never have the spending power to buy products. Therefore, though food and manufactured products were available, people did not have access to ready cash to buy them; this he called, "poverty in the midst of plenty." Douglas suggested that governments should distribute "social credit" – cash – to people so that they could enjoy goods and services without incurring exorbitant credit charges from banks.

The theory was taken up by William Aberhart, the principal of Crescent Heights High School and founder of the Calgary Prophetic Bible Institute. Through his radio broadcasts and Social Credit study groups, Aberhart spread the message of Social Credit. His mixture of Social Credit philosophy and evangelicalism proved popular with many people in Alberta. Aberhart's promise of a $25 dividend to all Albertans also helped convince voters to give Social Credit a chance. In August 1935, Aberhart received a mandate to put the theory into practice: Social Credit took fifty-six of sixty-three seats in the provincial election.

There were important consequences for schools in the Social Credit victory. In addition to the premiership, Aberhart took on the education portfolio in the new government. He had taught in Calgary schools since 1910, and as a well-known high school principal brought expertise and a familiarity with educational problems to the job of minister. In the government's first session, Aberhart introduced two important pieces of legislation which transformed education in the province: he improved the professional status of teachers by requiring all teachers to become members of the Alberta Teachers' Association; and he consolidated rural school districts in order to save money and improve the educational opportunities of rural children. Under Aberhart's supervision, the Department of Education also went ahead with the introduction of progressive reforms in curriculum that had been initiated by the U.F.A. government.

Aberhart's role in the curriculum revisions undertaken in the 1930s illustrates the limitations of the Minister in determining school content. Given Aberhart's religious beliefs, it is ironic that he supported the reforms introduced in the name of progressive education, a movement later criticized for its moral relativism and emphasis on materialism. Certainly Aberhart was familiar with the theories of progressive education and its American roots. He was a member of Calgary's Educational Progress Club whose educationalists studied and championed progressive reforms. On the other hand, there is little evidence that he thoroughly understood the implications of progressive education, let alone adopted its teaching approach.

While he rarely spoke publicly about the new curriculum, surviving newspaper accounts of his few speeches on this issue indicate that he felt progressive education offered an opportunity for character education. To the Home and School Associations in 1936, he explained that "We have attempted to make our schools so practical that we have neglected the higher standards of virtue. Smart Aleck cleverness is the chief characteristic of the output, not culture."[2] He regretted that schools had largely abdicated their character-building role. The progressives' emphasis on education for cooperation and for a more humane society seemed to Aberhart to signal a return to traditional virtues; it seemed to be a rejection of selfish individualism and a return to a healthier sense of community. This supports historian Ken Osborne's assertion that "this tendency to see citizenship as a matter of personality and character, to equate the good citizen with the good person, was reinforced by the version of Progressive Education that Canadian educators imported from the United States between the Wars."[3] In Canada, educators drawn to progressivism tended to emphasize John Dewey's writings about education as personal growth and downplay his, and other American progressives', assertions that schools should become instruments of social reconstruction.

There is certainly little evidence to suggest Aberhart employed progressive teaching methods in his own classroom. He has usually been described as a formidable teacher who dominated the classroom with his powerful voice and large physique. Historian David Elliott said, "Aberhart still adhered to the old-fashioned teaching method of analysis and repetition, and taught his pupils the value of an orderly mind. He taught them to absorb facts, but not the value of independent reasoning. One teacher under Aberhart described him as a dog-trainer and the school as a factory."[4] As a principal, he publicized Crescent's examination results and celebrated the accomplishments of scholars and athletes in the school. This is not to suggest that Aberhart was not an effective teacher or school leader; there is simply little indication that his familiarity with the rhetoric of progressive education was translated into practice.

Aberhart, however, certainly supported the efforts of the officials in the Department of Education in proceeding with progressive curriculum revisions initiated by the U.F.A. government.[5] The degree of cooperation between Aberhart and the officials in the Department is interesting given the hostility other ministers of the Social Credit government felt for bureaucrats. Generally, Social Crediters had a negative image of the state and of civil servants, seeing them as pawns of financial interests and therefore opposed to the best interests of the people. In contrast, Aberhart's relationship with the members of the Department of Education was extremely cordial. To some extent, his deference may have been due to a lingering respect he felt for men who had been his superiors. It may also have been a result of his respect for their graduate education. It was certainly a result of the personal rapport he felt for his Deputy Minister, G. Fred McNally.

Aberhart left many of the responsibilities of the Department to McNally because his business as Premier took priority over demands of the ministry. However, there is an indication that their long-standing friendship played a role in the way the Department was run. Aberhart had been an important ally to McNally when the high school curriculum revisions were undertaken in the 1920s. McNally respected his administrative abilities and was occasionally a guest in his home. Some have suggested that the respect they had for each other's work in their church communities also made their working relationship a rewarding one. T.C. Byrne, who later became Deputy Minister of Education, recalled that Aberhart respected McNally's work in the Baptist church, particularly his Bible classes.[6] In fact there is some indication that Aberhart's respect for McNally's faith background had an impact on his actions as Minister. When Aberhart was accused by coreligionists of not taking sufficient advantage of his position as Minister to inject new religious awareness into schools, it was McNally who provided the rationale for separating his religious faith from his public responsibilities.

Throughout his time in office, Aberhart received many letters from voters who criticized him or who claimed to be disappointed that a "man of God" hadn't done more to counteract the growing secularization of schools. One issue that arose frequently was the teaching of evolution. Many people wrote to Aberhart to tell him that, in the words of one correspondent from Carbon, "I have always wondered at you teaching the Radio Sunday School work and then undoing it through the week. You say evolution was taught before you took office. That is just the trouble, we thought a Christian man would change it, but instead it is worse now than then in spite of what you would like to think."[7]

By 1942, Aberhart evidently felt a need to address the issue more adequately. He wrote a pamphlet entitled "The Theory of Evolution: Can it Be Proven?" with Melvin Donald, an official with the Inter-Varsity Christian Fellowship. The pamphlet emphasized that the theory was based on assumptions that could not be scientifically proven because they were not immediately observable. After providing quotations from textbooks that described evolution in contradictory terms, and after quoting scientists who supported the Biblical account of creation, Aberhart concluded that "The facts disclosed by scientific enquiry in the fields of inorganic and of organic matter, far from supporting the Evolutionary Theory, in reality contradict and vigorously militate against it. All wide-awake students should recognize the fact and form their conclusions in accordance therewith." The pamphlet was signed, "William Aberhart, Minister of Education."[8]

When Aberhart told McNally that he wanted the Department to publish the pamphlet and distribute it to all schools in the province, McNally responded in a carefully worded but lengthy memo. He suggested that it would be unwise for the Department or the Minister to produce or distribute this material for several reasons: most Albertans were not aware of the controversial nature of the theory and probably would not even be able to define it, it would cause a controversy and make the minister vulnerable to charges of interference in the teaching of the schools, and the Ministry does not take sides in issues of this nature but rather allows the truth to emerge over time. And in case Aberhart considered using other avenues to pursue its publication, McNally reminded him that while it may be better to have the Bible Institute publish and distribute the pamphlet, critics of the government would still see it as a case of ministerial interference.[9]

Aberhart accepted McNally's assessment. When Mabel Giles, a teacher at Crescent Heights and colleague in the creation of the pamphlet, asked Aberhart about its status, he responded with a verbatim summary of McNally's memo. In his response, Aberhart added that he could make little effort to intervene in any element of curriculum building because "I might be charged with using my office as Minister for the sake of propagating my strange theories."[10]

And so the Minister did not interfere in curriculum policy. Officials in the Department of Education took the leadership role in creating and implementing a progressive program in Alberta's schools. In fact it was with this progressive revision that educationalists took formal control of curriculum building. Officials in the Department of Education and education instructors at Normal Schools and later Faculties of Education at the universities were recognized as educational experts; they were publicly acknowledged as those best able to define curriculum policy.

## PROGRESSIVE EDUCATION IN CANADA

In the 1930s, jurisdictions across Canada experimented with various reforms described as "progressive." Canadian historian R.S. Patterson describes the years 1930 to 1945 as "the halcyon days of progressive thought in Canadian education," years after criticisms of these reforms had already arisen in the

United States.¹¹ Just as in the United States, curriculum revisions that were identified as progressive were rooted in many different ideas about children, schools and the nature of the societies they serve, but they tended to be described as "activity" programs, "child-centred" education, "learning by doing," and "democratic education." In the 1920s, experiments with individualized study methods such as the Winnetka and Dalton plans were undertaken, but wholesale curriculum reform was not attempted until the early 1930s.

Saskatchewan and Nova Scotia introduced activity-based elementary school programs in 1932 and 1933. Both described the importance of initiating learning experiences based on the children's interests. Both emphasized the importance of schooling that was clearly relevant to the real lives of children.¹² Alberta's progressive revision, characterized by the adoption of "the Enterprise" in the elementary grades and social studies at the secondary level, followed in 1935 and is described in detail later in this chapter. British Columbia, though it had first raised the prospect of progressive reforms with the Putman-Weir Report in 1925, finally introduced curriculum revisions under the direction of H.B. King in 1936. Ontario followed with a new elementary school course of studies in 1937, also grounded in the activity approach and calling for the social development of the child to be the fundamental aim of schooling.¹³ Ontario drew heavily on the Alberta program, even plagiarizing large sections, so that Alberta's Supervisor of Schools, H.C. Newland, commented with some satisfaction that "This is the first time on record that the good old province of Ontario saw fit to import an educational procedure from the West."¹⁴ The trend continued with Manitoba, New Brunswick and Protestant Quebec also introducing activity programs by 1940.

R.S. Patterson characterizes the progressive education movement in Canada as moderate and selective in its policy changes. In his words, "there was no recognition or acceptance of the underlying philosophy behind the movement."¹⁵ For the most part, educationalists across the country saw in progressivism the opportunity to adopt teaching practices that would better suit the needs and interests of children, and introduce curriculum more relevant to the communities which their schools served. That said, Canadian educationalists turned to the American theorists and researchers of progressive education for assistance in theorizing and implementing new programs. Patterson suggests that it was only natural for Canadians to turn to Americans for assistance: American researchers and educators published widely and their work was readily available to Canadians and, since many leading Canadian educationalists received their graduate education at American universities such as Teachers' College Columbia, the University of Chicago and Stanford, they drew on the ideas they had been introduced to in these programs.[16] In some cases, curriculum-writing committees drew heavily on existing progressive programs in the American states. Alberta's program was modeled on one in the state of Virginia, despite the fact that official curriculum documents made reference to the Hadow Report from the U.K., used the British term "enterprise" rather than the American "project" or "activity", and the program was widely promoted as "home-grown."[17] When Alberta teachers were introduced to the program, American university instructors and school teachers were brought to the province to teach summer sessions. In 1939, nine members of the American Progressive Education Association traveled to the province to address the annual teachers' convention.[18]

For the most part, historians argue that reforms attempted in Canadian schools in the name of progressive education were not terribly successful and were largely abandoned by 1945. Poorly educated and overburdened teachers were not able to implement the programs with the few resources provided to them. As much as the economic and social crises of the 1930s seemed to call for innovative social programs, including new school curricula, the public preferred predictability and stability for their children. Within the context of World War II, school programs that implied a rejection of tradition were vulnerable to attack from conservative educators and politicians. Historian Robert Stamp argues convincingly that the election of the provincial Conservatives in Ontario under George Drew signaled the end of progressive education in that province.[19] The same was true across Canada, with the notable exception of Alberta, as we shall see. In this province, the legacy of progressivism resonated for many years, in rhetoric if not always in reality.

**PROGRESSIVE EDUCATION IN ALBERTA: THEORY**

The progressive educationalists were led by Hubert C. Newland, appointed Supervisor of Schools in Alberta in 1935. Newland was born in Ontario but moved to Saskatchewan as a young man and completed his teacher training at the Regina Normal School under D.G. Goggin. After several years teaching, he entered the University of Toronto and received an Honours B.A. in Philosophy in 1910. He taught and served as an administrator in several rural schools before settling down at Victoria High School in Edmonton, where he taught Latin from 1915 to 1928. While teaching, he earned an LL.B., an M.A. and a B.Ed. from the University of Alberta. In 1928, Newland moved to the Edmonton Normal School, where he taught psychology until taking a leave to complete his doctorate. In 1932, Newland was awarded a Ph.D. by the

Hubert C. Newland, Supervisor of Schools, around 1940. Provincial Archives of Alberta, A13992n.

University of Chicago. When he returned to Alberta, he served briefly as a high school inspector and as Chief Inspector of Schools before being appointed Supervisor of Schools.

In addition to his teaching duties and his studies, Newland was involved in the young Alberta Teachers' Alliance and was a founder of the Canadian Teachers' Federation. Through his association with the Alliance, he served as president of the Edmonton high school teachers' local, teachers' representative on the Edmonton Public School Board, Alliance president, editor of the A.T.A. *Magazine*, and managing director of the Alliance's Bureau of Education (a bureau intended to serve as a research body for the Alliance). He loosened his ties with the Alliance after conflicts with J.W. Barnett, but continued a long and profitable association with the Education Society of Edmonton for many years. He also served on the executive of the American Progressive Education Association.

By all accounts, Newland was extremely intelligent and determined to modernize Alberta's school curriculum. Dr. T.C. Byrne, later Deputy Minister of Education, provided his impressions of Newland in an interview in 1977: "Newland, to me, personified intellectualism and freedom of thought. He was a socialist, a critic of educational traditionalism, an espoused progressivist, an avowed democratic thinker – a man of great intellectual capacity. He was very much interested in social justice."[20] In contrast to most Canadian progressives, Newland was profoundly influenced by American George Counts and the stream of progressivism historian Herbert Kliebard labelled "social meliorism."[21] The influence of these ideas on Alberta's curriculum revision will become apparent in the description that follows.

Colleagues respected his obvious intelligence, his energy and his social commitment, but found him austere and difficult to work with. In contrast to the affable McNally, Newland did not consult with his peers in the Department. Instead, he preferred to work closely with like-minded educationalists he selected. Historian John Chalmers describes Newland as a "one-man Curriculum Branch."[22] This is probably overstated, but he did devote a considerable amount of time and energy to curriculum reform. He served as the head of all curriculum review committees and carefully delegated contacts from the Education Society of Edmonton to the committees that actually wrote the new course of studies. The personal responsibility he took for the program led others to see him as authoritarian. W.H. Swift, who served as Chief Inspector of Schools while Newland was Supervisor, recalled one occasion when Newland has been particularly forceful in imposing his views on curriculum revision on a meeting of school superintendents: "He [Newland] spoke to them very authoritatively about what they had to do, and so on. Without that much discussion about it or anything, just that this was what you were to do. I happened to walk out the door with McNally for lunch. McNally said, 'It takes a good socialist to be a good authoritarian.'"[23] There is some evidence to suggest that Newland's lack of consultation in his work, his rigidity and his political leanings all led to his being passed over for promotion to the Deputy Minister's position when McNally retired in 1946.[24]

Among the people chosen by Newland to create the new elementary school program was Dr. Donalda Dickie. Details about Dickie's educational and professional background appeared in newspapers of the period in order to emphasize to the public the level of expertise of those in charge of the revision. The *Edmonton Bulletin* reported in 1936 that Dickie, like Newland, was born in Ontario and educated at Regina Normal School. She taught in rural Saskatchewan schools before returning to university to earn an M.A. from Queen's. In 1912 she came west and accepted a position at the Calgary

G. Fred McNally in 1963. Provincial Archives of Alberta, Pa654.1n.

Normal School. She eventually served as an English and History instructor at all three Normal Schools in the province. She did postgraduate studies at Columbia and at Somerville College, Oxford. She was awarded a ph.d. by the University of Toronto.[25] In addition to her teaching duties, Dickie prepared textbooks for use in elementary schools in history, geography and reading. In later years, she was awarded the Governor General's Award for her 1950 children's history textbook, *The Great Adventure*. After her involvement with the introduction of "The Enterprise," as the progressive education reforms in elementary schools were called in Alberta, she wrote *The Enterprise in Theory and Practice*. It became the standard text on progressive education used in teacher education programs across Canada.

Alberta educationalists, like others across Canada, were heavily influenced by the ideas of American progressives. That said, rather than analyzing the American roots of progressivism, it is more important here that we understand how Alberta's educationalists came to understand and apply those ideas in the province's schools.

While the intellectual elite of previous generations had accepted that the primary aim of schooling was the acquisition of knowledge, Dickie insisted that "education, when all is said, has just one purpose: to help people to learn how to live happily together in the world."[26] She argued that this could only be done by encouraging people to be self-confident and by assuring them of acceptance within the social group. The school, she said, must take the responsibility of developing within the child a well-balanced personality capable of happy citizenship. In other words, education no longer referred to the development of an individual's intellectual abilities; progressive education emphasized training in social behaviour. To that end, progressive educationalists in Alberta based their curriculum revisions on specific understandings of three principles underlying schooling: the nature of the pupil, the nature of the learning process, and the nature of the society the school served. Each one of these theoretical principles had specific implications for classroom practice.

Progressive educationalists in Alberta and elsewhere defended their reforms with references to research in psychology, particularly research related to child development, in arguing that schooling needed to be better suited to the nature of the pupil. They spoke and wrote about the contributions of psychologists such as Lewis Terman and the importance of intelligence testing. They summarized Jung's research on personality types and Maslow's and Mittelman's work on personality growth. From these psychologists, Alberta educationalists learned that the level of instruction in schools must be individualized to suit every student, and that instruction should be directed to the level at which the student operates, not the level which the teacher feels is suitable.

The emphasis on meeting the needs of the existing child, rather than the future adult, was central to progressive education as Alberta educationalists conceptualized it. Donalda Dickie contrasted the traditional approach with the new child-centred approach when she wrote:

> The modern teacher thinks of himself as teaching, not a subject, but a child. The teacher who teaches a subject – arithmetic, or history, or science – naturally thinks first of his subject. His purpose is to ensure that the subject is clearly and completely understood, and his attention is devoted to organizing and presenting it in a logical way. The teacher who teaches a child thinks first of the child; of what he needs; of what means he has to work with to fulfil his needs; of how he, the teacher, can best help him to use the means at his disposal to satisfy his needs. This change in the teacher's point of view is the basis of the changed procedure used in the modern school.[27]

Dickie, and other Alberta progressives, argued that schools should be reorganized to put children and their interests at the centre of the educational endeavour. The American progressive, Harold Rugg, provided specific guidance as to what these child-centred schools should look like. He wrote: "these schools visualize the curriculum as a continuing stream of child activities, unbroken by systematic subjects, and springing from the interests and personally felt needs of the child."[28] Theoretically, child-centred schools abandoned instruction in traditional subject disciplines in favour of activities chosen by students in order to answer questions they raised or explore issues of interest to them.

Progressive educationalists then put motivation at the centre of their understanding of the learning process. They insisted that children have innate curiosity; learning is fun for them. Rather than doing everything in their power to emphasize the seriousness of learning, teachers should spark students' interest with attractive classrooms and take advantage of children's natural interests. Lest this be misinterpreted, University of Alberta education professor K.F. Argue assured readers of the *Alberta School Trustee* that teaching to student interest did not imply catering to students' whims. He said that education "need not, however, be drudgery. The essential reason for having more interest in school is not so much that the children are made happier thereby as because they learn better that way. It should perhaps be emphasized that having children like what they do is a position very far removed from that of having them do what they like."[29]

Argue went on to assure trustees that the new teaching methods of Alberta schools were rooted in the newest advances in the science of psychology. From the behavioural psychologists at Columbia, educationalists had learned about the importance of environmental causes of certain behaviour. This understanding of psychology – as an exploration of the science of behaviour rather than an analysis of the mind – had an extraordinary impact on schooling. In the 1930s and 1940s, it meant that educationalists believed that a carefully crafted school environment could create a specific kind of child. They began to adopt techniques of "behaviour modification" and the language of "behavioural objectives" for classroom lessons. They accepted that learning occurs when pupils undergo experiences. Therefore, pupils must actively participate in learning exercises led, but not controlled, by a teacher. The emphasis in progressive education on enterprises, group work and activity-based interdisciplinary projects was a result of the acceptance of the principle that students must experience a lesson in order to assimilate it.

An emphasis on learning as total experience also came from the Gestalt school of psychology. From them, educationalists learned that individuals react to total situations; learning does not occur in sequential stages nor are lessons limited to what the teacher ostensibly teaches. Argue pointed out that "when students are studying a history lesson, for example, they are at the same time learning a host of other important things: habits, attitudes, likes and dislikes, loyalties and antagonisms, methods of work and many general behaviour patterns."[30] These by-products of teaching – methods of learning – were increasingly seen to be as important as the factual material that had dominated the content of the course of studies.

Classroom practice was also affected by the progressives' understanding of the nature of society and the role of schools in that society. They celebrated democracy and emphasized the role of schools in preparing future citizens to take an active role in shaping their democracy. They maintained that only students who had experience in governing themselves, rather than having discipline imposed upon them by outside authorities such as teachers, were adequately prepared for participation in a democracy. Their argument that progressive education was central to democracy was made frequently during the World War II. Professor Argue insisted that:

> The meaning of the word "democracy" is rather vague. On close examination it seems here to demand that the same high regard for the worth of the human spirit should be shown for children as is desired for adults. That is, education should not stifle the latent creative initiative in youth, but rather should liberate and facilitate its expression. This kind of liberty, in fact, is the basic adult right for which we are fighting abroad today ... For we may no longer delude ourselves that training for freedom and democratic living is unnecessary.[31]

Progressive educationalists insisted on democratic classrooms, characterized by student freedom. The minds and spirits of children could only be liberated when their legs were freed from desks and their voices freed to speak. They would only learn how to live with their fellows if they learned how to work cooperatively with them in school. In essence, progressive educationalists saw the school as a kind of laboratory in which children gain an understanding of democracy and practice the skills necessary for group living or real life.

## PROGRESSIVE EDUCATION IN ALBERTA: PRACTICE

The new program was accompanied by structural changes in the school system. The province adopted a new division of grades: six elementary, three intermediate, and three senior high school grades. The elementary grades were further divided into two divisions, allowing rural teachers to teach combined grades and promoting students only after the completion of each division, i.e., from Grade III to IV, and from Grade VI to VII. Grade IX was moved to the intermediate level, later part of the junior high school, and examinations were eliminated at Grades X and XI. The six-diploma high school course introduced in 1921 was replaced by one general diploma that required English, the new Social Studies, physical education and a wide range of options in order to maximize students' flexibility in creating a course of studies suitable for them. Promotion in high school was dependent upon a "credit" system, where one credit equalled a certain amount of instruction time. The innovation meant that students could no longer obtain standing in courses by writing departmental examinations: the one hundred credits needed for graduation represented time spent in the classroom (presumably experiencing important learning activities and engaging in group living) in addition to content mastered.

The revision at the elementary school level consisted of the introduction of "the Enterprise." According to the new program, the enterprise was "a series of purposeful activities arising out of the pupils' needs and interests and revolving around one central theme." Out of the chosen theme, for example "Food," students would undertake activities that would lead to learning in the subject areas of social studies, science, health, language and possibly several of the fine arts. While very specific guidelines were still provided for "tool" subjects such as reading, handwriting and arithmetic, specific content or skill requirements in the other subjects disappeared from the course of studies. Instead, general objectives were listed that emphasized the development of students' social skills, emotional stability, academic skills and personal character (see Appendix 1).

The revision committee, consisting of Donalda Dickie, Olive Fisher and William Hay, spent a year examining the curricula of various American states and completing the new course of studies. In autumn 1935, a group of seventy-five teachers, all carefully selected, piloted the new program. It was declared a success and extended to all elementary schools in the province in 1936. It remained a recommended program until 1940, when its use was mandated by the Department. At that time, a more detailed description of the enterprises was provided, but specific content in the integrated subject areas was rarely provided. For example, regarding history and geography, the program said only that "if a teacher has exercised good judgment in her choice of enterprises, the pupils leaving Division II [Grade Six] should have acquired a fair working knowledge of the past and present of Alberta, and of a few of the outstanding geographical features of Canada."[32]

At the secondary level, specific curriculum guidelines were provided for vocational subjects that were now more widely available to students. Junior high school students, for example, could choose among optional subjects such as farm and home accounting, elementary bookkeeping and junior business, typewriting, general shop and home economics. Senior high school students could receive training in woodwork, metalwork, automotives, electricity, printing, homemaking and textiles. These courses were intended to speak more directly to the skills average students would need upon school leaving than the traditional academic subjects had.

The philosophy of progressive education was best reflected, however, at the higher grades by the abandonment of courses in history and civics and the adoption of courses in social studies. The program defined social studies as those investigations "whose subject matter relates directly to the organization and development of human society and to man as a member of social groups." But since the function of all schooling was to fit the child for social living, social studies was the hallmark of progressive education. For those traditionalists who feared the loss of instruction in history and geography, the new program assured them that the new social studies course

[w]ill introduce to the pupils the problems of modern civilization in their historical and geographical setting. As its name implies, it is socially directed, dealing essentially with the "here" and "now," and subordinating the "there" and "then." It is in no sense an attempt to camouflage history, geography and civics. When the content of these formal subject categories sheds any light on the problems under study, it is then introduced.[33]

Since the social studies courses introduced in this period were later characterized as abandoning the teaching of history altogether, it is appropriate to point out that this was not the intention of the curriculum writers. They saw history as it was taught in schools as largely irrelevant for children, but they did not, strictly speaking, support eliminating the teaching of history. Rather, they drew on ideas that had long dominated the debate among history professors and educators about "new teaching"; they advocated a new philosophy of history.[34] They argued that history was not about memorizing facts, it was about understanding and explaining trends in the past. It was about using information about the past to make sense of current issues. History, as they understood it within the context of social studies, would allow teachers to use historical background to solve problems. What advocates of social studies failed to recognize was the problematic nature of historical "facts" and the unique nature of historical thinking. American historians James Harvey Robinson, Charles Beard and Carl Becker had raised the debate within their own academic and professional communities about the problem of objectivity and its relevance for historical inquiry.[35] They challenged their colleagues to acknowledge that facts in history were not facts in the sense that they could be empirically proven true for all time. The task of historians, as they saw it, was to assess the validity of historical facts, interpret their significance and use them to build our understanding of ourselves and our world; in other words, to think historically. The creators of Alberta's social studies curriculum assumed that historical facts could be discovered, interpreted and applied to some current problem in the same way that scientific facts could be discovered through experimentation and applied to new situations. This understanding of the discipline resulted in substantial changes in curriculum.

The social studies program for intermediate grades was written by Normal School instructor W.D. McDougall. In his memoirs, McDougall said he became involved in the curriculum revision through the Education Society of Edmonton. In 1935, he made a presentation to the group in which he outlined a new course of studies for the junior high schools based on American Harold Rugg's approach to the teaching of social sciences.[36] As the meeting ended, Dr. Newland approached McDougall and asked him to develop his ideas into a formal proposal for curriculum revision that could be presented to the newly appointed curriculum committees for approval. McDougall presented his draft of the revisions to the Society several times in order to get feedback. Only after it had been refined by these educationalists, was it presented for approval. The Grade IX social studies course was not even reviewed by the committee before it was presented in draft form to the Easter Convention of the A.T.A. in 1936. McDougall wrote the course outline over a weekend after consulting Newland. Newland presented the course to teachers at the convention, where it was favourably received.[37]

McDougall's independence in creating the new program is particularly striking when one realizes the extent to which he modified existing courses. The Grade IX course, for example, had consisted of ancient and medieval history. According to McDougall, "in the midst of a world wide depression and in a period when the war drums were again throbbing in Europe, it did not seem realistic to have the final year in the social studies concentrated upon the problems of ancient Egypt, Greece and Rome."[38] Accordingly, he created a course entitled "The World of Today," in which students examined current problems such as the impact of industrialization and technology on modern living and the various political experiments undertaken by postwar governments to solve political and economic difficulties.

History maintained its dominant place within the new social studies courses for senior high school, but the lack of Canadian history content was striking. Social Studies 1 (Grade X) consisted of the study of man to 1500 within the context of many different civilizations: Egypt, Babylonia, Phoenicia, Greece, Rome, the Arab Empire and China. The course for Grade XI continued the story to 1914 within the context of western civilization. Social Studies 3 (Grade XII) included an examination of international history since 1914 so that students could better understand the roots of contemporary global problems. As indicated previously, though the courses looked like traditional history courses, progressive educationalists in creating social studies had in fact adopted a new philosophy of history. Gone was the belief that the past was worthy of study for its own sake or even because of what it could tell us about the present. History had to be useful, and it was useful only insofar as it could demonstrate a direction for the future. The new courses were intended to provide the pupil with the opportunity "to relate his findings to present-day problems with a view to discovering how we may cope with these problems." It also required new teaching methods. It was supposed to give the pupil the opportunity "to get some experience in democratic leadership and co-operation so that he may adequately discharge his social responsibility later in life."[39] How were teachers prepared for this shift in philosophy, content and method?

The educationalists who wrote the new progressive program also trained new and experienced teachers in the approach and provided resources to help them in their classrooms.[40] Normal School instructors who had written the new courses prepared their students to implement them. W.D. McDougall explained the new curriculum to students and he modeled the techniques the future teachers were expected to use. He chaired forums for his students on topics such as "What Democracy Means to Me."[41] The Edmonton Normal School modified its program to give students experience with independent and cooperative learning. Formal classes were restricted to the morning so that students could use their afternoons for optional courses, field trips and student committee meetings.

While introducing prospective teachers to the new program was relatively straightforward, the task of familiarizing practicing teachers with the aims and methods of progressive education was much more daunting. The Department of Education devoted summer sessions and teachers' conventions over several years to the theme of the enterprise and progressive education. Attendance at summer schools was essential for teachers wanting to upgrade their teaching certificates. There, they were taught by Donalda Dickie and W.D. McDougall, who helped them plan for the new courses. Successful enterprise teachers, such as Belle Ricker from Edmonton, submitted course outlines, activities and step-by-step instructions for use by other teachers. The Department also brought in many American experts. Boyd H. Bode, Harold Rugg, Hilda Taba and Ralph Tyler all spoke at teachers' conventions. Speakers at the 1938 summer session included Lillian Gray from San Jose State College, Edna Reed, an elementary school teacher from Scarsdale, New York, and Tompsie Baxter, a teacher at one of the practice schools associated with Teachers' College at Columbia.

Alberta teachers also turned to the *A.T.A. Magazine* for more information about progressive education. The magazine reprinted keynote addresses given at teachers' conventions by prominent American progressives such as Dr. Bode from Ohio State. It also reprinted articles that addressed criticisms of progressive education. A 1942 article reprinted from the journal *Progressive Education* provided teachers with ready responses for parents who were worried that the new program lacked academic rigor and encouraged lax classroom discipline.[42]

*A.T.A. Magazine* also provided tips for teachers struggling to implement enterprises. The magazine introduced a regular "Teachers' Helps" department edited by W.D. McDougall. The column consisted of practical suggestions for teachers as well as summaries from important books and articles about progressive education. The magazine also reprinted lectures given by school inspectors on new classroom procedures. School inspector J.F. Watkin contrasted the progressive social studies classroom with the traditional history classroom when he advocated that teachers create "a place where students come willingly to explore, to investigate and to do things, rather than a mere classroom where they come unwillingly to sit in desks and listen."[43]

Teachers putting the theory into practice in their own classroom shared ideas with colleagues across the province. They were encouraged to make use of new technology such as slides, movies and radio programs like the Department of Education's own "These Make History" program that introduced pupils to high-profile political and military leaders. Student research projects were described. In 1938, a teacher from Ryley explained how his class collected pictures and created scrapbooks to illustrate the topics of the Grade IX social studies course. Under the topic "New Materials Result in Better Homes," his students pasted samples of wallpaper and rugs, booklets on paints and advertisements for Johnson's Wax. He even included practical tips for teachers: "A little advice as to the proper use of glue will be of particular value to boys who naturally want clippings saturated with glue before pasting."[44] In October 1940, a teacher from Etzikom described an ambitious cooperative research project that allowed his Grade X students to prepare detailed timelines of entire civilizations and share them with their peers.

Activities such as these demonstrate one of the difficulties of translating progressive theories of education into classroom practice. Teachers tended to fill time with activities of little educational value, such as scrapbook work. This was hardly suitable for fourteen-year-old students. As early as 1936, school inspectors noted that while many teachers seemed to have grasped the aims of the new program, others "have mistaken the means for the end and have allowed the pupils' activities to degenerate into pure manual exercises."[45] In 1941, they recognized that "unless the teacher takes time to plan carefully, the activities tend to lean too heavily in the direction of art or manipulative procedures."[46] By 1945, a divisional superintendent complained that "there is a tendency for pupils to waste time in random activities which are not on their plane of experience, which lack any coherent sequence and which result in the formation of no positive skill associations."[47]

Teachers who grasped the spirit of the program and planned more active learning experiences, still faced difficulties in evaluating students' progress. The purpose of the enterprises and courses in social studies was the creation of responsible citizens. Teachers were simply at a loss to measure the extent to which students met this objective. Stanley Clarke, a teacher in Two Hills and a member of the Progressive Education Association, designed a test intended to evaluate his students' citizenship skills after they had completed high school social studies courses. His test was reprinted in the *A.T.A. Magazine* in September 1939. Each question presented students with a separate problem; a dilemma was described and three solutions offered. Students were asked to rank the solutions in order of preference though they were not asked to explain or defend their rankings. Some of his questions seemed to test teachers' commitment to progressive education rather than students' skills or understandings:

One of the boys in the Sociology class is a Red – a definite Communist. Many students are not yet well informed and are easily influenced.

(a) The teacher should cut him short every time he starts to say anything in discussions.
(b) The teacher should argue with him and show him where he is wrong.
(c) The teacher should keep in the background as far as possible and let him and the other members of the class discuss all matters freely.

Other questions failed to ask anything at all:

There is an election for officers of the Students' Union at your school. One student says he isn't going to vote. Another says he ought to. Consider these reasons which were given for not voting.

(a) It doesn't make any difference which side gets in.

(b) I don't know any of the candidates or what they stand for.
(c) We ought to have a director of each activity (say a teacher) instead of the Students' Union sponsoring and controlling it.

Not surprisingly, Clarke asked for readers' help in creating a correct-answer key for his examination.[48]

Teachers trying to implement the new progressive programs also faced difficulties finding suitable resources. Very few school boards had the money to buy slide and movie projectors. Few could even buy the long list of textbooks and reference books recommended by the Department of Education for enterprise and social studies teaching. Many teachers apparently made use of the ready-made enterprise units available from the Western Canada Institute in Calgary because by 1937 inspectors warned teachers to avoid prepackaged activities: "Prepared helps in enterprise work have proved an obstacle to efficiency, originality and teacher progress. These so-called aids may serve to provide the teachers with suggestions, but when the plans given in the manuals are slavishly followed, the very spirit of enterprise work is lost and pupil activity is seriously impaired."[49]

Teachers who were accustomed to teaching with and from texts found it extremely difficult to transform their classrooms into buzzing hives of student activity. When the new program was introduced, the Department provided lists of minimum, secondary and supplementary books rather than authorizing one textbook. When it became clear that teachers needed more direction and that school boards could not provide libraries full of reference books, textbooks were produced. However, when the authorized textbooks were released, teachers were reminded that the texts did not represent all the course content. For example, a review of W.D. McDougall's Grade VIII social studies text (called a guide book rather than a text book) asserted that the text did not provide all pupils should learn about British Africa. Rather, "in the pursuit of these problems and studies, teacher and class are intended to forage abroad among the conventional text books, geographical magazines, industrial advertising booklist and adventure stories (perhaps even among modern films like 'Sanders of the River' or 'King Solomon's Mines') in order to fill in the main facts about the interplay of human and natural forces in the Dark Continent."[50]

Surviving samples of student work suggest that, particularly in intermediate and senior high school, teaching tended to remain text-driven. Though the courses were designed to facilitate discussion, debate and research, student notebooks demonstrate that teachers took advantage of the new textbooks and assigned portions of the text and asking students to answer the questions now conveniently located at the end of every chapter. A Grade VIII

A "progressive" classroom: Riverside School, Medicine Hat, 1947. Provincial Archives of Alberta, A7096n.

social studies notebook from Edmonton's Parkdale school in 1944–45 shows how closely the teacher followed the text, *Our Empire and its Neighbours*. The notebook is divided into the seven problems required by the curriculum. The questions at the end of every chapter are duly answered and all the special projects completed.[51]

But while teaching remained text-centred, the texts had changed. Gone were the chronological historical surveys that had dominated school texts in earlier years. The intermediate social studies texts, written by W.D. McDougall and Gilbert Paterson, covered every required topic of the curriculum thematically rather than chronologically. No topic was covered in great depth; every chapter concluded with questions for students to answer, suggestions for further research projects, and a resolution for them to debate. The texts were written in a conversational style that directly addressed the readers and was intended to appeal to children. They tried to enliven dull passages by making connections to the students' own experiences. For example, after introducing the topic of Canadian fisheries, they added, "What boy does not enjoy fishing!

Girls are not so keen about the sport, – they don't like the flopping trout and the wriggling worm."[52] Many of the texts of the period were notable for their liberal use of exclamation points, as if punctuation alone could encourage student interest.

The high school texts were generally still very long but also incorporated reading aids to help students make sense of the material. Chapters frequently began with short summaries of important ideas; boldface headings helped students remember main ideas or locate specific information. Each chapter or section of text concluded with names and terms to remember, suggestions for further reading, and projects to undertake. Review questions sometimes asked students to recall main ideas in the text, but often they were more complex questions, asking students to think critically about what they had read. Students were asked to apply what they had learned to the modern world. The social studies text used in Grade X from 1939 to 1950, for example, asked students to "compare the political and economic position of the Egyptian and Babylonian labourer with a Canadian workman," and to "compare the social and cultural position of the modern woman with that of the woman in Athens."[53]

**NEW IDEAS; NEW IDENTITIES**

While it is doubtful that many teachers really adopted progressive teaching methods in these years, the resources they used did reflect new ideas about history, identity, society and citizenship. Progressive educationalists created new courses and new resources that would prepare students to take up their responsibility for restructuring society along more rigorous standards of social justice. They sought to create social activists, familiar with local issues and committed to social change. They redefined the qualities of good citizenship. Fostering individual virtue was insufficient; the modern world would require citizens capable of diagnosing problems and engineering solutions. What new messages did the curriculum and textbooks provide?

Because this was the first time curriculum support materials such as textbooks were written by local authors, it is not surprising that it was also the first time local issues were prominently featured in schools. Students were encouraged to define themselves as citizens of a region as well as a nation. They were encouraged to take interest in economic and political issues of special concern to Albertans. For example, the social studies texts by McDougall and Paterson presented Alberta's regional grievances in a particularly provocative manner. Their Grade VIII text equated the position of Canada's prairie provinces with the agricultural south of the United States prior to the Civil War. After a brief examination of Canada's industrial expansion, students were asked, "Would Canada be better off to-day if there had been no tariff barrier to trade between Canada and the United States during the last fifty years?" The conclusion of the book made Alberta's point of view very clear:

But the eastern manufacturer has persuaded the Canadian government to place heavy customs duties on all such goods coming into Canada from abroad, thus raising the price of foreign goods and leaving the western farmer no choice in the matter. Under such conditions it might be expected that the Canadian government would regulate to some extent the prices charged for necessary implements of production, for winter clothing and other essential goods, but unfortunately no such safeguards have been attempted...

This "economic imperialism" (as it is sometimes called) of the East over the West has caused a great deal of discontent throughout Alberta, but because the population of the province is small, it has not very many members in the Dominion Parliament, and the East continues to control the government.[54]

Their Grade VII text asked students to debate the wisdom of giving so much western farmland to the C.P.R., discuss whether Montana might be a more natural trading partner for Alberta than Ontario, and decide whether every farmer should belong to a cooperative buying and selling organization.[55]

It should be noted here, however, that World War II returned a national focus to social studies courses in Alberta. A national call for better Canadian history teaching resulted in the creation of the Committee for the Study of Canadian History Textbooks by the Canada and Newfoundland Education Association in 1943. The Committee expressed grave concern about the difference in content between French and English history texts. They felt this illustrated an important reason for the increasing gulf between French- and English-Canadians. They called for a pan-Canadian curriculum that emphasized Canadian unity.[56]

Officials in Alberta's Department of Education addressed the growing demand for a curriculum that would nurture national unity. Deputy Minister G. Fred McNally recognized the urgent need for schools to bring together the diverse elements of the Canadian population. In June 1944, he wrote that "all agree that we must rely on the school as the most significant agency for the bringing about of this sense of national solidarity, this spirit of mutual confidence, this pride of national accomplishment and disposition to good neighbourliness so much to be desired."[57] Accordingly, the Department increased Canadian content in all social studies courses in Grades VII to XII though they did not change the social studies approach.

One idea in the new curriculum for "social activism" World War II affirmed, rather than challenged, was a belief in the efficacy of government intervention in the economy. W. Stewart Wallace's civics text, used in junior high schools, went beyond the traditional treatment of Canadian political institutions. Only one of the three sections of the book dealt with the machinery of government, the traditional summary of the responsibilities of the various levels of government. Instead, the book focused on the public services provided by the levels of government. Wallace also suggested how governments might deal with contemporary problems. For example, he advocated government support for those unemployed because of the Depression: "But perhaps the commonest and most heart-breaking of all the causes of poverty is lack of employment. There are few things more terrible than the situation of an honest, able-bodied, and hard-working man, with a family dependent on him, who cannot make a living because, through no fault of his own, he cannot find employment. To provide for such victims of misfortune and to try to prevent their misfortune, is the plain duty of society."[58]

Authors recognized the risk in encouraging governments to take on greater social responsibilities, but within the context of the 1930s, most of them advocated greater government involvement and planning in the economy. George Brown, in his Canadian history text, argued that "only by planning and by the action of large masses of people can evils such as unemployment, distress, and want, be banished in the midst of a world that could give security and plenty."[59] While admitting that balancing government planning and individual rights would be challenging, he insisted that the Canadian government was well able to combine strong planning with a respect for the liberty of its citizens.

This enormous faith in the efficacy of government planning – a hallmark of American Progressives like John Dewey and George Counts – was also demonstrated by other textbook authors. V.P. Seary and Gilbert Paterson advocated radical solutions for social problems in their Grade X social studies text. In *The Story of Civilization*, they maintained that capitalism encouraged people's selfish instincts; goods were produced for a profit rather than for the good of society. Since the purchasing power of the poorer classes would have to be increased for industry to survive, they confidently predicted that "the future undoubtedly will see profound changes in the existing system, probably along the lines of state supervision and restraint. There may also be many extensions of the socialistic idea, perhaps in directions not at present foreseen."[60]

Other authors celebrated the positive interventions government had already made. F.R. Scott's *Canada Today* was used in Grade XII social studies. The book outlined a wide variety of Canadian "problems" and "conditions" such as the nationalist movement in Quebec and the role of Canada in the Commonwealth. In the chapter on the Canadian economy, like other authors of the period, Scott supported government intervention. He stressed the role of government policies such as the National Policy in the development of the country. He insisted that given Canada's size, state involvement in transportation and resource development was necessary. Moreover, its proximity to the United States and relationship to Great Britain necessitated the development of protectionist trade policies.[61]

Before World War II, there was a sense of urgency in textbook authors' recognition of the need for government intervention in the economy. After the war, the texts reflected a kind of calm public confidence in legislators and in governments to deal with all social problems. The successful handling of the war effort seemed to prove to many that governments were capable of intelligent planning and of solving social problems. School texts assured students that even in the new atomic age, governments could address problems effectively. They reflected the prevailing optimism in human nature – the belief that human ingenuity could solve any problem if it was appropriately directed. George Brown reminded students that "if modern science puts instruments into the hands of dictators, it puts them also into the hands of the democracies." Students should not be distressed by the scientific developments of the war because "there is no proof whatever that people are incapable of controlling the things which they create. For centuries men have been creating things which they have had the choice of using wisely or unwisely."[62] Brown implied that given the choice, men would always act rationally.

Many texts explicitly or implicitly supported the belief that people act reasonably if given suitable information and appropriate training; they maintained that this information and training would come from the social sciences. Textbook authors compared the knowledge and training of social scientists to natural scientists, thereby stressing the legitimacy of social science expertise and its importance in improving society. Authors James Quinn and Arthur Repke, whose text was used in junior high schools, explained, "when we are sick, we go to the doctor; when our automobile does not run, we go to the mechanic. When society is sick, why not go to the social scientist? He specialized in the causes and cures of social maladies." They stressed that society's problems can only be solved through investigation and planning – a process they described as scientific: "As in the case of all forms of engineering, the social engineer starts with a problem and attempts to work out a scientific conclusion."[63] The comparison of social science with engineering is indicative of another message in the new curriculum: that science was an essential tool in the reconstruction of society; that the citizen activist must think "scientifically."

The celebration of scientific and technological progress was well articulated by educationalist A.L. Doucette in an address to the A.T.A. on the new science education. After emphasizing the importance of scientific literacy for the emerging generation, he stated that "science has made us realize that man need have no inferiority complex. Science has given man confidence in his ability to control nature for his purpose. He is no longer a terrified cringing individual. He is great, because his works are great."[64]

The new science curriculum for elementary schools reflected this confidence: "it is now generally recognized that man *can* and *must* control his environment for his welfare and happiness."[65] The old nature-study approach was criticized for its tendency to anthropomorphize nature and encourage wonder. The new Enterprise curriculum was intended to do away with superstition and magic and, instead, train children in the use of the scientific method. But just like in social studies, specific guidelines of subject content in science were downplayed in favour of teaching the "scientific attitude" or "intelligent enquiry." Indeed, the enterprise technique itself was held up as a living example of the scientific method in action. According to the 1940 curriculum:

the enterprise technique ... is the scientific method, consisting essentially of a problem with a *purpose*. During the process of solution, materials must be available and a plan of attack agreed upon. Revisions will be made in the light of observations and conditions arising out of the activity, and a final conclusion will be reached. Science *may* and *should* have a contribution to make toward the solution of the problem, and if such is the case, science comes into its own.[66]

At the junior and senior high school level, too, emphasis was placed on problem-solving in science, because "the scientific method, once mastered, gives one a way of thinking that can be applied to all walks of life."[67]

The new social studies program and its resources celebrated the scientific and technological advances of the modern world. Minimum requirements in Grade IX social studies included "an appreciation of the effect of the Industrial Revolution on the great world powers," and "an appreciation of the part played by the automobile, the telephone, the radio, and the press, in developing a superior type of rural and urban culture."[68] A recommended text for Grades X and XI social studies also reflected this celebratory attitude toward technological innovation:

The Industrial Revolution was the greatest step of progress that mankind ever made. Nature, before which man had crouched in terror and helplessness, became a kind and bounteous benefactor ... Progress had become the order of the day. No longer does man fear change, trembling lest it should spell disaster; he now welcomes new methods, new things, new ideas, as the harbingers of a life better worth living.[69]

In at least one case, the celebration of technological progress led to sinister predictions about the future. Seary and Paterson touted the potential of the science of eugenics. They explained that Saskatchewan, Alberta and several American states had laws in place to prevent those with defective tendencies from reproducing. While admitting that the laws of heredity are sufficiently complex to require years of scientific research, they expressed the hope that abnormal children might be cured with new treatments and that a better society may thereby be created:

As the organization of society becomes more complex, a new type of man is required, more tolerant, more adaptable, with better social as well as intellectual gifts and training. Every advance, however, leaves its train of stragglers, the feeble-minded, the criminal, the incompetent. It is quite certain that the future holds great promise for the control and improvement of these types.[70]

Most educationalists and authors, however, did not go to such menacing extremes. They associated scientific and technological progress with a growing connection of people. To them, improvements in technology provided opportunities for increased communication and therefore greater understanding. One resource used in elementary enterprise units outlined improvements in communication over centuries. The author assured students that they "shall see how speedier ways of sending messages have made the world smaller, and its people neighbors and friends."[71] Canadian texts also stressed that improvements in technology had contributed to the growing national feeling in the country. F.R. Scott assured readers that despite the great size of the country, "the radio, the aeroplane, the railways, the motor-car and the telephone have reduced the vast size of the country to manageable proportions."[72]

Ironically, while arguing that technological advances brought people together, many authors continued the tradition of judging some racial and ethnic groups very harshly. For example, while earlier historians had criticized aboriginal groups and the regime of New France because of their "uncivilized" and "nondemocratic" ways, authors now criticized these same groups for fighting the inevitable march of material and technological progress. Scott was critical of the French-Canadian suspicion of technology. He explained that "the French Canadian, because of the character of his religious education, tends to believe that a high standard of living is proof of 'materialism' and a dangerous influence on society."[73] McDougall and Paterson, in their Grade IX text, argued that struggle for responsible government in Canada would have been easier if only the French could have been convinced to abandon their outdated traditions. Regarding the Quebec Act, they regretted that "Undoubtedly the scheme achieved its purpose, but with the result that the old French civilization, which might have been gradually mingled with the English, was preserved for generations to come."[74]

Aboriginal groups continued to be treated harshly. McDougall and Paterson attributed the ease of the European defeat of aboriginal groups in the settlement of Canada to technological superiority: "Where the Indians lived on lands desired by the Europeans they were soon driven out, because guns were better weapons than bows and arrows."[75] The curriculum guidelines for an enterprise unit on The Canadian Nomad Community required that students attribute their lack of technological innovation and civilization to the "improvidence of the Indian."[76]

The critical appraisal of racial and ethnic groups was not limited to Canadian history texts. Races were judged according to "impartial" or "scientific" standards of material achievement in progressive texts. For example, races were categorized according to their suitability for immigration to Canada based on characteristics that might contribute to the economic advancement of the country. McDougall and Paterson described Germans as "hard-working and well-educated people. They are not as inventive as some peoples, but are exceedingly clever at putting the ideas of others into practice." In the review section at the end of the chapter, students were asked, "What personal qualities do Germans possess which make them very satisfactory settlers for Canada?"[77] On the other hand, students were also told that Chinese workers were content to work for very low wages and that after the railways were built, they competed with white workers for jobs in coal mines and other public works. Students were then required by the program of studies to engage in an open forum answering the following question: "Should Oriental immigrants be permitted to enter Canada?"[78]

In language strikingly similar to earlier texts, McDougall and Paterson attributed Britain's commercial success and imperial expansion to superior personal qualities. They described the British as "industrious and energetic, and this fact, combined with their favorable situation, has made the British Isles a world centre."[79] An enterprise unit on London was called, "A Very Modern and a Most Progressive Community."[80]

The persistence of racial stereotypes was justified by pointing to more rigorous standards of "scientific progress." On the other hand, these same standards were assumed inadequate to the task of proving the superiority of particular political systems. Indeed, in the period before World War II, text authors and educationalists seemed to equate a scientific turn of mind with dispassionate appraisal. They seemed to believe if they were more tolerant toward other countries and different political systems, they were scientific in their approach.

The new social studies program specifically required that teachers provide students with an objective look at the variety of new regimes in Europe and consider the implications for Canada. Even in junior high school, McDougall and Paterson warned students to be careful in judging Russia. They asked students if Canada could learn any lessons from Russia.[81] The new "scientific" approach also meant that historical events were interpreted in a way that was intended to demonstrate tolerance toward other nations. Explanations for the outbreak of World War I apportioned blame among all the Great Powers. W.R. McAuliffe, whose Grade XII text was used throughout the 1940s, described the greed and blind ambition of all nations at the turn of the century:

During this time, each of these countries was doing its best to outstrip the others: to gain more land in Europe or more colonies over the seas; to train a better army or build a stronger fleet; to possess greater factories, more railways, and richer coal mines than the rest. Statesmen thought only of their own country, and of how best to make it stronger, and therefore more important. It did not matter how much others suffered so long as some little triumph could be achieved, or one of the other nations set back a pace or two in the race for gain.[82]

These interpretations ended with the outbreak of World War II. Textbooks used after the war reinterpreted events according to insights gathered from the war experience. For example, authors of general history texts blamed Germany for the outbreak of World War I since they had confirmed their "aggressive tendencies" by starting a second war. R.O. Hughes in *The Making of Today's World* offered a typical assessment of the responsibility for World War I: "The Germans will never admit that Germany and her allies were entirely responsible for it. The willingness of German leaders to start another war twenty years later, however, cast doubts on the explanation she has offered in her defense for the earlier conflict."[83]

W.D. McDougall's sympathetic treatment of the future enemies of Canada made him the target of controversy. His *World of To-day* came under fire during the Calgary municipal election in the fall of 1939. Independent Candidate E.H. Starr held it up as an example of the propaganda being taught in Alberta schools under the title of social studies. Of particular concern to politicians and to those who wrote to the Department of Education was the explanation given in the text for the Germans' acceptance of Nazism. McDougall and

Paterson blamed the harsh peace treaty of 1919 for the frustrations of the German people. In the context of the fall of 1939, many read the explanation as an apology or justification for the Nazi regime. Starr further criticized the book for degrading the British army by suggesting that it did not defeat the Germans, and for painting too gloomy a picture of conditions in postwar Britain.[84] Other critics demanded the withdrawal of the text because of its "leftist tendencies." To support their accusations, they pointed to the following passage: "Some people feel that the capitalist (competitive) system is out of date in this modern world, and should be modified or replaced entirely by a system better fitted to deal with the problems of today. Three of these plans are especially interesting: the Communist (as in Russia), the C.C.F. and Social Credit."[85] Newspaper editorialists dismissed the criticisms, but the Department of Education faced tremendous pressure to revise or withdraw the book.

H.C. Newland assured the public that the text was one resource among many and not the sole text for the course. Moreover, he defended the tone of the text, arguing that "courses in Social Studies must in their very nature, raise controversial issues and it is the great value of education in a democratic society that such issues can be raised."[86] Under increasing public and government pressure to clear up the controversy, Newland called a joint meeting of all the Department's social studies committees. Though the meeting passed a resolution supporting McDougall and Paterson's approach, it recommended that some changes be made to the text. Committee members thought that the text tended to disparage Canada's economic and political system too severely. To Premier Aberhart, the committee reported that:

a few instances were found where the choice of a particular word or heading might be considered unhappy or inappropriate or even provocative; one or two instances where exception might be taken to the strict accuracy of statements of fact; and likewise, one or two instances where questions had been phrased in such a manner to suggest answers rather than to leave the answers to be found after study and investigation.[87]

The text was revised by a committee that did not include McDougall, who was by then the social studies instructor at Calgary Normal School. Later he remembered that the controversy surrounding his text and the accusations to which he was subject was "not the kind of experience I would wish to repeat."[88]

These reactions demonstrate the extent to which democracy had become the unquestioned "good" of public education, the vaguely defined end or purpose of public education. Before the war, progressive educationalists were prepared to consider the virtues of undemocratic political systems and the problems with democracies. In 1937 Stanley Rand, an instructor in the

University of Alberta's School of Education, compared the Alberta school system's uncritical promotion of democracy to fascist or communist propaganda. He challenged the notion that democracies represent the highest form of political development. He argued that democratic governments in the West were simply a product of their historical development, just as totalitarian regimes in Italy, Germany and the Soviet Union were the logical outcome of their past experiences.[89]

This line of reasoning was rejected during the war. In 1942, Dr. Clarence Sansom, Professor of Education at the University of Alberta, spoke for many when he challenged the relativism of earlier progressives and asked: "Should we believe that goodness, beauty, and truth are *real*, or that they are merely *relative to the mind*? And if they are merely relative to the mind, what are we fighting Hitler for?"[90] Educationalists knew what the conflict was about and were committed to fighting for democracy on the most important battleground: the school. In 1941, H.C. Newland described the progressive teacher as "an evangelist for democracy and a social engineer."[91]

Textbook authors, too, stressed the urgency of the problems facing western democracies, and emphasized the peril facing those that failed to solve these problems. In *Contemporary Problems*, L.A. Bagnall warned:

During the last twenty years, in a score of countries, social and economic problems have proved too complex for solution by their governments. Science and industry have advanced, but distribution of goods has broken down. Crops are destroyed, and men go hungry. Some men are overworked, other are unemployed. Further, no government is able to protect its people from fear of war. In the face of these failures, men have turned from democracy to some form of dictatorship. If democratic government and individual liberty are not to perish from the earth, Mr. Average Citizen must be brought to realize that these problems are his concern.[92]

"Education for democracy" became a statement of faith for educationalists. They saw the establishment of democracy as the purpose of society; they failed to understand democracy as the political framework that allows the largest number of people to seek the good life. They saw democracy as the end or purpose of society, rather than the means to an end.

The new curriculum for "social activism" redefined virtue. Educationalists and the school materials they produced emphasized the qualities of initiative and imagination that would encourage students to participate in the process of social reconstruction. The Department of Education's 1942 *Annual Report* outlined the views of numerous working groups who had been given the task of defining the fundamental objectives of secondary education in Alberta. The groups defined democracy as "equal opportunity for all," and they agreed that "training for citizenship in a democracy, or in other words, training for social responsibility, is one of the three most important objectives, if not the most important objective, of the high-school programme."[93]

These qualities of good citizenship were further defined in specific curriculum documents. The decline of the language of virtue is striking. In the junior high school curriculum documents, competence in citizenship included solving public issues, taking political action, and practicing consumer skills. No reference to the personal attributes of good citizens was made; the Department only required that students should develop "democratic attitudes and behaviour in all social situations."[94]

The Edmonton Public School Board made a serious attempt to define good citizenship by listing the personal qualities associated with good citizenship and then requiring teachers to evaluate those qualities on report cards introduced in 1947. Significantly, the characteristics of good citizenship were restricted to behavioural traits. Growth in citizenship skills was equated with "personality development," and students with poor ratings of these skills were characterized as "poorly adjusted." The "Guide for Evaluating Growth in Citizenship" that accompanied the new report cards defined the traits teachers were looking for: emotional control, creativity and initiative in enterprises, a scientific attitude that would be demonstrated as "open-mindedness," cooperation with peers and obedience to authority, dependability and courtesy.[95] This mixture of psychological adjustment, critical thinking skills and traditional virtues reflected the eclecticism in the progressive curriculum regarding the nature of good citizenship.

Responding to a request by Premier Aberhart, in 1940 the Department prepared a memorandum on "The Ethical Content of Alberta School Programme." Officials pointed out that ethical aspects of the elementary school curriculum included "the promotion of social adjustment and the development of desirable attitudes, ideals, and appreciations." They reminded the Premier that these goals were reached by indirect teaching and by example, rather than through specific lessons. Some indication of the future direction of "character education" was given in the outline of the aims of the high school program. Here, officials explained to Aberhart that "the High School Programme offers special opportunities for boys and girls in their later adolescence to understand the importance of sound mental health and wholesome sex adjustment. There is provision for a special course of training in Guidance. There is also a special course in Psychology which emphasizes the study of behaviour, especially towards others, and the main patterns of approved social conduct."[96]

Ministers of Education who followed Aberhart echoed the Department's insistence that appropriate psychological guidance could improve students' character. In 1947, R.E. Ansley announced to school trustees that the Department had appointed its first Guidance Officer. He explained that "the work of his office and his associates is going to be far more than vocational guidance. You may expect him to do a great deal towards guidance that will help bring about better moral and character development of the boys and girls in our schools."[97] In 1952, Ivan Casey explained the nature of character development of schools to a correspondent who asked why no time was set aside in schools for teaching moral conduct. He was probably not reassured by Casey's reply that courses in Health and Personal Development were being developed for Grades VII to X that would give students practice in cooperation and the opportunity to research the "problems of boy-girl relationships."[98]

Textbooks used during the progressive years made fewer direct references to good character and traditional virtues than earlier texts. Historian Robert Stamp describes the approach to the teaching of morality in school readers used in this period in Ontario: "The search for moral values was now more open-ended, with the correct response in any given situation dependent not so much on Judaeo-Christian absolutes but on what a later generation would call situation ethics."[99] The same was true of readers used in Alberta. The new *Highroads to Reading* series included stories with lessons that had more to do with consumer awareness and public safety than traditional character development. For example, Book Two included the story, "Peter Learns a Lesson." In the story, Peter, a young farm boy, resents doing the chores around the farm. One day as he walks to school various farm animals cross his path. As he tells each animal to go away, the egg and the bottle of milk in his lunch, and even his sweater, disappear. He learns how much he depends on the things around him. In the same book, a foolish little boy uses a match to find his skates in the dark attic. He forgets to blow out the match and the attic goes up in flames. Children were reminded that it is much safer to use a flashlight.[100]

The speeches and writings of progressive educationalists indicate a profound shift in their understanding of good citizenship and good character. Educational experts in earlier years emphasized traditional virtues that they felt helped society function smoothly. The intellectual elite that dominated public education believed in virtues that lent a certain civility to governance, public discourse and social interaction. They had a deep respect for previous ages and eternal truths. The new understanding of good character, in the case of educationalists, was largely rooted in personality development and the acceptance of behavioural psychology. Officials in the Department of Education and members of Faculties of Education accepted that good character was essentially a well-balanced personality. They argued that character education could not consist of teaching traditional virtues; it should guide students to correct behaviour through personality adjustment. They accepted that individuals and therefore society could be improved. The corollary was the assumption that the experience of the past was irrelevant.

In 1934, H.C. Newland announced that one of the most important aims of education was "releasing the present from the paralyzing hold of the past."[101] In part, he meant that traditional methods of teaching and learning must give way to new methods and new ideas about schooling. Donalda Dickie repeated the refrain of progressive educationalists when she told school trustees in 1939 that old education was not suitable for life in the new world: "It seems, therefore, no more than common sense to say that if the world we live in now is different, there's no use trying to teach the children – to bring them up and train them – for life in the old world. It's only common sense to say we must teach them to live successfully in this new world."[102] Progressive education denied the validity of educational traditions and insisted on new teaching techniques for the new world.

But progressive education did more than reject tradition in pedagogy; progressive education questioned the value of the study of the past. In 1943, Solon Low, the Minister of Education, told the Alberta School Trustees' Convention that some misguided teachers refused to accept the validity of the new ideas about education. He explained that "it is far easier for them to tell their students about the motionless past that it is to join with them in trying to understand the moving present that has to be studied afresh at the beginning of each new day."[103] H.E. Smith, an education professor and the president of the A.T.A., ridiculed those who criticized falling academic and cultural standards in schools by challenging them to identify the "golden age" in the past. He argued that it was

[s]urely not in Old Egypt, with its poverty, cruelty, false gods, and wholesale slavery; surely not in the days of David and Solomon with their butchery, serfdom, and irreligion; surely not in the palmy days of either Greece or Rome with again universal slavery, flagrant vices, paganism, and political corruption. If anyone suggests the England of Queen Victoria, surely he has not read Charles Dickens or Sidney Webb."[104]

To progressive educationalists, history was a catalogue of human failure and misery. What they sought through social studies instruction was a recognition of the possibility of human triumph. Social studies defined a goal society should achieve and in essence tried to emancipate society from its history.

A.L. Doucette omitted any historical content from his list of required knowledge which he outlined in speech to the University Women's Club in 1950. He said that

[c]hildren must know about the United Nations, of Hitler and Mussolini, of the Berlin Air-lift, of Social Security, of Sulpha Drugs, of Penecillin [sic], of Wheat Agreements with Britain, of Rural Electrification, of the St. Mary's Irrigation Project, of Polar War, of Hemispherical Defence, of Isotopes, of Radar, of Television, of Radioactivity, of Ultra-violet rays, infra-red rays, of gamma rays, of Vitamin B-12, of atomic energy. These are all foreign to the days of Greece in 500 BC, or in the days of Thomas Aquinas, Martin Luther, Herbert Spencer, of Dr. Banting.[105]

He argued that schooling which encourages an appreciation of history condemns society to an outmoded way of thinking and living. In 1947, he asserted that "to concentrate merely upon the passing on of the social heritage is to make education serve only as a recapitulation of the past, to attempt to secure stability, and to preserve the status quo in a world which refuses to remain stable and to keep the status quo. We cannot stand still or we may slip backward."[106]

Progressive educationalists rejected the notion that historical understanding was useful in the modern world. The extent to which they rejected the authority of tradition was reflected in their statements about the abilities of children. Time and again, they celebrated the "insights" of children and ridiculed teachers who were detached from the realities of the modern world. Doucette maintained that "when topics in Latin and History must deal with 'How the Wooden Horse Saved Troy' and 'How the Battering Ram was Used in the Siege of Babylon', youth squirm with disinterest because they know more than the Latin or History teacher about supersonic fighters and jetpropelled missiles."[107] H.C. Newland insisted that teachers give up control of the classroom because "we parents have no right whatever to expect our children to conform to our personalities, or our creeds and beliefs." He justified this abdication of responsibility by explaining that "we are on the western summit, they are rising with the sun."[108] The Department of Education's own statement of educational philosophy rejected the legitimacy of adult claims to authority based on experience and knowledge. In *Foundations of Education*, the Department lamented that "too often the urchin who peddles newspapers on the streets knows more of social reality that the teacher who sets the History examination which this same youngster fails to pass."[109]

The abandonment of the attempt to know the past represented a tremendous shift in the content of school knowledge. As inadequate as earlier curricula had been, they had always reflected the belief that an understanding of the past was central to defining ourselves. Progressive educationalists sought to emancipate children from the past in order to create a better society. They rejected the notion that a society must root its sense of belonging within its historical experience. They sought to develop a sense of citizenship and identity through the common problem-solving exercises of the enterprise and social studies, rather than through an inquiry into the meaning of the past. Students were not led to discover who they were through an examination of what they had been; they were set to the task of self-definition by imagining who they would like to become. But the public dissatisfaction with schools after World War II ensured that once more, Albertans would reassess the aims of public education and the meaning of citizenship and history.

# 4

## AN EDUCATION FOR UTILITY: DEFENDING DEMOCRACY IN THE COLD WAR ERA, 1945 TO 1970

Alberta emerged from the Second World War with a new premier and a new maturity. Ernest Manning, Aberhart's young lieutenant, took over the premiership upon the death of Aberhart in 1943. He served as premier for twenty-five years, seeing the province through years of prosperity and tremendous population growth. He also led the Social Credit Party through its transformation from a radical movement to a conservative defender of free enterprise.[1]

Manning presided over a government with a reputation for fiscal prudence through times of relative prosperity. Despite the fears of many that war would again be followed by economic recession, the late 1940s and early 1950s instead ushered in an era of opportunity because of the oil boom. The strike at Leduc No. 1 brought many American oil companies to Alberta and signalled the beginning of financial good fortune for the province. The frantic search for oil resulted in the discovery of more natural gas reserves. The drilling, production and transportation of the valuable resources put thousands of people to work and attracted many more to the province.

In 1946, there were 803,000 people in Alberta; within five years, the population had grown to 939,000.[2] Newcomers arrived from the United States, Europe and other parts of Canada. The vast majority of people moved to Alberta's cities. While the agricultural sector was healthy after the war, technology transformed farm work. The population shifted from rural to urban areas. Between 1951 and 1956, 75 per cent of the province's population increase was accounted for by the growth of Calgary and Edmonton. The remaining 25 per cent was the growth of the province's seven smaller cities.[3] This growth put demands on the housing industry and other community services. The overwhelming desire of returning veterans, Albertans who had experienced the war at home, and the new immigrants was for an opportunity to enjoy the new economic prosperity and the lifestyle it could provide.

Civic governments undertook massive expansion of hospitals, libraries and parks. In fact, provincial politics during the 1950s were dominated by disputes between municipal governments and the provincial Social Credit government about the financing of these facilities. While Manning's government generally practiced fiscal conservatism, it also collected the highest per capita revenue in the country, and therefore had the money to spend on programs it could justify ideologically. Most of the province's budget during the 1950s was divided among health, education, public welfare, and highway construction. The government's spending priorities seemed to reflect the will of most Albertans. In 1956, the Social Credit League polled Albertans about their concerns. Education was identified as the area of provincial responsibility most in need of improvement.[4]

Throughout the 1950s, Alberta had the highest per capita spending on education in Canada. Despite this apparent commitment to education, or perhaps because of the significant level of public spending, there was considerable public debate about schools. Issues of concern included the provision of secondary education for rural students and the development of composite high schools which would offer academic, vocational and commercial programs under one roof; the severe shortage of teachers at every level of schooling and the salaries and working conditions that continued to discourage promising candidates from entering the profession; and the necessity for better school facilities to accommodate the burgeoning population of school-age children.

But to a remarkable degree, people were interested in what was going on inside Alberta's classrooms. There were public debates about philosophical issues such as the aims of education and the intellectual and moral principles embodied in the curriculum. The successful prosecution of the war and the tremendous feat of planning that victory had entailed convinced the public that the same effort could be brought to bear on domestic problems. Public education was seen to be central to the task of reconstructing and reorienting society to face the new world. Schools and teachers had to do the job right. Public schooling, therefore, was scrutinized, and many critics were not happy with what they saw.

## THE ATTACK ON PROGRESSIVE EDUCATION

Most of the Canadian critics of public schooling in the period immediately following the Second World War were university professors. In 1948, John M.

Ewing, principal of Victoria College of the University of British Columbia, published a critique of progressive education in *Saturday Night*. The same year in *Maclean's*, Queen's history professor Arthur Lower bemoaned the lack of culture among his students and the preparation they had received in public schools. In the early 1950s, newspapers and magazines of all descriptions addressed the educational failures of the nation. In 1953, Sidney Katz outlined "The Crisis in Education" for *Maclean's*. In the same year, Hilda Neatby, head of the History department at the University of Saskatchewan, published *So Little for the Mind*. Her searing indictment of Canadian education in general, and progressive education specifically, caused a furor and led to public debates about the merits of public schooling. Critics pointed to her book as the proof they needed for the degeneration they suspected had occurred within classrooms. In Alberta, Classics professor W.G. Hardy echoed many of Neatby's points in a series of articles he wrote for four major newspapers in the province.[5] Politicians and the general public took up the debate and professional educationalists were forced to defend the reforms they had made.

Problems with the implementation of the progressive curriculum were acknowledged from the beginning. Inspectors complained the school boards did not have enough money to buy the required resources to support enterprise and social studies teaching. Normal school instructors lamented teaching candidates' poor academic skills and their inability to understand the theory of progressive education. Veteran teachers were criticized for their stubborn adherence to outmoded methods. In 1945, when H.C. Newland retired, the new Chief Superintendent of Schools, W.H. Swift, acknowledged that "the present status of activity and group techniques is far from encouraging ... we have neither the school plants, equipment nor competent teachers necessary for their successful application."[6] Rather than give up on the approach, however, the Department updated the programs of study to give teachers more direction in terms of course content and standards of achievement expected of students. They continued to use the rhetoric of progressive education, and this may explain why there was so much public dissatisfaction with schools over reforms that educationalists (and historians) insisted were never really implemented. The public education debates of the early 1950s in Alberta were largely debates about the principles of progressive education rather than an examination of actual classroom practice.

What were the criticisms of progressive education? In 1946, the editorial writer for the *Lethbridge Herald* argued that recent high school graduates were losing jobs because of their poor command of the three Rs. He pointed out that "it does not impress a prospective employer to receive a letter of application which has words misspelled or sentences badly constructed."[7] Letters to the editors of all Alberta newspapers complained about students' failure to master basic academic skills. Dr. Hardy referred to a survey asking Edmonton businessmen their impressions of the high school typewriting course. They replied that "it would have been better if the students concerned had spent their time at English grammar and at learning how to spell."[8]

Social studies was specifically singled out as academically inadequate. Professor Hardy saw these courses as deficient and argued that one "is inclined to feel that a reasonable knowledge of the history and geography of, at least, Canada and the British Commonwealth of Nations is still of real importance to children when they step out of school."[9] Betty Horton, in her reminiscences about her experience in Edmonton in the 1950s, remembered that there was considerable parental concern about the lack of content in elementary enterprises, "so that a student could study Holland or Switzerland twice, and never learn about most of the rest of the world."[10]

Alberta's politicians joined the chorus. Since many of the members of the Legislative Assembly had been teachers or school administrators, debates about schooling were often lengthy. Opposition members criticized falling academic standards and progressive influences; government members defended the educationalists in the Department of Education and the philosophy of education they had embraced. As a result, very conservative and moralistic Social Credit members often found themselves defending the theory of progressive education.

For example, in 1953, Liberal Hugh Macdonald advocated the establishment of a permanent education commission that would guard the academic credibility of the provincial school system and recommend changes. That he advocated a fairly traditional view of schooling was reflected in his choice of members for such a commission: the president of the University of Alberta and others in the arts and sciences faculties, rather than the new generation of educationalists.[11] Progressive Conservative member, and former teacher, Percy Page chastised the government for granting high school diplomas to Grade 12 students with a C standing in courses, which meant the student received between 40 and 49 per cent in the course.[12] In 1954, Conservative W. (Cam) Kirby suggested that the government had intentionally lowered matriculation standards and reduced the emphasis on mental discipline in schools for reasons of political expediency: "He suggested a poorly-educated populace is 'conducive' to the Social Credit government remaining in power and possibly this was the government's aim."[13]

The Social Credit members of the Legislative Assembly defended the underlying principles of the progressive reforms and characterized the Opposition members as out of touch with modern educational research. In response to

Opposition criticisms of modern teaching methods, Education Minister Ivan Casey recited three stanzas of "The Ancient Mariner" which he said he'd been forced to memorize when in school, and concluded that "he didn't think this method of studying literature was education, adding that he had learned to hate history because of having to memorize dates."[14] M.L.A. Lee Leavitt, formerly a guidance supervisor in Banff, told the Legislative Assembly that he could not support "any idea which advocates changing our curriculum back towards the good old horse and buggy days."[15] Russell Patrick, a school principal in Lacombe, accused critics of outdated thinking, saying, "the very statements they make indicate that they have not made any attempt to keep up with educational developments of the last 20 years, so that they themselves might have grown educationally."[16]

Critics of progressive education said that in trying to educate all children, schools had developed programs that demanded little of any of them. In 1947, Paul Bracken, vice-principal of Crescent Heights High School, described the high school program as "uniform mediocrity" in an address to the Knights of the Round Table organization that was covered by the *Calgary Herald* and reprinted in *The Alberta School Trustee*. He condemned progressive education reforms and suggested that the elimination of most of the traditional compulsory high school subjects had resulted in a decline of academic standards for a generation of Alberta students.[17] Dr. Hardy echoed his concerns, insisting that the elimination of all compulsory subjects in the high school program with the exception of English and Social Studies, meant that students entered university inadequately prepared for a true liberal arts education. As a Classics professor, he was particularly concerned about the loss of Latin from the high school curriculum.[18]

Politicians warned that there would be serious consequences for the unfortunate democratization of high schools. In 1958, Liberal M.L.A. A.L. Sims attacked the government's continued support for progressive education. He noted "two generations of young people have been 'exposed' to it." This has resulted, he maintained, "in the lowest percentage of matriculants of any nation providing education facilities."[19] His colleague Richard Hall acknowledged that graduates had polish and confidence, but decried their lack of mental discipline and their materialism.[20]

Professor Hardy argued that education for democracy did not mean that children should be given the same schooling or the same courses. He stressed that democracies need leaders who are knowledgeable about the past and who are able to think constructively and critically about the future, in other words leaders who have received a traditional liberal education. He recommended the establishment of special classes for the gifted that would employ more traditional methods of instruction and a more rigorous academic curriculum.²¹ The same suggestion was made by two groups that presented briefs to the 1954 Standing Committee on Education of the Legislature. Both the Citizens' Committee on Education from Calgary and the University Women's Clubs demanded an enriched program for gifted students.²²

Some critics of progressive education labelled it as "amoral," or at least deficient in training children in traditional virtues. In *So Little for the Mind*, Hilda Neatby argued that pragmatism, the philosophy upon which progressive education was based, eliminated standards of right and wrong; it encouraged children to become self-centred and provided no reason for them to deny themselves for the good of others.²³ In essence, she asserted that despite its rhetoric about cooperation, progressive education encouraged children to be selfish. Professor Hardy agreed, saying, "children have quite enough ego without being encouraged to regard themselves as special cases."²⁴

He was also particularly critical of the progressive emphasis on fun in the classroom: "Learning in my experience, isn't necessarily 'fun', unless you consider hard work, 'fun'. To learn is hard work."²⁵ The editorialist in the *Lethbridge Herald* made the same point: "Too often the logic of hard work on subjects which are perhaps not so attractive is forgotten in the more flowery frills of education. After all, it takes work to learn to do sums correctly and to spell correctly and to use good grammar."²⁶ To that writer, the hard work of schooling is good preparation for much of the drudgery of work in adult life.

Other critics called progressive education amoral because it was irreligious: it rejected the notion that the aim of education must be tied to the purpose of life itself, which was not to improve oneself or live in a community, but to walk with God. L.A. Bond, in a letter to the editor of the *Calgary Herald*, warned, "this progressive education has much in common with the rationalism which was propagated in the German schools, universities and modernistic pulpits. It says little of sin, but much of man's supposed ability to lift himself up by his own bootstraps. Progress! Instead of lifting himself up, man has about blown himself up!"²⁷ He advocated Bible teaching in the schools as an antidote to dangerous modernism.

The Protestant clergymen and church organizations who expressed concerns about progressive education did not, however, advocate Bible teaching as the sole force to counter irreligion in the schools. Angus MacQueen, the minister at Robertson United Church in Edmonton, attacked progressive education in the *Alberta School Trustee* in 1948. While he suggested that Bible teaching was an important element of true education, he also stressed the need for an educational philosophy that would permeate the entire curriculum and transcend the rampant materialism of modern society. In his view, the progressive curriculum contributed to the spiritual impotence of the time.[28]

The Edmonton diocese of the Anglican Church also called for a complete reassessment of the principles underlying the public school program. In a brief on Christian education submitted to the Minister of Education, it argued that the public schools were, in effect, indoctrinating children in a pagan religion, in a superficial and materialistic philosophy of life. The schools, by concentrating on preparing children for earning a living, were abdicating their responsibility for preparing children to live a full life in the Christian sense.[29]

Roman Catholic Bishop Carroll in Calgary was equally alarmed by the progressive influence on schools. In 1937, shortly after the introduction of the progressive curriculum, he insisted that all teachers in the Calgary Separate School Board take his catechetics class. In these classes, he criticized the prevailing attitude toward religion in the public schools: "Religion is treated as something that binds man to man. 'I don't steal, or lie, or murder. I give every man his just due' – says that modern man. 'That's my religion – as for God – He can take care of Himself.' But that's an entirely false conception. From the beginning, religion concerns first and always our relations toward God."[30] Roman Catholic education in Alberta was grounded in the understanding that schools should bring children into a right relationship with God. This Catholic theory was defined and explained in Pius XI's 1929 encyclical letter, *Divini Illius Magistri (On Christian Education of Youth)*. It certainly stood in opposition to the progressive understanding of human nature and the purpose of schooling, particularly with regard to moral and religious training. How did Catholic educators react when the progressive program was mandated by the province?

Certainly the intelligentsia of the Catholic church understood that their view of Christian education and the progressive philosophy underlying the new curriculum were incompatible. Critical appraisals of the new ideas in education began appearing in the *Western Catholic Reporter* in the early 1930s. Bishop Carroll stressed the unique responsibility of Catholic schools in the face of the new mandate to teachers, trustees and Catholic parents. As time went on, he increasingly contrasted the aim of Catholic schools with that of secular schools. In 1947, he addressed the first meeting of the Catholic Education Association. He told the meeting that Catholic education includes two elements of true education omitted by progressive education: it addresses the whole man with his physical, intellectual and spiritual needs; and it reflects the understanding of the child as a child of God. The consequence of this was that "Catholic education consists essentially in preparing man, not so much for what he must know, but for what he must do and what he must be here in the world in order to attain the sublime and for which he was created."[31]

The trustees of the Catholic school boards, while they likely failed to appreciate the nuances of the theological debate surrounding progressive education curriculum, were ambivalent about it and quick to remind concerned parents where the responsibility for creating curriculum lay. At the annual meeting of 1943, the Education Committee of the Board reported that "with certain features of the courses of study particularly at the high school we are not entirely in agreement but these courses are prepared by the Department of Education and our teachers must follow them with no discretion on their part or on the part of this Board."[32] In 1944, the Committee said, "when parents of pupils see reason to find fault with any aspects of what is taught in our schools or the methods by which it is taught, it should be remembered this Board has no discretion in these matters and if there be any room for criticism, this should be directed at the Department and not at the teaching staff of the schools of the Board."[33] In 1952, Fred Kenny, the Chairman of the Board, acknowledged that revisions to the course of studies for junior and senior high schools had caused much public comment, but insisted, "it is not within the competence of this Board to say whether progress is being made or whether the course of study is being watered down to the point where we cannot turn out scholars any more."[34]

In the face of this barrage of public criticism, supporters of progressive education lashed out. Education Minister Ivan Casey argued that schools could hardly be held solely responsible for declining academic and moral standards. Bad habits were learned at home, he insisted, and the schools faced an insurmountable challenge in countering the influence of comic books, radio and television, which "were enough to put any youngster on the wrong track."[35] Calgary teacher Jennie Elliott argued that the failures of the progressive revision were the fault of citizens who refused to adequately fund classrooms and thereby failed to provide necessary resources and well-trained teachers.[36] She was supported in this argument by the Alberta Federation of Home and School Associations, who blamed not only the lack of financial resources for schools, but, like Casey, the "general lack of discipline in society which is reflected in the schools and which increases the difficulties of the teacher" for the failure of schools to recognize all the benefits of the progressive approach.[37]

Educationalists, too, argued that teachers were facing children seriously deficient in self-control. Indeed, they argued that schools were fighting a rearguard action in emphasizing important social virtues in the face of declining moral standards. In 1950, Morrison Watts, Director of the Curriculum Branch in the Department of Education, described the radio and other modern technologies as "fifth column" interventions in the efforts of the schools. To the Home and School Associations, he said that "movies, the radio, the newspaper, slick magazines and cheap comics provide us with a large part of our information and tremendously influence our patterns and conduct, our values and our ideals."[38] He added that since families were incapable of battling these forces, schools needed to meet the physical, emotional, social and spiritual needs of children.

H.E. Panabaker, Supervisor of Guidance for Calgary Public Schools, agreed with him, saying, "at a time when commercialized amusement and sport are setting up false standards of value, and when many other factors are robbing the home of much of its effectiveness, the school seems to be the only agency left with enough contact with young people to give them adequate skill for coping with life's varied problems and a sense of purpose and value to direct their application of that skill."[39] Dr. M.E. LaZerte concurred that the old-fashioned emphasis on academic skills alone was inadequate preparation for the modern world. In 1955, he wrote, "Parents are no longer satisfied to have the '3 R's' as the major part of the school's curriculum. The school has been forced to take over many responsibilities from the family, the church, the community, the office and the factory."[40] But whether schools were responding to society's needs or assuming responsibilities better left elsewhere was very much debatable.

Comments like those of Watts, Panabaker and LaZerte indicate that educationalists seemed to hold contradictory ideas about the relationship between school and society. They argued that schools should be updated to meet the demands of modern society; they also maintained that external social forces undermined the efforts of schools to improve students. Many educationalists, for example, defended the need for progressive curriculum revisions along the lines argued here by F.G. Buchanan:

> The school curriculum, its content and teaching methods, are determined in a large measure by the ideals and ideas that control a society at any particular time. In a period of rapid change in the social, economic and political beliefs, educational practices are challenged and there arises an insistent demand that the curriculum of the schools be brought in line with accepted ideas of the society which they exist to serve.[41]

In fact, Deputy Minister of Education W.S. Swift insisted that the progressive curriculum had been introduced "because of the vocal demands of society."[42] In short, they said that schools generally reflect public opinion. At the same time, however, they insisted that schools represented virtues and standards of behaviour that challenge modern society. H.E. Smith, the Dean of Education at the University Alberta, argued that "the school supports the ideals of universal peace, Christian brotherhood, cooperation, simple living, and high thinking. From these it is a far cry to the actualities of commerce, nationalism, and much of applied science."[43]

The fact that educationalists argued both that schools reflect society's expectations and are often at odds with society's expectations demonstrates the frustrations they had faced in introducing progressive education reforms. The optimism of educationalists who, in 1935, saw education as the key to social transformation had been tempered, by the early 1950s, by their realization that a large section of society did not support their vision. Now they called for a synthesis or balance of traditional and modern visions of schooling in order to help students take advantage of the economic opportunities the province could offer. The balance would be found in a curriculum that was practical. The best of each approach to education could be adopted with a view to creating the most useful curriculum possible.

## THE "USEFUL" CURRICULUM

Much of the public debate pitting traditionalists against progressives masked their fundamental agreement about the aim of schooling: that schools should produce modern workers with skills and attitudes that would benefit the modern economy. Opposition politicians who criticized progressive education in Alberta's schools called for new programs in mathematics and science in order to produce the technicians the province needed. Liberal Richard Hall and Conservative Cam Kirby agreed that the province would need "an almost unlimited supply of competent, well-trained engineers, business executives and leaders."[44] In their calls for a new curriculum, they sounded a lot like the Education Minister who committed his ministry to creating graduates who would "build a bigger and better Alberta."[45]

Educators also reflected the prevailing belief that schools should create competent technicians. Their messages in yearbooks of the period are full of assurances that great opportunities are available to students with appropriate technical education. The Superintendent of Schools in Lethbridge, in his 1956 message to the students of Hamilton Junior High School, celebrated the growth of job opportunities in the growing industries of Alberta and assured them that the petrochemical plants under development in the region would provide jobs for every well-trained boy and girl.[46] The principal of Bassano High School told his students that the development of Alberta's wealth would require "large numbers of qualified personnel in the designing, construction, operation and maintenence [sic] of a wide variety of plants and industries."[47]

The principal of Bow Valley Central High School in Cluny warned his students that they should buckle down and study hard, because "the aspirant without education has reduced his share of Alberta's abundance to the dregs left by those with sufficient foresight to equip themselves adequately to meet the challenge."[48]

Educators were convinced that parents supported this emphasis on useful education. In 1960, T.C. Byrne summarized the history of curriculum development in Alberta for the annual convention of the Alberta Home and School Association. He concluded his speech with his understanding of the public's expectations of schools: "It is quite evident that for the people of Alberta the high school exists by and large as an institution for upward mobility in society. I mean by that, that parents are concerned that their children take those courses which will lead to positions in society which provide a status and income beyond the average."[49] Many Albertans in this era believed that the primary purpose of schooling was to ensure that graduates could benefit from and contribute to the affluence of the province.

In 1957, there came another reason to emphasize the importance of technical skills in Alberta's schools: the launch of Sputnik 1. The Soviet achievement came as shock to North Americans. To critics of progressive education, it was proof of the weaknesses of the progressive theories that had dominated curriculum development in North America for about twenty years. Children across North American had clearly been allowed to fall behind. Across Canada and the United States there were calls for the reform of the public school curriculum, for higher academic standards and for a strengthening of math and science education.[50] In Alberta, the province appointed Senator Donald Cameron to lead a Royal Commission on Education. The Commission had a broad mandate to investigate many issues regarding public schooling in the province, but it is significant that the first two priorities listed in the terms of reference for the Commission were curriculum programs and the attainment level of pupils.

In 1959, after many months of consultations and investigation, Cameron told his colleagues in the Senate why curriculum reform was imperative in all Canadian schools. He maintained that the country needed skilled workers not only in order to take advantage of important economic opportunities, but because the superiority of the technical training in the Soviet Union and the People's Republic of China would ensure that those countries would outpace the West in economic development. This economic superiority would then convince developing countries of the superiority of the Communist system.[51] This Cold War rhetoric was also used in the provincial legislature. Cam Kirby insisted that Alberta's school system must improve because "we are living in an age in which a battle is being waged for the minds of men. Every blandishment, every trick of sophistry, every known form of deceit employed to advance that evil thing Communism must be met by minds capable of resisting the insidious indoctrination of the mind with subversive ideas."[52]

The task of building a curriculum to ensure the economic growth of the province and to protect the hearts of students from dangerous foreign ideologies was given to a reformed General Curriculum Committee. In 1945, H.C. Newland resigned his position as Supervisor of Schools, apparently because he was passed over for promotion to Deputy Minister in favour of W.H. (Bill) Swift. Upon his departure, the positions of Supervisor of Schools and Chief Inspector were eliminated. Instead, the Chief Superintendent, working under the Deputy Minister, was given responsibility for a Division of Instruction that oversaw all activities directly related to classroom instruction. Included in the Division of Instruction were the Examinations Branch and the Curriculum Branch.

The Curriculum Branch was responsible for all curriculum development undertaken by its four advisory curriculum committees. The General Curriculum Committee oversaw the entire process of curriculum development. There were three other general committees, one for each of the three levels of schooling in the province. Subcommittees were established in order to write programs of study, suggest textbooks and propose changes in policy for specific courses or subject areas. By 1952, there were thirty-two subcommittees working under the high school, junior high school, and elementary school curriculum committees.[53]

From 1945 to 1952, the curriculum committees were composed of department officials including high school inspectors and divisional school superintendents, representatives from the Faculty of Education at the University of Alberta, school board administrators and principals from Calgary and Edmonton, and several teachers. The General Curriculum Committee also included representatives from the Alberta School Trustees' Association and the Alberta Federation of Home and School Associations. Traditionally, the Department appointed teachers nominated by the Association to the various subject-area and grade-level subcommittees. Few, if any, teachers served on the high school, junior high school, elementary or general curriculum committees. To these committees, the Association nominated prominent members, usually high school administrators; as a result, there were no practicing classroom teachers on the policy setting committees of the Curriculum Branch. This reflected the prevailing opinion, even within the profession, that teachers were not appropriately educated, nor were they suitably situated, to undertake the complex task of writing curriculum.

In the wake of the tremendous criticism of schools in the late 1940s and early 1950s, the Department restructured its curriculum committees in 1953 to include wider representation of lay groups. The official duties of the General Curriculum Committee continued to be to review and indeed to initiate proposed curriculum changes. The membership was broadened to include not only representatives from the Department, the University of Alberta, the Alberta Teachers' Association and three school superintendents, but also representatives from interested organizations like the Alberta Federation of Home and School Associations, the Alberta School Trustees' Association, the Alberta Federation of Agriculture, the Alberta Women's Institutes, the I.O.D.E., the Associated Chambers of Commerce, and the Alberta Federation of Labour. The Department hoped that by adding representation from public organizations and decreasing the academic representation, it would be better able to anticipate public criticisms. What role did these groups play in the actual construction of the course of studies?

The Department felt that the General Curriculum Committee was best used as a sounding board for curriculum initiatives that originated with Department officials. The Committee did not actively participate in curriculum development; it was restricted to an advisory role. While lay groups were occasionally asked to poll their membership regarding curricular matters, none of the issues the representatives brought back to the GCC were acted upon. The I.O.D.E. representative reported that their local organizations recommended compulsory examinations in Grades X and XI and a review of the high school courses in mathematics. The report was filed for information but never addressed at subsequent meetings. The representative from the Alberta Federation of Home and School Associations called for a return to a more traditional approach to the teaching of basic skills at the elementary school level. The issue was never included for discussion on the agenda of the GCC.

The lay groups represented on the committee recognized the limitations of their influence on curriculum development. They realized that they would have to make it clear to the public that representation on the GCC did not imply support for all the curricular initiatives of the Department of Education. In March 1955, a former vice-president of the Alberta Federation of Home and School Associations, Dr. A.G. McCalla (also Dean of Agriculture at the University of Alberta), criticized the tendency of Department officials to announce that curriculum innovations were endorsed by the lay groups represented on the committee. He told Home and School members that "the comparatively minor role we play in determining the educational program being offered our children carries with it a heavy responsibility. It is essential that we know exactly what we are asking for and why and also that we know exactly what we are being asked to endorse, or we may find ourselves credited with approving a program of which we really disapprove."⁵⁴

Publicly, educational professionals recognized the consultative role of lay groups but emphasized the need for practicing professionals to make informed curriculum decisions. In February 1956, the Faculty of Education of the University of Alberta, Calgary Branch, presented a discussion, called "Facing the Problems of Curriculum Organization," on CKUA radio. Listeners were told that the job of curriculum building was so complex that it could not be done by the Department of Education alone. The professors of Education explained the committee structure of the Department and insisted that while the General Curriculum Committee oversaw the whole process of curriculum development and ensured the support of the public, the actual writing of the programs of study was done by subcommittees for each level of schooling.⁵⁵ Listeners were assured that this specialized work was left in the hands of practicing teachers. In fact this was rarely the case.

The three subcommittees representing the three levels of schooling were composed of school administrators and dominated by Department of Education officials. The subject subcommittees, who wrote the programs and chose resources, included more teacher representatives. However, while teachers were represented on these committees, there is some indication that curriculum development was dominated by the Department officials who chose the teachers and set the agendas for the meetings.

A debate about the role of Department officials in setting curriculum erupted in the Legislative Assembly in March 1958. Liberal Opposition member Harold Tanner, a high school principal, said that teachers who disagreed with the Director of Curriculum were being removed from the senior high school curriculum committees.⁵⁶ Education Minister Anders Aalborg responded that the curriculum was not determined by the whims of individual officials. The fact remains, however, that many teachers and university professors involved with curriculum building also felt that Department officials virtually dictated policy. In this, they were not alone. They reflected a growing sense across Canada that a gap was growing between the academics who had long been part of the curriculum development process, and the officials in department bureaucracies who were making curriculum policy.

Senior officials in Departments of Education across Canada defended the practice of limiting real decision-making in curriculum development to trained educational professionals because curriculum building was seen as a "scientific" task. In the 1952 Quance Lectures at the University of Saskatchewan, H.L. Campbell, Deputy Superintendent of Education in British Columbia, argued that teachers and lay people tended to be conservative in designing curriculum. He maintained that "in these days of scientific study and research, well-trained curriculum personnel, from a central office which is able to give broad vision, has much to contribute to the building of desirable curricula."[57]

So while the Department of Education claimed to be listening to public concerns and committed to increased public involvement in the curriculum-building process, the lay organizations on curriculum committees had no real power to effect change. All the curriculum committees were dominated by officials from the Department of Education and by professors of Education from the University of Alberta. These experts defined the role of schools, the aims of education, and prepared the courses of study designed to meet those aims. To them fell the challenge of finding a middle ground between the progressivism they believed in and the traditionalism demanded by the public. They created a program intended to help students meet the challenge of building a modern, affluent and democratic province. What kind of curriculum did they create?

In 1954, Dr. W.H. Swift, Deputy Minister of Education, predicted that the next curriculum revision would be characterized by a synthesis of traditional and progressive approaches to schooling. The new program could not, however, reconcile approaches and philosophies that were essentially mutually exclusive. Instead, it addressed specific public concerns regarding the rigor of the program and teachers' complaints about clarity. The commitment of educational experts to progressive aims in education remained unchanged.

Educators involved in curriculum revision continued to insist that schools should broaden children's interests and meet the psychological and vocational needs of all children. Indeed, they defined these needs very broadly. A.L. Doucette, head of the Calgary Branch of the University of Alberta, told student teachers that "boys and girls must learn rather similar tasks, such as personal care in dressing, in keeping clean, getting along well with age-mates, learning the basic fundamental skills in school, developing a keen sense of right and wrong, behaving in a tolerant manner." He further stressed the importance of teachers' awareness of the world of modern students: "Teachers must be modern and sense that boys and girls of today are growing up in a 1953 culture of automobiles, wurlitzers, going steady, coffee parties, rumpus rooms, fraternities, petting, and bygone chaperones."[58] Clearly, progressive educators such as Doucette continued to believe that schools should help students adjust to their social world.

When the Department of Education redefined the aims of senior high school education in 1957, it identified four very broad objectives: personal development, growth in family living, growth toward competence in citizenship, and occupational preparation. Maintaining that the "prime aim of the

Deputy Minister of Education, W.S. (Bill) Swift, 1963. Provincial Archives of Alberta, A7096n.

school is to assist each Alberta youth in his growth toward maximum self-realization," the Department downplayed academic skills and emphasized the responsibility of schools to address all aspects of preparation for life. Goals that once formed the basis of the curriculum and could properly be described as intellectual, were limited to one of six subcategories under the objective of "personal development." Here the ability to think rationally, to understand the scientific method and the principles of mathematics, appeared beside "the development of suitable recreational and leisure time activities."[59]

### CITIZENSHIP AND SOCIAL STUDIES

Citizenship education as described by the Department encompassed a wide range of desirable outcomes, from "displaying democratic attitudes and behavior in all social situations" to "developing consumer competence." The belief that schools should prepare students to share in the affluent society was also reflected in the emphasis on occupational preparation. Schools were specifically directed to help students develop marketable skills and prepare for more specific vocational training.[60]

The Enterprise in elementary schools and social studies in the secondary schools remained the major vehicles for citizenship education and remained a progressive bastion within the curriculum. It was simply impossible to find a synthesis of traditional and progressive approaches in a subject area that was progressive by its very nature. The new elementary Social Studies–Enterprise program introduced in 1963 was an attempt to address public criticisms of the program, but the guide to the program clearly stated that the program "attempts to effect the changes as recommended by the Royal Commission and by the 1957 survey insofar as these changes appear practical and in line with recent research and theory."[61] The objectives of the program were quoted directly from American progressive educators James Quillen and Lavone Hanna. Policy makers, rather than transform the program, addressed the concern that social studies was not intellectually rigorous. They specified the content of the courses but the objectives remained broad in scope and often vague.

The Department provided a sequence of topics for social studies–enterprise from which teachers were free to choose. Students in Grades I and II were introduced to topics such as Our School, Our Homes and Families, or Community Helpers. Students in Grades III through VI completed four enterprises a year, one with an historical theme, one on an economic theme, one on a geographical theme, and one that emphasized the social impact of scientific and technological progress. For example, students in Grade VI completed one enterprise on an ancient civilization such as Egypt. They then turned to an economic theme such as Canadian Primary Industries or Conservation in Canada. Within the geographical theme, teachers could feature the West Indies, Indonesia, New Zealand or Portugal. Finally, students studied the development of the St. Lawrence or the Columbia River Project in order to grasp the "contributions of science to social progress in Canada and the United States."[62] The potential for the development of research skills and other important academic skills was present, but not clearly required by the curriculum. Some local school boards provided more specific direction for teachers. Edmonton Public School Board, for example, created social studies–enterprise units for all six elementary grades that were widely used and even requested by teachers throughout the province. The Edmonton Board also introduced standardized tests in social studies, science and spelling.

Grade Three students with their Jungle Enterprise, Strathearn School, Edmonton, 1954. Provincial Archives of Alberta, ws38n.

The new social studies program at the secondary level was also extremely broad in scope. Here, curriculum developers tried to emphasize the development of students' critical thinking skills within the social studies. The Department reminded teachers that the modern world required citizens that could understand the personal relevance of changes occurring around them. The secondary social studies program was redrawn around themes intended to be of interest to students and to help them understand the relevance of political and technological changes in the modern world. Most of the themes were stated as "problems" for students to solve, such as the impact of industry on our way of living, or the rise of nationalisms in the nineteenth century. The Department insisted that "this program proposes the more modern viewpoint of providing meaningful situations in which pupils must think through a series of problems. The teacher's function is to provide the meaningful situation, to set the stage, to arrange conditions so that children may learn *with understanding*."[63]

The fact remains, however, that it was extremely challenging for teachers to create meaningful and student-directed learning activities given the amount of material the new program required them to cover. The three junior high school social studies courses centred around an examination of Canada and her relationship with her neighbours. The Grade VII course covered Canadian geography; primary and secondary industries in Canada; Canadian history from New France to the early nineteenth century; the development of Western Canada; and local government. The Grade VIII course ostensibly covered Canada's role in the Commonwealth but included a wide range of material: economic development in Europe from the Middle Ages to the Industrial Revolution; the geography and political development of all Commonwealth members; the constitutional development of Great Britain from feudal times to the interwar period; and a wide-ranging examination of many institutions in Canada modeled on those in Britain, from the family to fair trade practices. The Grade IX course was the most diverse. It centred around the theme of Canada in the western hemisphere but consisted of six seemingly unrelated topics. Students learned about the physical geography of the western hemisphere. Economic and technological problems were covered through an examination of the impact of the industrial revolution on businesses, homes and community living. Historical content was included in the examination of the settlement and development of Latin America and the United States from the time of the first European settlers. Traditional civics was covered in a unit on the machinery of Canadian government and constitutional development. The course concluded with the various cultural organizations and institutions that would cultivate students' "appreciation for the beautiful and the good."[64]

The senior high school social studies courses were equally lacking in coherence. Historical topics maintained an important place in the program, but a narrative approach or chronological treatment of historical themes was strongly discouraged. The Grade X course (now Social Studies 10) included a fifteen-week unit covering the beginnings of human civilization to the fall of Rome. The other two required units were citizenship and local government, and an eight-week unit on consumer education. Teachers were then encouraged to select two other optional units out of a broad range of choices. The Grade XI course (Social Studies 20) included the Renaissance, Reformation, Scientific Revolution, Enlightenment, Rise of Nation-States and the Development of Parliamentary Democracy. Teachers were reminded to include a summary at the end of each unit that clarified the application of the concepts students had learned to the modern world. The Grade XII course remained virtually unchanged from a 1954 revision. Its examination of "Canada in the Modern World" included its geography, the nature of its trade, participation in twentieth-century conflicts, the growth of Canadian nationalism from Confederation through the creation of the modern Commonwealth, and an outline of the responsibilities of citizenship.[65] After his unsatisfactory involvement with the curriculum revision, University of Alberta historian Lewis Hertzman wrote that "the conception of social studies as imagined in the Alberta curriculum is beyond the wisdom and knowledge of an Arnold Toynbee to devise; it is beyond the capacity of a Socrates to teach."[66]

While they may not have been able to live up to the example set by Socrates, Alberta teachers did get teaching advice from the Department of Education. The Curriculum Branch advocated the use of the "unit method" of teaching. In this method, teachers were not simply to disseminate information; teachers were to guide or direct the learning process while allowing students to engage in group and individual research projects. Leaders in social studies education, such as Dr. John Chalmers and G.L. Berry, provided specific guidance for teachers implementing the new program. They advocated the use of many different teaching strategies: lectures, discussions, reading assignments and group work. They recognized the need for a wide variety of teaching materials: movable desks, chalk boards, maps, recordings, and plenty of reading material. They stressed that factual knowledge was an important element of social studies, but that the ultimate aim of the program was to use those facts to understand problems.[67] The junior high school curriculum guide specified that students should identify and plan the committee research projects most appropriate for the required unit or problem under study. It also recommended that teachers spend fifty per cent of their class time teaching formally or directly, and forty per cent using socialized procedures such as student reports, class discussions and debates. The remaining ten per cent was to be used for testing.[68]

There is some evidence that during the 1950s and 1960s, teachers were slowly incorporating some of the new techniques in their classrooms and improving their handling of old ones. In 1957, the Department of Education reported that "an improvement in enterprise instruction has been made during the past few years. Many teachers have, through experience, become more proficient in managing and carrying through class work on enterprise themes. Recent graduates of the Faculty of Education have shown good capability in developing teaching and learning situations in the enterprise field."[69] Secondary school teachers, while using a greater variety of teaching resources, continued to overemphasize factual knowledge and underemphasize understanding, according to Department officials. In 1958, High School Inspector J.C. Jonason reported that older teachers with strong academic backgrounds in one of the content fields in social studies (read "history"), and younger teachers with little academic background, tended to overemphasize the memorization of specific content rather than teach critical thinking skills.[70]

Other comments in the Department's annual reports suggest that many teachers continued to make extensive use of required textbooks in social studies classes. In 1959, Morrison Watts, Director of the Curriculum Branch,

High school instruction, Edmonton Public Schools, May 1966. Provincial Archives of Alberta, Pa3646n.

reported that the social studies curriculum had been revised to more closely mirror the primary reference book used for the course.[71] In 1960, T.C. Byrne, Chief Superintendent of Schools, praised the extensive use of community resources in social studies classes and the willingness of teachers to employ a wide range of student-centred activities. However, he acknowledged that teachers had expressed concern about the social studies courses for Grades VII and VIII because the texts did not adequately cover required course content.[72] To clarify the connection, the junior high school program published, in 1963, specified applicable textbook pages for each required problem or topic in the curriculum.[73]

In the 1960s, the first research studies were undertaken to determine exactly how social studies teachers were teaching. Researchers used teacher surveys and classroom observations to conclude that the most frequently used teaching procedures were lecturing, question and answer, class discussion and written exercises. Field trips, panels, debates and guest speakers were used least.[74]

They also noted that classroom discussions were usually centred around material presented in textbooks.[75] When A.B. Hodgetts conducted the research for his National History Project in Alberta classrooms, he commented that "[t]he situation in Alberta is compounded by the fact that social studies courses are divided into units, each with a recommended time limit. Time and again teachers from these provinces explained to us that they simply had to lecture in order to get through the course and get students through the examinations."[76] Indeed, he concluded that "The incidence of lecturing found in Alberta was 26 percent greater than the national average."[77] Despite years of teacher education, in-servicing and curriculum revisions, the textbook remained central in Alberta social studies classrooms.

The textbooks used in the 1950s and 1960s retained the reading aids and the conversational style first seen in the progressive texts of the 1930s and 1940s. Maps, charts and photographs illustrated the texts; boldface headings and questions at the end of the chapters helped students learn from text. Authors used a conversational style that they thought would appeal to children. One example illustrates this approach: the Grade VII Canadian geography text, *Canada and Her Neighbours*, was written in the form of a travelogue, following a train journey across the country. Parts of the text were written in the form of dialogues among characters. In this case, two boys explain why it is important to learn about Canada:

*John.* "What do you suppose Billy? They say we are to study Canada in Geography this year. We had such fun learning about how people live in faraway lands, and now this year we have to study Canada. I don't see what fun there can be in that. I would like to learn about China, or India, or some other country that we don't know all about anyway."

*Bill.* "But Canada, that's our *own* country; we ought to know a lot about it."[78]

But if the approach of the textbooks was still progressive, the themes related to history, identity and citizenship embodied in them changed to suit the ethos of Alberta's new, affluent, postwar society.

## THEMES IN THE "USEFUL" CURRICULUM

The curriculum of the 1950s and 1960s was dominated by the theme of utility. The public, politicians and educators still talked about creating "good" citizens, but virtue was redefined: it was equated with the skills and attitudes necessary for employment. Lee Leavitt, Social Credit M.L.A. for Banff, remarked during a debate in the Legislature about educational standards, that "the time has come when we could very well add another group of Rs to our list of fundamentals – not as a substitution but an addition: reliability, responsibility and resourcefulness would give you another three Rs and, Mr. Speaker, these three Rs represent respectable words."[79] School trustees also stressed virtues of responsibility and reliability. A. Froebel, a trustee from Lac Ste. Anne School Division, challenged the view that the purpose of schools was to develop the personalities of students. He said that "personality development is an indirect process, furthered by difficulties and a certain amount of frustration. It thrives on old fashioned virtues such as industry, neatness, a high regard for your duties, a higher regard for the other fellow's rights and the ability to concentrate."[80]

Clearly these statements reflect concern for the character of the future citizens of the province. All of the qualities politicians and educators mentioned – hard work, responsibility, reliability, persistence – are virtues. But they are the virtues that among other things, are associated with successful employment. They failed to mention qualities such as creativity, initiative and independence. Indeed they seemed to value conformity above everything else.

In 1961 Robert Warren, Superintendent of the Calgary Public School Board, explained in the *Imperial Oil Review* how his board's laggard policy – its policy for dealing with non-attending or failing students – demonstrated its commitment to creating citizens with good habits of industry and effort. He stressed the importance of preparing students for the world of work but indicated that the affluence of the province had in some ways made the job of schools more difficult. He explained that in the past few years wages had risen faster than individual productivity in the workplace so that "among many workers the 'good life' has come to mean 'more money for less work.' Getting something for nothing has become a virtue in some circles." Expelling students with poor attendance or who neglected their schoolwork was intended to emphasize the board's disapproval of the "respectability of failure."[81]

The 1963 elementary school program explicitly called on teachers to develop in students the understandings and attitudes valued by an affluent, modern society. Students were required to understand the significance of "man's increasing knowledge of social development and social control," and "man's increasing control over nature." They were further required to develop attitudes of "self-control – marked by control, discipline and direction through his own initiative," and "social concern – marked by earnest effort to implement whatever desirable ends his group may seek."[82]

In 1964 the Director of Curriculum, Morrison Watts, identified the trends apparent in the school curriculum in Alberta. In addition to the cultivation of good work habits, Watts singled out the utility of high school programs for special consideration. He said that the emphasis on utility was reflected in the greater number of technical and vocational courses available, in the growth in second language programs and in the inclusion of consumer education in the social studies curriculum.[83]

The "usefulness" of knowledge was a dominant theme in the social studies. The consumer education unit in Social Studies 10 mentioned by Watts introduced students to practical skills such as making a budget and familiarized them with the meaning and use of credit. The Grade VIII social studies course introduced students to practical topics such as the nature of banking and emphasized the virtues associated with employment. Students were specifically required to develop understandings or appreciations such as pride in work, acceptance of trade unions, and the responsibility of management for the welfare of workers.[84] Topics or problems were included in the program only if they could prove their social utility or relevance. Historical content, for example, was included if it would help students solve problems, problems that were often philosophical or political in nature. It was not treated as an exciting story and of intrinsic interest to children. Like the 1935 progressive revision, history within the social studies was not seen as an inquiry through which students might define themselves. It only provided factual information that might be useful in the discussion of current issues.

For example, the writers of one of the required texts on ancient history used in Grade X asked students, "Is all effort to make the world a better place quite useless? Or is the world, in spite of temporary setbacks, becoming better and standing now on the threshold of a brighter future than has been known before? The story of the past helps to provide an answer."[85] Authors tried to demonstrate the relevance of historical study by drawing parallels between the events covered and present day conditions. Another ancient history text compared ancient Sparta with Nazi Germany.[86] University of Alberta Classics professor W.G. Hardy, in his ancient history text, asked students to "Explain how the empires such as the Assyrian or the Persian tended to eliminate differences between peoples. To what extent has World War II led to the same result?"[87]

The Grade XI text explained that the study of history would help students understand why recent wars happened and understand the tensions that threaten world security. The Grade XII text assured students that in a young country like Canada, history increases in importance the closer you get to the present day. In other words, recent history is the most relevant history.

In addition to the theme of utility or relevance, social studies courses and resources stressed the importance of cooperation, in history and in the modern world. Cooperation had been a theme in citizenship education after World War I, but there was a new urgency in the tone of textbooks used in this period as authors called for greater understanding among all groups to avert another, potentially cataclysmic, global conflict.

J.W. Chafe and Arthur Lower, in their Canadian history text, identified the cooperation of French and English as a hallmark of Canadian history. They acknowledged the differences between the two cultures, but stressed the unique political solutions that emerged when the two peoples cooperated. After outlining the attempts of reformers to modify the colonial government of the early nineteenth century, for example, Chafe and Lower concluded that "their solution, a compound of English and French persistence, tolerance, compromise and statesmanship, they called Responsible Government."[88] They attributed conflicts such as the conscription crisis to differences in attitude and culture; they celebrated conciliators such as Baldwin, LaFontaine, Cartier, Macdonald and Laurier.

*The Story of Canada*, used in Grade VII, maintained that the generous treatment of the French by the British after the Conquest set the pattern for the tolerance that would characterize their relationship in the decades to follow. The authors' criticism of Lord Durham reflected the lesson students were intended to learn from Canadian history: "Lord Durham failed to understand how deeply French Canadians cherish their own speech and ways. To-day, we realize that Canadians, even though they speak different languages, can get along together if they will try to understand each other's point of view."[89] Their emphasis on the lessons of tolerance and cooperation in Canadian history presumably accounts for their failure to include examples of many conflicts that have marked Canadian history: the treatment of aboriginal people, the Winnipeg General Strike, the Japanese internment, to name a few.

Canada's historical relationship with Great Britain and its role in the Commonwealth were also celebrated as examples of cooperation among nations and mutual respect. Some traces of the earlier "Anglocentric" emphasis in the curriculum remained. The Social Studies 20 course required that students understand parliamentary democracy as Britain's great contribution to world civilization.[90] W.D. McDougall's text on the Commonwealth stressed the liberating influence of British rule in the colonies and portrayed imperialists such as Cecil Rhodes as visionaries and men of peace. He told students that "if the Commonwealth continues to be a symbol of freedom and justice to all men throughout the world you and your generation will not have played an insignificant or ignoble role upon the stage of history."[91]

The most significant example of cooperation was, according to textbook authors of the Cold War era, Canada's close relationship with the United States. Across Canada in the 1950s, American content in geography, history and social studies courses increased significantly.[92] These courses stressed Canada's identity as a member of the community of American nations. Geography courses in the intermediate or junior high school included an examination of the physical regions of the United States and their industries. In history, the traditional British history courses declined in favour of an examination of western civilization and courses in North American history. In western Canada, new courses moved away from Canada's historic connection to Britain and emphasized her modern role as a member of the community of American nations. Even in Grade VIII, a year given to the study of the British Commonwealth, students were required to consider the United States' relationship with the Commonwealth and how British influence on Canada was modified because of its proximity to the U.S.. In the intermediate and senior grades, textbook authors stressed the importance of Canada's relationship with the United States in its evolution as a nation. George Brown explained that in his book, "a serious attempt has been made to correlate the story of our own country with that of the United States, and to impart sympathetic understanding of our relations with our neighbour."[93]

The courses and texts detailed the many disputes about borders, fisheries and trade that had characterized Canada's relationship with her neighbour in the past, but authors asserted that the lesson to learn from such conflicts was that disputes could be solved peacefully through cooperation. A Grade XII text on contemporary world problems asserted that "the tradition of a peaceful adjustment of disputes is now so well established that any other course is unthinkable."[94] A Grade IX text included a lengthy chapter on historic disagreements between Canada and the United States. The author, however, was careful to downplay the seriousness of these disputes:

Perhaps what has been said in the preceding pages will have left you with the impression that during the hundred years following the American Revolution, Canadians and Americans were scarcely on speaking terms. Such a picture is far from true.... Canadians were going to the United States to live, and Americans were crossing the border to settle in Canada. The occasional outbursts of ill-feeling were much like the backyard spats which occur between neighbors, something like the happenings between Dagwood and Woodley in the cartoon *Blondie*, but on a more dignified level.[95]

The texts celebrated the cooperative efforts of the North Atlantic alliance during World War II and stressed Canada's continuing role as mediator between the United States and Great Britain. They were careful to include photographs of Canadian Prime Minister King standing between Churchill and Roosevelt. Texts by Brown and by Chafe and Lower described Canada as "the child of divorced parents" who reminds them of the importance of their historic and current relationship.[96]

That Canada was ready to play a role in maintaining global cooperation was also addressed in social studies in this period. The role of world organizations, such as the United Nations, in that process was more contentious. According to the Department of Education, students were required to study the work of the United Nations in the class time devoted to the discussion of current events. A significant portion of the Social Studies 30 course consisted of a study of conflict in the twentieth century and the role of world organizations in those conflicts. A conflict about the nature of these organizations flared up in the provincial legislature and indicated the high emotional pitch of discussions about Canada's place in the world.

In March 1954, Conservative M.L.A. Paul Bracken quoted anti–United Nations statements in Social Credit publications and he expressed concern over remarks made by Social Credit M.L.A. W.E. Cain. Cain was reported to have said that he would use "every power he had to see that reference to the United Nations is removed from the textbooks over the province."[97] Cain asserted that Social Crediters were "opposed to the infiltration of Communist ideas and the infiltration by Communists of high posts in the UN governments and educational institutions." He added, "it is the duty of every man in here to expose Red infiltration."[98] Politicians such as Cain seemed to associate the message of cooperation and tolerance in many textbooks with being soft on Communism. In reality, most texts emphasized the threat to world peace posed by Communism and stressed the need for security.

The Social Studies 30 program defined the point of view teachers should take in their treatment of world security issues in the classroom:

The search for security is man's major problem in the twentieth century. A half century of warfare and competitive struggle for power has brought mankind to the edge of an abyss – a void filled with the horrors of self-destruction. Weapons of war have become fearful agents of self-annihilation. Modern science has explored and conquered secrets of nature that will require man's noblest efforts to control for the common good. The politics of power have been removed from the area of national self-interest, they operate now at a level that involves the existence of mankind.[99]

High school texts addressed the precarious nature of world peace and clearly advocated the establishment of effective world government. In contrast to the textbooks used during the progressive era, Chafe and Lower provided a relatively pessimistic view of the future:

So far man has misused almost every gift that science has given him, wresting it to purposes of destruction. Today, with the atomic bomb, he is like a child going about with a loaded revolver. Will he develop restraint enough to prevent his firing it off and killing himself? Not unless he can organize peace through some form of world government. The clashing sovereignties of the great world powers can only mean more war, and more war can only mean mankind's destruction.[100]

The positive view of science, the belief that technology could provide answers for man's problems, appeared less and less in school texts in this period. The decline of the myth of the infallibility of science is one of the most striking characteristics of the curriculum of this period.

The Grade XII textbook, *Canada in the Modern World*, explained what impact the spread of Communism would have on Canada. Edgar McInnis described Communist expansion in southeast Asia, the Middle East and Latin America. He identified the danger to Canada of the 1954 Communist infiltration of Guatemala: "The danger lies not in the power of any American republic to commit aggression, but in the possibility of involving the Rio Pact nations in a hemisphere struggle that would give the other half of the world over to Communist infiltration and domination."[101]

Educators took up the call for citizenship education that would protect children from Communism. Frank Baer of the Calgary Branch of the University of Alberta wrote in the *A.T.A. Magazine*, "Today, when we are engaged in an ideological war of a magnitude unknown to previous generations, we must indoctrinate our pupils with the fundamentals of democracy and seize every opportunity provided by our studies to make those fundamentals lucid and to juxtapose them with the intolerable ideologies of non-democratic countries and communities."[102] Statements like these became representative of the renewed debate about the nature of democracy and the role of social studies in educating students for citizenship in a democracy.

The progressive notion of democracy as a "state of mind" still appeared among educators. The Edmonton Public School Board, for example, stressed the need for children to experience democracy through cooperative learning, particularly through enterprise work.[103] High schools often emphasized the importance of student councils in giving students experience in democratic citizenship. Generally, however, the approach to education for democracy in the late 1950s and 1960s was more "hard-nosed" than the experiential approach of the progressive era.

V. Gable, writing in the *A.T.A. Magazine*, attacked the progressive idea that democracy must be lived, not learned: "What unmitigated cant and idiotic nonsense! ... Democracy is a form of government with certain fixed essential principles, and certain simple but indispensable procedures which citizens must perform to make it function successfully. The most disastrous fault of education has been its failure to recognize and teach these procedures!'"[104] He rejected the teaching of ancient and medieval history in "this disturbed and dangerous world" and advocated instead teaching about the machinery of government and the responsibilities of citizenship.

The elementary school curriculum reflected a "tougher" approach to democratic education. It no longer accepted the progressive view of democracy as cooperation; it stressed the free market of ideas and the need for students to be prepared to make difficult decisions. The curriculum guide explained that

[t]o participate in the decision making process, citizens will need skills which will enable them to deal quickly with difficult problems. They will need to be able to think clearly and to evaluate critically, while potential leaders battle for control of men's minds and emotions. They will need to be able to distinguish between emotional persuasion and intellectual reason. They must be able to do logical thinking and since this can only come with practice it must begin early.[105]

Despite the call for the development of critical thinking skills, however, the curriculum reflected a very traditional approach to civics education. Units outlining the purpose and structure of government and the responsibilities of citizenship were included in every year from Grade VII to XI. Their emphasis on the machinery of government and the importance of conformity offered few opportunities for debate and critical thinking. Instead, civics education seemed to reflect a concern for the fragility of democracy, as if students could not be trusted to develop habits of democratic citizenship and still think critically. In the 1950s and 1960s, educators were no longer so convinced that democracy was the natural outcome of history, that communities would naturally be led to democratic, progressive regimes. The curriculum reflected the growing conviction that only people who conducted themselves appropriately could adequately defend democracy. In this sense, the curriculum incorporated some echoes from the past.

The curriculum called specifically for students to cultivate good taste and good manners. For example, the Grade IX social studies curriculum required students to develop an "appreciation for the beautiful and the good." Teachers were reminded to introduce students to the improving cultural opportunities available at their local art galleries and museums; students were expected to understand beauty expressed through art, music, drama and literature.

The issue of religion in schools was raised again. In the 1950s and 1960s, there was a kind of Christian ethos in the curriculum, but the teaching of religion remained a contentious issue. Despite considerable pressure from religious groups to mandate Bible teaching for credit in schools, Premier Manning and his Social Credit government left religious instruction to the discretion of the school boards. The Edmonton Public School Board, for example, limited religious instruction to the last period of the day once a week. Only teachers were allowed to provide this instruction, and they were directed to books of Bible stories approved by the Board. Teachers were also allowed to open the school day with a reading, without explanation or comment, from the approved books, and were allowed to recite the Lord's Prayer.[106] Many schools in the province began the day with scripture readings and the Lord's Prayer.

While specific religious instruction was rejected, the curriculum did make references to the importance of a spiritual dimension in schools. The 1963 Program of Studies for elementary schools identified behavioural goals each child should reach. Under the category of "Attitudes" was "Reverence – marked by a conviction of Diety [sic], and a regard for His supreme handiwork, mankind."[107] The Grade VIII social studies program included a study of a variety of western traditions, including "Christian Traditions: (1) Sunday observance as a day of rest and recreation; (2) Respect for the Christian Church; (3) Freedom of religion."[108]

The senior high school curriculum was also intended to foster respect for the Christian tradition, but became less explicitly Christian from the mid-1950s to the 1960s. The 1955 curriculum included a Grade X unit of study on "The Christian Church and its Contributions to Our Civilization."[109] By 1962, the texts used in classrooms tended to emphasize the role of religion generally, and Christianity in particular, in fostering a sense of cooperation and responsibility for the community. In the words of the authors of the Grade X text, "the spirit of true religion is a power that could bind together all peoples, and make all men brothers."[110]

Clearly, religion in the public schools continued to be seen as Bishop Carroll had described it in the 1930s: as the bond between men rather than an understanding of man's relationship with God. However, the curriculum probably reflected public opinion in its emphasis on religion and morality as social forces. In 1959, the Cameron Commission reported that public schools should inculcate basic values such as "honesty, truthfulness, integrity, self-discipline and reliability."[111] These values were described as "basic" precisely because of their social utility. Notable for their absence were virtues such as temperance, fortitude or humility, virtues which occasionally put individuals at odds with social expectations or which define the individual's relationship with God.

The theme of "utility" in the school curriculum of the 1950s and 1960s was a reflection of the anxieties of the period. Educators, politicians and the public were concerned that Alberta be prepared for technological and ideological competition. Themes in social studies education such as the cooperative nature of Canadian society and its historic relationship with the United States were intended to define the country's role in the new global order. Students learned about the machinery of democracy so they would be able to resist the ideological inroads of totalitarianism.

Ultimately, the schools reflected the belief of educators and of the public that the best defence of the Canadian way of life was to prepare students to take advantage of the economic opportunities available in a prosperous society. Students were treated as future workers. The virtues associated with conformity and hard work were stressed. Students were expected to develop attitudes and skills that would help them contribute to and share in the affluence of the post-war society.

Toward the end of the 1960s, these conservative messages about citizenship were, however, delivered within the context of school systems that were increasingly experimental. Vocational programs and technical education had grown enormously throughout the province. The semester system had been introduced in high schools to give students greater flexibility in programming. School culture had become much less authoritarian. Dress codes were dropped, behavioural expectations relaxed. Mathematics and science courses had undergone major reforms. New courses in Family Life and new programs in drug education were introduced. Large school boards like Edmonton Public Schools experimented with a new kindergarten program and introduced the "Continuous Progress Plan" into elementary schools to allow children to advance at their own rate rather than to complete a specific grade at a specific pace.

Within the context of this kind of experimentation and flexibility, conservative messages about virtue, citizenship and identity in the curriculum seemed out of date. Schools that emphasized conformity were seen as institutions of social control. Again, there were calls for curriculum reforms that would prepare children for the future, a future increasingly defined by the need for people able to adapt easily and quickly to a rapidly changing political and social landscape.

# 5

## CITIZENSHIP AS SELF-ACTUALIZATION: NEOPROGRESSIVISM IN THE 1970S

When Ernest Manning retired in 1968, he accepted appointments to the boards of directors of many corporations, including a national bank. This symbolized the transformation of Social Credit, or at least of Manning, from an advocate of economic radicalism to the champion of free enterprise. He won seven elections because he was recognized as a trustworthy steward of the province's resources. Albertans supported his government's policy of encouraging private-sector investment, largely American, in the province's oil and gas industries. He opposed the federal government's expansion of social welfare programs, but presided over a provincial government that spent more than the national average on social services. He had an intuitive sense and real skill in leading the province's economic modernization of the 1950s and 1960s. However, he remained a social conservative and within the context of the late 1960s, his opposition to Sunday openings of movie theatres and the liberalization of liquor laws seemed out of date.

Albertans in the late 1960s were ready for change. Baby boomers, now emerging from colleges and universities, were tired of being governed by a rural and conservative party. By 1966, 69 per cent of Albertans lived in urban centres. Edmonton and Calgary were the country's fastest-growing cities. The Social Credit government, still dominated by rural representatives and rural attitudes, seemed unwilling to accommodate the fiscal demands, and political demands, of city governments.[1]

The Social Credit government made some attempts to speak to the concerns of groups within the province who felt they were the victims of injustice. In 1966, they passed the Alberta Human Rights Act. Critics correctly pointed out that the act was entirely symbolic and a variety of groups continued to press for recognition. Aboriginal people challenged racist laws and attitudes. Feminist writers and activists pointed out how sexist attitudes limited the educational and professional opportunities available to women. In 1968, many Albertans supported the election of new Liberal Prime Minister Pierre Trudeau, who had made his reputation as Justice Minister by liberalizing divorce laws and decriminalizing abortion and homosexuality.

In 1971, Albertans elected a new Progressive Conservative government more in tune with its urban, middle-class and secular leanings. Under the leadership of Premier Peter Lougheed, the province went through a decade-long boom as a result of high worldwide oil prices. The province became the wealthiest in Canada, with the highest per capita income in the country and a GDP that grew from just under $8 billion to $47.2 billion by 1981.[2] The economic boom attracted people from all over Canada and the world. Changes in federal immigration law in 1967 meant that the province now welcomed people from many parts of the world: China, South Asia, Korea, the West Indies and Latin America, to name a few. Alberta became not only multicultural, but increasingly multiracial.

Along with increased wealth for the province came an increasingly acrimonious relationship with the federal government. The 1970s and 1980s were characterized by a series of disputes between the provincial Conservative government and the federal government. Federal Liberal initiatives on bilingualism, metrication and the patriation of the Constitution were relatively unpopular with Albertans. Liberal energy policies were extraordinarily unpopular. Together, they gave rise to a sense of western alienation that differed from earlier conflicts with the federal government in that the province had the wealth and confidence to defend its interests vigorously.

Despite the provincial government's insistence that federal energy pricing policies deprived the province of billions of dollars, the Conservative government spent lavishly on attempts to diversity the province's economy, on cultural and recreational facilities, and on research and education. In its willingness to finance expansion of educational facilities and programs, it continued a trend that had already been established for decades.

The 1960s had seen an enormous expansion of school facilities and programming. New elementary schools were built with large, open areas to facilitate "open learning," groups of students sitting at tables working cooperatively on projects often supervised by teams of teachers. In order to stem the tide of students dropping out at Grade X, new programs were introduced at the junior high school level. In contrast to the comprehensive high schools created in the 1950s, new junior high schools, such as Van Horne and Shaughnessy in Calgary, provided only the specialized "Junior-Academic Vocational Program" for students who were not succeeding in the more traditional academic program. Traditional ideas about gender roles determined students' curricular path. Boys were directed into carpentry or small motor repair while girls took courses in beauty culture and child care. Both were provided with an academic training suitable for their future employment, at least the employment path their guidance counsellors had determined was most appropriate for them.

The emphasis on vocational preparation also had a huge impact on courses available at the senior high school level. In fact, throughout the 1960s, the federal government provided special funding for the expansion of vocational programs through the Technical and Vocational Training Assistance Act. Vocational high schools such as James Fowler were built with federal financial assistance. Composite high schools were able to offer courses in everything from cosmetics to electricity. When the funding came to an end at the end of the decade, however, the programs remained.[3]

Vocational programs, the new libraries, theatres, specialized facilities for music and art teaching, athletic equipment, and outdoor education programs were all very expensive to provide. So was an educational bureaucracy that grew enormously in order to take on responsibilities for curriculum policy, implementation and evaluation. School boards increased school taxes and spoke often about the need for increased funding for schools. Increasingly, politicians and the public were wondering just where the money was going and what exactly was going on in schools. When the Social Credit government appointed Walter Worth to lead a Commission on Educational Planning in 1969, it surveyed the changes that had already happened in education, and attempted to provide direction for reforms to come.

Alberta was not alone in Canada in undertaking a major study of its education system. Between 1960 and 1970, every province in the country examined its systems of elementary, secondary and post-secondary schooling. Quebec and Newfoundland completed studies that recommended modernization and resulted in the gradual secularization of their school systems. Ontario's 1968 Hall-Dennis Report supported the development of a huge range of educational programs designed to meet the needs of all learners, of every age, every interest and every ability. Its focus on child-centred instruction signaled an attempt to revive the progressives' ideas about the nature of children, schools and society.[4]

Alberta's Commission report, released in 1972 and usually referred to as the Worth Report, echoed many of the themes of the Hall-Dennis Report. It described two possible scenarios for the province's future. One was called the "Second-Phase Industrial Society" and was characterized by the continued expansion of the production and consumption of goods and a social hierarchy with the need for conformity that would support that growth. Education in this scenario would be dominated by preparation for work and authoritarian teaching strategies. The other, clearly preferred by the Commission, was the "Person-Centred Society." This society would subordinate the needs of the industrial system to the human need for self-fulfillment. In this society, technology would be directed by human needs, not industrial needs. More time would be given to leisure and the healthy pursuit of self-actualization. Education would be a life-long process. Schools would put less emphasis on credentials and grading, and more on facilitating "self-learning skills."[5]

The Commission made a huge range of recommendations covering everything from early childhood education to post-secondary education. It suggested reforms to all areas of education: curriculum development, program delivery, student evaluation, teacher education, teacher remuneration, education financing, school choice, and educational technology. One major impact on school curriculum came in its emphasis on "valuing" and the importance of helping students consider alternative values rather than simply accepting traditional morality. Another important element was its insistence that the future could be shaped and planned according to a specific design. While the progressives of a previous generation had been optimists in their belief that schools could reshape society to address social ills, the neoprogressives represented by Worth's report were utopians. They insisted that schools could equip citizens to solve the problems of society, even the world, and provide all individuals with an avenue for self-fulfillment that would last a lifetime. Not surprisingly, this was a vision that dominated educational policy more in terms of rhetoric than reality. But the community of social studies educators in the province had been busy for several years already revising curriculum and creating resources grounded in their understanding of the "New Social Studies," an approach that they thought would help children consider alternative values and shape a better global future. When the Worth Report was released in 1972, it reported that a social studies curriculum revision was already well underway. In this sense, the Report with its emphasis on alternative values and reconstructing the future reflected rather than initiated the fundamentally new understanding of citizenship and history education within social studies.

## THE "NEW SOCIAL STUDIES"

In the late 1960s as curriculum revisions in social studies began in Alberta, educators across North America were trying to implement the "New Social

Studies." This was an approach to social studies teaching that drew on the ideas of Americans Jerome Bruner and Edwin Fenton among others. Bruner developed a psychological and educational rationale for a more intellectually demanding curriculum at a time when American education was being criticized for its lack of rigor. He argued that the process of thinking is essentially the same regardless of the level of thought or the age of the thinker. For example, the child solving problems in mathematics class is engaged in essentially the same process as the mathematics scholar. That process, he said, is defined by the structure of the discipline.

Bruner applied his understanding of the structure of knowledge to the improvement of teaching and curriculum. He argued that children must be introduced to the structure of the disciplines. They could only learn mathematics by learning the structure of mathematical principles; they could only learn science by becoming scientists and engaging in scientific inquiry. A curriculum that taught children to think for themselves, that allowed children to use the methods of disciplined inquiry to explore concepts in all domains, was the only curriculum that could truly create rational citizens. Bruner's theory was particularly attractive to curriculum reformers seeking to restore academic rigor to mathematics and science programs in the late 1950s. As Canadian curriculum historian George Tomkins indicates, Bruner's book, *The Process of Education*, became "a manifesto that set the terms of curriculum debate through the 1960s" as every province took up the challenge to implement "discovery learning."[6] Alberta revised its mathematics and science curricula in the 1950s according to American models of inquiry-based programs.[7]

Educators in English, History and the social sciences found Bruner's ideas challenging to implement. Northrop Frye, who chaired a joint committee of the Toronto School board and the University of Toronto to revise curricula, was unconvinced of the relevance of Bruner's theories because of the difficulty in defining the structure of disciplines like English.[8] The advocates of the New Social Studies, too, faced a considerable challenge in determining the structure of the discipline of social studies. Social studies incorporated many different disciplines: history, geography, economics, sociology, political science and anthropology, among others.

Edwin Fenton, a historian by academic background, not only wrote extensively about the theory of the New Social Studies; with the support and financing of the Carnegie Institute of Technology, he also developed curriculum materials used in schools that helped teachers put the new inquiry-based teaching into practice. In his book, *The New Social Studies*, he stated that schools must aim to prepare students to live in the future and, given the pace of social, economic and technological change, this meant that schools needed to teach children how to continue learning for the rest of their lives: "[U]nless students also learn a method of inquiry, they cannot continue to learn independently once the classroom door shuts behind them for the last time."[9] He argued that in order for students to learn the structure of a discipline, they must understand the concepts and generalizations central to the discipline, and the process by which those concepts are developed or proven.[10] Accordingly, in one of the experimental teaching units he and his colleagues designed, students were led through an inquiry into the nature of history as a discipline before embarking on a year-long examination of the origins of western civilization. The inquiry unit required students to read a wide variety of primary and secondary sources in order to discover how historians classify information, how they hypothesize, how they cope with the tentative and interpretative nature of historical facts, how they determine valid and appropriate research questions, and how they appreciate the unfamiliar mentality of people of such different times.[11] In other words, students were led to complex and penetrating conclusions about the nature of historical inquiry before being asked to apply those conclusions to their further study.

Bruner's and Fenton's approaches were taken up by Alberta teacher educator Evelyn Moore, who taught at the University of Alberta and the University of Calgary in the 1970s. She coauthored *Teaching the Subjects in the Social Studies* with University of Victoria's Edward E. Owen. They stated the purpose of their handbook clearly in the Introduction: "[W]hat distinguishes this handbook from other works is that the authors accept, as a major purpose of the social studies, that elementary school children should begin to learn the thinking patterns, or the structure, of the social sciences."[12] The handbook went on to provide a sound theoretical grounding and examples of the practical application of the inquiry approach in the teaching of geographical and historical concepts to young children. After a detailed introduction to historiography and a review of the thinking skills crucial to historical inquiry, Moore and Owen provide a long list of resources and materials useful in the teaching of history: names of historic sites and museums for field study; local archives and other sources of primary documents and historical artifacts and photographs for children to use to gather data; names of historical paintings and sources of historical maps that would be useful for children to interpret; important titles of historical narratives and periodicals that teachers should consult for further information. Their suggested teaching strategies emphasized the "doing of history" rather than the "reading about history" so common in elementary school classrooms. Teachers were encouraged to have students read letters, diaries and journals of historical figures, to conduct interviews with grandparents and elders, to engage in role play and simulation exercises, and to make timelines to demonstrate change over generations. While some of the questions for inquiry they suggested were relatively traditional – "How will Wolfe invade Quebec?" for example – they provided active and challenging teaching strategies that would make history meaningful and relevant for young children.

However, other theorists were not as convinced of the central role the discipline of history should play within the New Social Studies. They did not see the study of the past as an appropriate focus for social studies instruction. Americans Byron G. Massialas and C. Benjamin Cox, in *Inquiry in Social Studies*, listed five major areas of conflict in the United States and globally that schools urgently needed to address: racial conflict; crime and delinquency; family disorganization (i.e., the increasing divorce rate); the need for government involvement in social affairs to solve problems with urbanization, public health and so on; and world social problems such as the population explosion and the nuclear arms race.[13] They stressed that in its commitment to solving these problems, "social studies today incorporates more concepts and data from the social sciences and fewer from history."[14] While history was descriptive, the social sciences were analytical. Only inquiry into social issues through the social studies could prepare students to take on the task of "progressive reconstruction" that changing values and social divisions had made imperative. They argued that "the single, most important goal of education should be the reflective examination of values and issues of current import," and of all subjects in the school curriculum, only the social studies could speak to that goal.

As Alberta educators grappled with social studies curriculum revision, they consulted American leaders in the New Social Studies and debated the relative importance of history vis-à-vis the social sciences in social studies. Frank Simon, a teacher at Victoria Composite High School in Edmonton who became involved in writing the new program, asked, "Can history teach students how to think?" In essence, he answered, "No." Citing American historian Henry Steele Commager's acknowledgement of the tentative and interpretative nature of historical facts, Simon concluded that history as a discipline was therefore unreliable and its conclusions invalid. The only intellectually sound basis for the social studies in his view was obviously the social sciences: "[T]he curtain is being rapidly drawn on the teaching of lore. The basic ingredient of the social studies curriculum of tomorrow will be *process*, the process of social science, our most effective means of preparing students how to think and do in the realm of human behaviour."[15]

Other Alberta educators went one step further and clearly distinguished between the process of the social sciences and the nature of social studies as a school subject. G.L. Berry, head of the Department of Secondary Education at the University of Alberta, clarified the distinction between the nature and purpose of the social sciences and the social studies in his book, *Problems and Values*:

Each of the latter [i.e., the social sciences] undertakes the formal organization of large bodies of knowledge in a particular subject or discipline, but, like all the sciences, they are concerned with seeking factual truth, that is, with the discovery and definition of existing situations. They do not consider the value question at all. They do not ask, "What ought the situation to be?" or "What is desirable?" Such questions of value cannot and should not be avoided in the school. Indeed, they enhance the significance of the social studies in the school program, providing an opportunity to discuss the social environment in which we live.[16]

For Berry, the focus of the social studies had to be on clarifying the values upon which social, economic and political decisions were made. Only by defining their own values and appreciating the validity of others' could students be prepared to tackle the serious issues facing the globe and guide appropriate social change. Half of Berry's book, an introduction to the design of the senior high school social studies course, explained the nature of values and value systems. He concluded with a call for the development of modern systems of values for western societies currently seeing the consequences of widespread anomie in the disintegration of families and widespread drug use among youth.

The new direction of Alberta social studies was set by a conference sponsored by the Department of Education in June 1967. The Department was already in the midst of a revision of the Social Studies 30 course with the notable cooperation of members of the Faculty of Arts at the University of Alberta. The success of that revision along the lines of an inquiry-based, process-oriented curriculum, and the decision of the provincial Social Studies Council of the A.T.A. to develop their own curriculum framework, motivated Department leaders to embark on a more general revision.[17] Morrison Watts and J.S.T. Hrabi, his successor as Director of Curriculum, invited twenty representatives from the Department of Education, the universities, board administrators and social studies department heads or coordinators to attend the two-week meeting. Byron Massialas was invited to address the conference four times and the recommendations that emerged clearly indicated the acceptance of his vision of social studies.

Dr. T.C. Byrne, Deputy Minister of Education, opened the conference with an address in which he signaled his willingness to oversee profound change in social studies education. He applauded the current interest in pupil inquiry but seemed to downplay the academic rigor implied by Bruner's structure-of-the-disciplines approach to the New Social Studies. Instead, he "argued the desirable social studies curriculum should be discovery-oriented and should focus on issues that are real to students."[18] He suggested drugs and urbanization as examples of such issues.

The Conference made a wide range of recommendations for the new social studies program: it should be problems-oriented with a focus on inquiry into social issues; content in courses should not be mandatory but left to the discretion of the teacher to develop with input from students; no textbooks should be prescribed; help should be provided teachers in the form of collaboration with university departments and the development of appropriate resources.[19] All of these recommendations were taken seriously by the educators who went on to design the new program. The so-called "Committee of Five"[20] that was delegated by the Department's Social Studies Coordinating Subcommittee to write the program used four sources: the recommendations of the June Conference, curriculum guides from the United States, the yearbooks of the National Council of the Social Studies, and the writings of Massialas and Fenton.[21] All of these influences were obvious when the new program emerged.

## NEW CURRICULUM FOR A NEW ERA

The neoprogressive curriculum, introduced in 1971, grew out of the belief among educational leaders in the Department of Education and the faculties of Education that students must be prepared to solve global problems. It also reflected their conviction that the social issues of the day could only be addressed by citizens with appropriate values. The aim of the new curriculum, therefore, became the development of students' value systems. It was not intended to inculcate in students values acceptable to the community; it was to enable students to discover their own belief system through the process of "values clarification."

The "valuing process" adopted by the new program came from *Values and Teaching* by Americans Louis Raths, Merrill Harmin and Sydney Simon.[22] They argued that the greatest problems facing American society were the apathy of citizens in general and the lack of direction among youth in particular. They insisted that the purpose of life could only be discovered through a clear set of values, so the task of schools should be to help students discover their values and thereby determine a purpose in life and come to a sense of self-fulfillment. They said that students who were used to having values imposed upon them failed to develop qualities of rational judgment. Schools needed to teach students a process by which they could weigh alternatives and determine their values. They called this process "values clarification." *Values and Teaching* outlined the process of values clarification by breaking the process into steps the authors described as choosing, prizing and behaving. This process became the basis of the new social studies program. Students were expected to choose a set of values after identifying the various alternatives, prize those values and then act upon their choices.

The new program specifically required teachers to use a problem-solving approach. The disciplines – particularly the social sciences – were the tools students were to use to solve problems: "[T]he Brunerian influence of the structure of the disciplines had an impact, but not to the extent that the discipline itself became the primary concern.... [T]he disciplines relevant to the solving of the problem were relegated to instruments with which the student attempted to gain insight into the nature of the problem and with which he endeavoured to solve that problem."[23]

The emphasis on problem-solving was certainly not new to Alberta social studies; indeed, it had been central to the thinking of the generation of educationalists who had created the original social studies program. That investigation and problem-solving had succeeded to some extent in penetrating elementary classrooms was confirmed by the fact that the educators responsible for the creation of the neoprogressive program simply reaffirmed their commitment to the Enterprise. Despite Evelyn Moore's insistence on a strong foundation for the elementary program in the concepts and processes of history and geography, the decision was made to go "interdisciplinary rather than multidisciplinary."[24]

Elementary social studies content was very vague; one-third of classroom time was left unstructured so that teachers could pursue inquiries of interest to the children. The required scope and sequence was organized according to the "expanding horizons" approach. Students in Grade One studied families, their own as well as those of other cultures and other countries. In Grade Two, students examined the nature of neighbourhoods, including rural and urban neighbourhoods and those in other cultures. In Grade Three, the content expanded outward again to include the comparison and contrast of students' own communities with unique communities in Canada such as the "Eskimo" (i.e., Inuit) and Hutterites, and with others around the world. In Grade Four, the historical, economic and geographic nature of Alberta was contrasted with similar areas around the world. Suggestions included Australia, Argentina, the U.S.S.R., the oil-producing regions of the Middle East and the western U.S.A. In Grade Five, students examined contemporary life in Canadian regions through case studies such as "people in an Atlantic fishing port" or "people in a French-Canadian mining town." Teachers here were free to include some historical background in their case studies. Students in Grade

Six undertook an anthropological analysis and social history of the "Roots of Man." They examined case studies of ancient civilizations in the Mediterranean, the Far East, the Americas and Africa.[25] The "internationalist" ethos of the program was intentional. The Worth Report applauded the new program for its recognition of the diverse, multiethnic nature of Canada.[26] Writers of the new program defended the structure of the topics that required children to consistently compare and contrast life in Canada with life in "non-western" communities because this would lead to greater international understanding and the recognition that all people share an identity as global problem-solvers. C.D. Ledgerwood, the leader of the curriculum writing team, asserted that "our international homogeneity is a product of the problems faced by all mankind."[27] He felt that students should to be taught to see themselves as part of this global, problem-solving community.

The secondary program had even less Canadian content. Though the program called for one-third of class time to be spent on "problems of current interest," there is little evidence that this actually happened. The scope and sequence of topics realistically gave little extra time for these projects driven by student interest. In Grade Seven, students examined case studies of "primitive, pre-industrial societies."[28] In Grade Eight, they considered Man, Technology and Culture in Afro-Asian societies using case studies selected from Africa, Asia, the Middle East and the Pacific Islands. The Grade Nine course continued the theme of the impact of technology on culture by examining case studies in western societies chosen from the Americas (not including Canada), Europe, the U.S.S.R., Australia and New Zealand.[29]

Grade Ten represented the only opportunity for the study of Canadian history at the secondary level. It was neither to be approached as a narrative of Canadian history nor as an historical inquiry into the nature of Canada. It was called "Canadian Studies," and teachers were directed to use data and processes from economics, sociology and political science as well as history to solve urgent problems facing Canada.[30] In Grade Eleven, students turned their attention to world problems, particularly overpopulation. They were also directed to spend half the year examining the history of western civilization from the Middle Ages to the beginning of the twentieth century in order to determine how man has coped with the problem of "tradition and change." Grade Twelve also included a history unit: an examination of twentieth-century history through case studies of "conflict and cooperation." Students were also introduced to basic political and economic theories through a unit on "Political and Economic Systems."[31]

The emphasis on "valuing" was obvious in the program. For example, the Grade Six study of ancient civilizations encouraged teachers to engage students in decision-making exercises, such as determining if the Aztecs deserved to be conquered. The Grade Seven course, which had consisted entirely of Canadian studies, became a study of pre-industrial societies around the globe. Children were then asked to answer "valuing questions," such as "Are all men equally human?"[32] Social Studies 10 became a study of Canadian "value issues" such as regional disparity, national unity and sovereignty. Students were encouraged to answer questions such as "Should the endowed and more advanced regions of Canada contribute to the less developed regions of Canada?" and "Should Canada 'massively' increase her foreign aid?"[33] Social Studies 20 (Grade Eleven) students grappled with a question the best adult minds could not answer: "Can the earth support its growing population?"[34] Social Studies 30 required students to answer "value issues" such as "Is war a legitimate means of settling disputes among nations?" and "Are supranational bodies the answer to international conflict?"[35]

The developers of the new curriculum recognized that secondary school teachers would have much more difficulty adjusting to the spirit of the new program than elementary school teachers. Many remained bound by the academic disciplines in which they had been educated and continued to use the textbook as the focus of their instruction. Attempts were made to help teachers understand the new program through the newsletter of the A.T.A.'s Social Studies Council. Between 1968 and 1972, many articles appeared in *One World* that explained and demonstrated what the inquiry method and the valuing process should look like in secondary classrooms.[36] Prototype units for inquiry and valuing were included.[37] Mindful of the call for help from the teaching force, the Department of Education sought to change teaching practices by resisting the adoption of a single text per unit and instead approved a wide range of suitable teaching materials.

**NEW WAYS OF TEACHING**

While the first progressive social studies curriculum had been supported by lists of recommended resources, the new neoprogressive program was accompanied by pages of acceptable titles. Rather than textbooks, the new program recommended that many resource books be available to support students in their guided inquiries. Canadian and American resources were approved. All were grounded in the inquiry approach: they provided lesson plans for teachers explaining the objectives of the lessons and the procedures to follow to identify the problem, hypothesize a solution, collect data and come to generalizations. The student materials contained some text from which students

New teaching methods with new technology in Calgary, 1971. Glenbow Archives, NA-2864-20435b.

could draw data. They were full of photographs, illustrations, maps, and diagrams students were asked to interpret.

Some of the resources were excellent, providing good factual information for children to provide a context for their study and requiring critical thinking in order to come to valid conclusions. Education professor Evelyn Moore edited a series of regional case studies called the *People and Places in Canada* intended for Grade Five. The materials reflected her solid grounding in the discipline of geography. The case studies in the series required teachers to develop appropriate inquiry questions with the children and facilitate open-ended exploration of a huge variety of pictures, maps, tables, charts, graphs and text. The units were written to help children define central concepts and come to valid conclusions; they embodied challenging, inductive teaching strategies. They also acknowledged that teachers would need to exercise professional judgment in selecting the most effective strategies for helping students reach the intended objectives of the lesson. For example, the teacher's guide for the series conceded, "teachers may wish to teach some of the concepts in the sample study by an essentially expository method. It is conceivable that some concepts are most efficiently or economically taught by expository means, and it is assumed that a varied program of teaching strategies will help awaken and maintain student interest."[38]

The American *Man and His World* series used in Grades One, Two and Six also tried to find a middle ground between the traditional transmission of information and the new skill-building approach. Publishers Noble and Noble called theirs a "transitional approach." They explained: "We have found that the most widely used new method – the *inquiry* method – has not been the panacea that so many had hoped for, but that elements of it do work with great success in classroom situations."[39] Their program, they explained to teachers, provided an adequate framework of knowledge for the generalizations children could be encouraged to come to through inquiry. At the primary level, many pictures were used from which children could draw information and which could provide a focus of teacher-guided classroom discussion. More textual material was added to the readers as children's reading abilities improved. The teacher's guides identified knowledge, value and skill objectives for each lesson, outlined a procedure for lesson development and suggested activities and critical thinking questions for students to discuss. For example, the book *People and Culture* asked students to examine photographs of artifacts from ancient cultures and consider their cultural impact: "What do you suppose ancient people used for storing and carrying things before they learned to make pottery? How would a people's way of life be different without the ability to store and carry things?"[40]

Other resources did not require quite so much in terms of content background and critical thinking skills. The *Ginn Social Science* series approved for use in the primary grades dealt in a very superficial way with diverse and seemingly unrelated topics. The Grade One program examined families of many different cultures from all over the world. In an attempt to address required value or attitude objectives, the student response book included activities like completing a crossword puzzle, titled "Living in a Slum." In the introduction to this activity, Grade One students read: "Poverty means not having enough of the things we really need. Many families in São Paulo live in poverty. They live in slums. On the next page there is a crossword puzzle. Below are clues to help you do the puzzle. The puzzle will help you to think about what it is like to live in a slum, too."[41] The Grade Two response book included activities that were equally as inane: making as many words as possible out of the letters in Korpilahti (the Finnish community being examined), using "creative lettering" to write words related to the Bedouin community, and writing or drawing anything the student "felt" about the various communities they studied. Again, the attempt to give young children opportunities to solve problems resulted in completely inappropriate exercises, such as brainstorming solutions to the Bedouins' problems of too much heat and too little water.⁴² Presumably, the desire to have children consider changing values led to the inclusion of this exercise in the students' response book:

In Korpilahti, we met the Nilsson family. We found out that Mrs. Nilsson was a skilled construction worker. Other jobs held by women in the community of Korpilahti are: baker, carpenter, bricklayer, dentist, and road supervisor. Make a list of jobs that you know about that women hold in your community. Put a check next to any job that you consider to be an unusual one for a woman. Write a short paragraph explaining why you consider some of these jobs unusual for women.⁴³

The "valuing" exercises suggested by other teaching resources might have resulted in some interesting conversations around the kitchen table after the school day. The Grade Eight authorized resource, *Through African Eyes: Cultures in Change*, included information about the daily life of young people among the Acholi of northern Uganda and southern Sudan. The teacher guide included the following assignment: "Write a paper on 'How My Parents Affect My Life.' Encourage students to discuss values as well as behavior, relating the two. Also ask them to compare their experiences with Acholi experience. Allow them to make value judgments. Give them freedom to express their 'beefs'; this makes for good discussion in class."⁴⁴

Some of the resources designed for use in history inquiries were excellent. Clarke Irwin's *Canadian Series of Jackdaws* provided a huge variety of primary sources and narratives for students to interpret. The *Ginn Studies in Canadian History* were designed for use with or without a basic textbook. The Teacher's Manual explained how to select and organize appropriate studies for whole class, small group or individual investigation. It demonstrated how the materials in the studies could launch problem-driven inquiries into the historical background to contemporary issues such as the federal government's treatment of "Indians" today. Guidance was provided for teachers who wanted their students to interpret photographs and paintings. There were appropriate cautions against simply drawing inferences based on the evidence in paintings. For example, accompanying a reproduction of the painting *The Seigneury of Longueuil*, which depicts Governor Talon visiting settlers, teachers are reminded: "His [the artist's] interpretation is that Talon visited and spoke with the settlers informally without a retinue of servants and officials in attendance, and without any subservience or deference being shown by the people. The validity of these assumptions can be questioned."⁴⁵

The *Gage World Community* series edited by Neil Sutherland also provided some excellent opportunities for teachers to engage young children in exciting and relevant historical study. *When Grandma and Grandpa Were Kids* brought the lives of children in the early part of the twentieth century to life. Included were photographs of home, school, chores and leisure time activities. Reproductions of pages from catalogues and from school books sparked comparisons and contrasts to the lives of modern children. Suggested activities included role playing, story telling, making diaries and interviewing grandparents.[46] Here were endless opportunities for relevant, challenging and powerful inquiries into the nature of the past and its impact on the present. Skills of historical thinking – interpreting evidence, drawing generalizations, considering change and continuity, assessing reasons for change – were all practised if the materials were used as intended by the writers.

The same was true for many of the resources approved for use in the senior high school history investigations. Bernard Feder's series *Viewpoints in World History* featured excerpts from primary documents and other source material. Also included were short narratives written by historians. The questions that followed asked students to consider the author's point of view and sources of information. Students are challenged to account for conflicting interpretations of the same material. The discussion questions provided at the end of the units, called "History Laboratory," often required students to critically examine the texts they were using in class. For example, the inquiry unit on feudalism approved for Grade Eleven asked:

Does your textbook explain how feudalism and serfdom developed, or does it merely describe them? *Should* a textbook interpret, or merely 'present the facts'? Explain, if an interpretation or explanation is given in your textbook, are other interpretations or points of view mentioned? Why would it be difficult for textbooks to present supporting evidence for all the generalizations made? What are some cautions with which textbooks must be approached? In what ways are they useful?[47]

Students who answered these questions in class would have had ample opportunity to engage in historical thinking and to appreciate the possibilities and limitations of the discipline.

Unfortunately, the opportunities to engage in serious historical inquiry were seriously limited by the content of the new program. In Grade Four, students were ostensibly required to consider the historical development of life in Alberta. Teaching materials like *Alberta: A People and a Province* made some interesting suggestions, such as constructing a time line or planning a play about pioneer life, but did not provide nearly enough information for students to use in order to make these meaningful or worthwhile activities.[48] In Grade Six, during which students examined various ancient civilizations, many of the approved resources were colourful, full of photographs and illustrations, but contained very little text. Since the resources were designed for use in the United States, where the topic typically appeared in Grade Four, the treatment was simply too brief and too superficial for eleven-year-olds.[49] That said, the teaching resources used to teach about culture, history and current issues all continued to embody powerful messages about citizenship, identity, values and the role of the individual in contemporary society.

## SOLVING THE WORLD'S PROBLEMS; SOLVING CANADA'S PROBLEMS

The recommended textbooks and other teaching units embodied many messages about the values and skills of good citizenship, the nature of the past and the obligations of individuals to solve the pressing social issues of the day. For example, they generally encouraged the consideration of a wide range of views rather than guiding students to appropriate conclusions about "value issues" or "global problems." Previous generations of students would have been astounded to read this introduction to a Grade Twelve text on global political and economic systems:

> It would presumptuous to put any answers into such a small book. It would be inappropriate to offer one answer in a textbook to be used by citizens of a free country, where each is expected to build his own answer on his own convictions.
>
> What is attempted in this book is the discussion of some aspects of the question as it applies to political and economic problems. The book describes the principal kinds of political and economic organization existing in various countries in today's world, and describes certain major problems in the realm of politics and economics. In other words, the purpose of the book is to provide positive information, to which the reader may add his own normative knowledge in order to reach his own conclusions about political and economic issues.
>
> By avoiding normative statements, the authors seek to avoid indoctrination in the classroom on current political issues.[50]

The assertion that texts – or teachers – lack authority to express an opinion about systems examined in the text, such as those in Nazi Germany or the Soviet Union, was a change indeed. The implication that students should come to their own conclusions about the most effective political and economic systems, rather than affirming the superiority of capitalist democracies, represented an enormous shift from the texts of the previous generation.

Resources for Grades Seven and Eight emphasized that studying other cultures broadens students' perspectives on the world and challenges their ethnocentrism. *Men Without Machines*, a text for Grade Seven, reminded students that "our own moral judgments, our own habits, our own sense of values, are largely the product of the culture in which we have grown up. Yet we often come to regard them as if they were 'naturally' right, and we are apt to judge how 'advanced' the customs and values of other peoples are by how close they are to our own."[51] The author was clear that even seemingly "primitive" cultures had something to teach the western world about living in harmony with their environment and within their communities. The teacher's guide for a Grade Eight text said that teachers and students must not mistake technological progress for moral or social superiority in their study of India and South Asia: "No educated Asian or African, for example, would deny that his continent is 'backward' with reference to the number of automobiles, amounts of electrical energy, and supplies of good food and medical services. He would resent, and rightfully so, the conclusion by inference that the value system of his culture is necessarily or equally 'backward.'"[52]

History textbooks addressed the curriculum requirements for an inquiry-based investigation that examined the values of cultures and countries. The history texts for Social Studies 20 included information about the arts, the social life and the religious beliefs of European countries in addition to tracing their technological, economic and political development. Authors tried to indicate how painting, music and literature reflected the values and worldviews of these cultures.[53] Authors also tried to frame their texts within the inquiry structure required by the program. *Our Western Heritage* began with the assurance that "your authors make it clear that it is not necessary to choose between sound narrative history and sound inquiry methods. Both are indispensable."[54] Regular features called "Inquiry Lessons" presented students with conflicting historical interpretations of the same event or development. They were asked to determine which is more convincing, though how, for example, they could have determined whether Carl Becker or Peter Gay was correct in his assessment of the nature of eighteenth-century Enlightenment thought remains unclear.[55] After an inquiry lesson that demonstrated that textbooks used in the 1930s in the United States, Britain, Germany and France all contained chauvinistic interpretations of the causes and events of World War I, students probably concluded that all historical points of view are equally invalid![56]

Attempts by the texts to reveal the methods of historians as well as communicate a narrative were generally half-hearted. Roselle and Young, for example, explained that historians have access to excellent data in order to write social and economic history of the nineteenth and twentieth centuries because modern governments collected and published important demographic statistics. They suggested that the data about life in seventeenth-century Europe needs to be approached with more care because it had been gathered by the Church, local governments, businesses and individuals and was therefore more diffuse and prone to error in the recording.[57] The fact that they did not question the motives of governments in gathering and organizing statistics indicates the limited attention given at least in this text to the nature and tools of historical inquiry. They might, for example, have simply asked students to observe what kinds of statistics governments collected and consider what the omissions might imply about government priorities and values. Moreover, the fact that the authors so rarely revealed the evidence on which they based their narrative, so infrequently addressed how they knew the story they were providing was the best possible interpretation of events, proves that they were more concerned with transmitting a story – albeit an entertaining one – than helping students engage in historical inquiry.

Teachers who preferred to stick with familiar text-centred instruction and telling the familiar stories of the past certainly were able to so with the approved texts in Social Studies 20 and 30. They were generally well written, full of information with a level of detail appropriate for students at this level. They included stories about important historical figures. Roselle and Young summarized the accomplishments of many European explorers, but said little about the crews that sailed the ships and nothing about the people they met. Great events were generally described as the work of specific individuals with little attention to social, economic, political or intellectual context. In the chapter on the Reformation, students were provided with a brief six-point list of social factors that contributed to the success of the Reformers, but the rest of the chapter detailed the life and thought of Luther, Calvin and other churchmen associated with the movement. Ricker and Saywell brought historical figures to life with intriguing detail about their lives, personalities and personal habits. Their section on Lenin began with a description of the hanging of his brother and Lenin's reaction. They continued:

Lenin was a hard-working man; he did not smoke and kept himself physically fit. He was fond of little jokes, and, like many Russians, played chess with a passion. His work – the making of a revolution – was the real purpose of his life. Although he was hard and calculating, he had a personal magnetism that could win him supporters in a single encounter. Lenin was a fanatic, a demagogue and an orator, and he had a mind like a steel trap. Altogether he was a dangerous man to the Russia of the tsars.[58]

The psychohistory popular in the 1960s and 1970s was integrated into the text's treatments of important figures. At the end of a chapter on Napoleon, students were asked: "Napoleon is often cited as an example of the person who 'overcompensates' for deep feelings of inferiority. Can you explain his behavior in these terms?"[59] Text authors pointed to Hitler's personal qualities rather than social, economic and political conditions in Germany for his rise to power. Ricker and Saywell stated: "Adolf Hitler was one of the most frightening personalities of our era. A little man with pasty skin and a ridiculous moustache, he nonetheless swayed millions with his oratory.... The key to his personality was hate, for which he had an unlimited capacity. Yet, he gained control of a great state and held the imagination of its citizens."[60] Roselle and Young also asserted that Hitler's persuasive speaking style as well as his ability to use the Sturmabteilung (SA, "Storm Troopers") to terrorize ordinary Germans were responsible for his rise to power. With little context and no elaboration provided, they concluded, "Finally, conditions in Germany and the world made some people believe that only a man like Hitler could 'save' Germany."[61] By interpreting historical events as the work of remarkable or remarkably dysfunctional individuals, text authors implied that history is not the story of ordinary people. Even when topics included economic, artistic and social life, the history in textbooks continued to neglect the way of life of ordinary people or the impact of important events on those who were not royalty or members of the elite. This "top-down" history provided some interesting, even entertaining, stories but it did not have much connection with the students' lives. It is easy to see how it could breed apathy among students about participation in public life rather than encourage them to see themselves as part of an unfolding historical drama, to see themselves as historical actors.

The alarmist tone of many of the texts in dealing with current global issues probably served to heighten students' anxieties about the future but did little to convince them they could find the solutions to these problems. The creators of the new program hoped that students would "think globally" and dedicate themselves to improving their world after thorough examinations of the myriad of problems facing mankind. Doug Ledgerwood wondered, "Can a child help but think internationally after he has confronted problems such as the production and distribution of food, the control of thermo-nuclear weapons, the exhaustion and/or pollution of the world's natural resources, and the loss of individuality in computerized society?"[62] They probably should have anticipated that children would probably just be fatigued and in despair after confronting these problems that were beyond the abilities of intelligent and skilled adults in national governments and international organizations to solve.

T.L. Powrie, a professor of Economics at the University of Alberta and author of the Grade Twelve text *Political and Economic Systems*, became involved with social studies revision in the late 1960s because "the traditional social studies was far too bland. It was not relevant. It painted the world in pink and glowing colours. What made social studies in high school so bland was the general unwillingness to accept the fact of human conflict whereas that is the exciting thing about social studies."[63] Arguably, the new program was about nothing but conflicts and problems, conflicts and problems not necessarily of interest to students, but to the adults who designed the program.

Not surprisingly, the texts and resources approved for use in the courses specifically centred on global problems provided exhaustive details and illustrations of the crisis facing the world because of overpopulation. Even the resources that employed inquiry strategies and provided source material for students to interpret were not particularly balanced in their presentation of the issue. Bernard Feder's *Can the Earth Support its Growing Population?*, approved for Social Studies 20, was frankly alarmist in its tone. In the section in which students were asked to rate the seriousness of the problem, five of the source documents talked about a "global catastrophe." Only the President of the International Bank for Reconstruction and Development offered some hope and even he conceded that "Population growth threatens to nullify all our efforts to raise living standards in many of the poorer countries ... Unless population growth can be restrained, we may have to abandon for this generation our hopes of economic progress in the crowded lands of Asia and the Middle East."[64] The booklet then went on to consider whether food production can be increased to meet the growing need, but again the documents led students to the conclusion that technological innovations were not going to help solve this problem. Moreover, the final word was a lengthy quote from Georg Borgstrom's *Hungry Planet* in which he criticized the United States specifically for spending 90 per cent of their research dollars on armaments, space and atomic research at the expense of medicine and public health.[65] The booklet concluded by examining the possible solution of population control, but again the treatment was so shallow and one-sided as to be completely misleading. The consensus of most of the writers of the documents was that population control could solve this problem, but the position of the Roman Catholic Church against artificial means of birth control meant that people in Third World nations were doomed to starvation.[66] No documents provided insights into cultural, political, economic and social factors that might make birth control an unrealistic and overly simplistic solution to such a complex global problem.

If the treatment of the issues in textbooks was not enough to trigger helpless anxiety in students, the tone of the texts certainly would. Even in the history texts, the authors' hyperbolic language could not have convinced students that there was much they could do to stop current trends that were clearly going to destroy mankind. At the conclusion of their chapter on the rise of modern industry, Ricker and Saywell provided this assessment of the problems facing the world today:

For the first time in perhaps 30,000 years we can no longer take our survival for granted. Armed with the power of science applied to technology, we ourselves, through pollution, exhaustion of irreplaceable natural resources, nuclear weapons and the population explosion, have become our own most formidable enemy. In our careless use of the earth's resources, we have come close to destroying air, water and soil, the very basis of life itself. At the same time, our complex world of production, trade and finance is spiraling beyond our control, bringing staggering wealth and yet leaving three-quarters of the world's population without a decent standard of living. Although successive scientific triumphs over the last century have resulted in a fantastic productivity, the achievements of our machines now seem hardly more impressive than the fantastic problems associated with them.[67]

This is not to suggest that the world was not facing serious problems in this era, or that school curricula should have continued to present a sanitized, bland treatment of current issues to students. It seems, however, unfair to present young people with a litany of tragic events and unsolvable problems and expect them to develop a sense of political efficacy and social responsibility by grappling with them with insufficient background and misleading information.

The few Canadian history textbooks used in schools in this period reflected some of the contemporary trends toward problem-centred instruction, but also retained some of the elements of traditional history texts. *Canada: Colony to Centennial*, written by two Alberta school principals, was primarily the story of Canada's political development. The sections of the B.N.A. Act were reproduced verbatim with explanations in order to help students understand the structure and responsibilities of the federal system of government.[68] It generally took a biographical approach to history, telling the stories of, and celebrating the men, who worked toward Confederation and greater Canadian sovereignty. The book covered the development of western Canada in more detail than was typical, but continued the practice of treating aboriginal groups very negatively. The chapter on the Red River, titled "They Claim to be a Nation," concluded the description of the Battle of Seven Oaks saying, "The bodies of Semple's men were stripped, mutilated, and left on the open field. Their bloodstained coats were washed in the Red River and carried off by the half-breeds."[69] The men who created the C.P.R. were lauded because "the building of a transcontinental railway would eventually bring civilization to prairie and mountain regions."[70] The questions at the end of the chapter describing the accomplishments of the North-West Mounted Police included the following: "In the 1880s the entire way of life of the Plains Indians changed. In a paragraph, explain why it had to change."[71]

Other textbooks simply ignored the historical experience of Canada's aboriginal people entirely, and instead concentrated on the pressing problem of Canadian politics in the early 1970s: Quebec nationalism. The text *Canada: Unity in Diversity* was celebrated at the time of its publication because it was the result of a collaboration between one Anglophone historian, Paul Cornell, and three francophone historians of the "Laval school": Jean Hamelin, Fernand Ouellet and Marcel Trudel. It was in fact published in both official languages and used in schools across the country. Eschewing the single narrative of Canada's political progress toward nationhood and the biographical focus of traditional history textbooks, the authors emphasized instead social and economic developments in every region of the country (except the north). Regional and cultural differences were acknowledged so that no chapter covered the entire country until the section on the post-1931 period. The message of the book was that technology and affluence had done what politics could not: unite diverse regions into one common culture: "Changing patterns of education and the emergence of new technologies ... have in the past couple of generations begun to put more emphasis on a milieu shared by all consumers wherever they are and common to one profession or skill no matter where it is practiced."[72]

Other texts seemed less optimistic about the prospect of fostering understanding and finding an accommodation between Canada's English-speaking and French-speaking populations. The Worth Report announced that "the builders of the new Alberta social studies program have opted for a new direction; a direction that asks students to attend to a global view that will allow them to perceive Canada as it honestly is with all her strengths and blemishes."[73] The blemishes, the problems facing Canada, certainly got more attention than they had in the teaching resources of previous generations. *Canada: Colony to Centennial* quoted Quebec separatist Marcel Chaput at length and acknowledged that "undoubtedly the Province of Quebec has some cause for complaint."[74] The Winnipeg teachers who wrote *Challenge and Survival: The History of Canada*, made it clear in the introduction that English Canada should not be complacent about its treatment of French Canada. Indeed, in their view, a better appreciation of the perspective of French-Canadians on the part of English-Canadians was critical to the survival of the country. Though the text generally focused on political developments, it used primary documents to present various points of view regarding turning points in Canada's past. For example, regarding the impact of the American Revolutionary War on the British North American colonies to the north, the authors stressed that Quebec's refusal to join the revolution should not be interpreted as a statement of support for the British regime. Rather, it was an indication of the ability of French-Canadians to make decisions that would best ensure the survival of their culture and language.[75]

In addition to the problems of regional and cultural division, Canada in the 1970s faced the problem of American political, economic and cultural domination. In contrast to the texts of the Cold War period in which the United States had been acknowledged as a leader of the free world, a model democracy and a good friend to Canada, the texts used in the 1970s stressed that Canada's close relationship with the United States came at a cost. After tracing increasing American investment in Canada after 1946, Cornell and his co-authors explained: "[E]ven the rapid expansion of Canadian industry seemed to be geared to north–south trade across the border, re-emphasizing the growing regionalism of Canada's economy and further disrupting her unity. Many Canadians feared the total loss of control of their own economic destinies in a creeping absorption into the American economy."[76]

A menacing tone was also used to describe American cultural influence. Using vocabulary that evoked the conduct of war, Cornell acknowledged that American culture had always had an influence on Canadians, but "television, adopted generally throughout Canada after 1950, added a new dimension to the bombardment of Canadians by American attitudes and values."[77] *Challenge and Survival* quoted Walter Gordon and John Diefenbaker at great length on the dangers of American economic and military influence. This was followed by a selection written by Gad Horowitz in which he compares Canada's relationship with the United States to Finland's relationship with the Soviet Union.[78] The idea that the liberal and capitalistic American democracy was equivalent to the obviously expansionistic and politically repressive Soviet Union would have been anathema to the previous generation of textbook authors. Even *Canada: Colony to Centennial* asked students to consider: "From what you have read, is there any reason to fear the United States of America?" For students who dismissed the possibility of actual invasion, the authors went on to hint: "How many TV programs which you watch each week are produced in the U.S.? How many magazines that you get at home are published in the U.S.?"[79]

In order to further distinguish Canadian values from American values, authors emphasized Canada's role in global affairs as a kind of helpful fixer. New heroes in Canadian history included Lester B. Pearson, who was an "outstanding diplomat" and, as Canada's Minister for External Affairs and its representative at the United Nations, served "with brilliance."[80] In contrast to the United States, which pursued a misguided, anti-Communist foreign policy,

Canada more pragmatically brokered agreements through the United Nations and the Commonwealth to pursue a more peaceful route to world peace. *Challenge and Survival* stressed that "in her efforts on behalf of the United Nations, Canada has made a special place for herself among the nations of the world."[81] *Canada: Unity and Diversity* acknowledged Canada's commitments to NATO and her efforts in Korea, but stressed that she continued to trade with Cuba and China despite the disapproval of the United States.[82] Canada's leadership role in the evolution of the Commonwealth was also celebrated: "Through Canada's efforts, Britain, Australia and New Zealand agreed to a modified formula that would allow membership to such nations [newly independent India, Pakistan, Ceylon and Ghana] in the Commonwealth.... Canada was responsible, to a large extent, for the transformation of the Commonwealth into a multi-racial association."[83]

Alberta students in the 1970s had reason to worry about all the problems facing the world and their country: overpopulation, nuclear proliferation, French-Canadian nationalism and American expansionism, to name a few, were covered in their school curriculum, but textbooks and other teaching resources encouraged them to recognize the validity of other points of view and other political systems. They suggested that their own values were the creation of their culture, not a reflection of eternal truths or a set of personal virtues critical for the progress of the nation. The rhetoric of relativism in the program became one of the reasons for its abandonment.

## ABANDON THE LIFE BOAT

Critics of the values-clarification approach, used in the United States as well as other parts of Canada, argued that it stripped the teacher, and indeed all social institutions, of any moral authority. It undermined the moral foundation of society and gave students the message that moral precepts could be adopted and shed like fashions of clothing. It seemed to these critics that schools were failing to prepare students for their responsibilities; they were simply encouraging self-indulgent behaviour.[84]

Indeed, in the Alberta program, teachers were discouraged from imposing their own beliefs on their students or even evaluating options presented to students. They were reminded that teachers who demonstrate "accepting" behaviour get better results from students; teachers who direct class discussion too closely "threaten" their students.[85] Soon, notorious examples of values-clarification exercises undertaken in classrooms were presented in the media. Teachers had asked children to write their own obituaries. Students engaged in a "self-awareness" exercise called the Life Raft that required them to decide which of their ten peers they would throw overboard from a raft designed for nine. Students were allowed to determine the situations in which cheating or stealing might be morally defensible.[86]

Criticisms of the values-clarification approach also came from within the educational establishment. Education Professor Donald Massey from the University of Alberta said, among other things, that expecting young children to step out of their own frame of reference and consider the values and perspectives of others was simply unreasonable, given the fact that they are at the preoperational stage according to Piaget's stages of psychological development.[87] Educational psychological Hugh Lytton from the University of Calgary mocked the phoney nature of the value choices presented to students in the program:

[O]n the one hand it insists that students choose their own set of values freely and on the other presents them with choices that are no choices, because the values concerned are so established in the western world that the answers are foregone conclusions. Examples are: "Should all individuals be considered equal?" "Should each generation preserve the earth's natural resources?" ... Would most social studies teachers view the answer "no" to the above questions with the same equanimity as the answer "yes"?[88]

While acknowledging that twelve-year-old students might have profitable discussions about personal values within the context of, say, group guidance class, he censured the social studies program because it "imposes on them a discussion of social, economic and philosophical, not personal, values and further denudes these of reality by relating them to different and often remote societies."[89]

The program was also criticized for its lack of Canadian content. In 1968, A.B. Hodgett's *What Culture? What Heritage?* was released. His in-depth survey of history teaching across the country revealed that students knew very little about their own country, and given the poor teaching to which they were subject, that was not going to change anytime soon.[90] His study received a lot of attention across the country from the media, from teachers and from educational leaders. In 1970, the Canada Studies Foundation was established in order to improve curricula, develop resources and educate teachers.[91] In 1972, the Worth Report acknowledged that Alberta teachers working with the Foundation and with Project Canada West were developing excellent resources that would engage students in meaningful local, regional and national studies.[92] But the fact remained that the social studies program provided very few opportunities to study Canada, let alone Canadian history. Some resources produced by the Canada Studies Foundation made their way into the Social Studies 10 course, but these were interdisciplinary inquiry units into current issues. In elementary school, Canadian studies were generally of the nature best described by historian Ken Osborne as "applied ethnic studies or cultural anthropology."[93]

As public criticism of the values-clarification orientation of the new program grew, as teachers continued to complain about the lack of helpful resources, and as politicians began to press for more Canadian content in social studies, the Department of Education responded by commissioning a major study of the 1971 program. The consultants, L.W. Downey Research Associates, discovered that teachers simply refused to teach the required curriculum. Their report concluded that one-third of teachers surveyed disagreed with the values approach and only one in five used the recommended values-clarification and decision-making exercises. It implied that it was simply unrealistic to expect a celebration of pluralism and diversity from teachers who were traditional and even closed-minded in their own values.[94] What was absolutely unique in this assessment was the acknowledgement that classroom teachers did more than deliver required programs; the report recognized that teachers ultimately had to be convinced of the theoretical orientation and efficacy of a revision in order for it to be successfully implemented in classrooms.

With the values-clarification approach for all intents and purposes abandoned, the Department began to increase Canadian content in the existing social studies program. In 1975, the federal government provided funds to education ministries to create classroom resources with significant Canadian content under a plan called the Canadian Content Project. In Alberta, several of these resources, really teaching kits, had already been produced when the provincial government announced the creation of the Alberta Heritage Learning Resources Project in November 1977. This project set aside $8,387,000 from the Alberta Heritage Savings Trust Fund for the creation of classroom materials for teachers to support new programs in Social Studies, Language Arts and Science.[95] These new resources were developed in conjunction with a new social studies program that was piloted over several years and officially implemented in 1981. Learning the lessons of the disastrous 1971 revision, the Department of Education spent a further $2 million to provide special training to ten thousand teachers in the implementation of the new program and the use of new multi-media teaching resources.

While "value objectives" and inquiry-based teaching strategies remained in the 1981 program, specific concepts and generalizations were identified to ensure that specific information was transmitted to students. Critical thinking skills, as well as the skills associated with subject disciplines such as geography, were also more clearly developed. History, however, continued to be a source of concern. Though the 1981 program of studies contained more historical content, it was "not in the curriculum treated as a model of inquiry but as a field of data."[96] Students were to collect information about "the past" in order to answer the kinds of questions historians never ask, such as "Should nations go to war," rather than "Why have nations gone to war?" It continued to ignore questions fundamental to the study of the discipline of history: what is history? How do historians formulate questions? What makes an event or person historically significant? What sources do historians use? How do they determine the validity of a source? What interpretations have historians made? What other interpretations are possible? While informed and interested teachers could use the curriculum to encourage students to think historically by doing history, there was certainly little in the program that required such an approach.

Criticisms of social studies teaching resurfaced in the 1980s and 1990s. Studies done across Canada in the 1970s and 1980s revealed the extent to which textbooks continued to portray aboriginal and other minority groups, defined by ethnic origin, class or political leanings, in stereotypical terms.[97] In Alberta, the Committee on Tolerance and Understanding, appointed by the provincial government and led by Ron Ghitter, examined textbooks and other teaching resources used in schools. As a result of their report, many textbooks and other teaching resources were revised or eliminated from classrooms.[98] Studies also criticized the portrayal of women in curricula and texts. They reported that in elementary school teaching resources, women were shown only in domestic roles. In secondary texts, particularly history texts, women's contributions were trivialized. They were typically portrayed only insofar as they supported the "more important" accomplishments of men.[99] Recently, feminist scholars have insisted that the very understanding of citizenship embodied by the curriculum, by stressing the relationship between citizenship and activity in the public realm and by privileging "rational" thought, has marginalized women and restricted our understanding of citizenship.[100]

As educators develop a new social studies program for the twenty-first century, they again face the challenge of creating a program that transmits shared values and ideas about what it means to be Canadian and an Albertan at the same time that it respects and enriches the increasing ethnic, cultural, racial, sexual and religious diversity of the people of the province. They continue to face a challenge in helping students come to understand the content and the nature of the various social sciences integrated into the social studies. They still struggle with the place of history in citizenship education. No doubt the program they create will again reflect and attempt to shape the beliefs of Albertans about themselves, their country and their world.

## CONCLUSION

Historian Douglas John Hall once wrote that periodically, societies go through a process of creating new images of themselves. What distinguishes one era from another, he said, was the different ways a community has understood what it means to be human and the various ways they have communicated those understandings: "Today we don't record our dominant images of man on tombstones; we put them into advertisements for Disneyland, Grade B movies, and school curricula."[1] School curriculum is one place where we tell ourselves who we are; it embodies our struggle to define who we as a society are and what we wish to become.

The school curriculum has always represented an important element of public thought in the sense that generations of Alberta children have been exposed to its themes and messages. It has always been written by an elite – an academic elite or a professional elite – that sometimes imposed their ideas about citizenship on schools, and at other times attempted to respond to the concerns of people in the province. In its attempt to embody the hopes of society, it has been characterized by different, often contradictory aims and messages. The messages of one period were not replaced by the next; traces of former aims and older visions remained so that by the end of the century, there were many different visions of society and citizenship reflected in the curriculum.

From 1905 to 1920, the intellectual elite constructed a curriculum that cultivated the academic talents of the few who would lead, and indeed serve, society. This "education for disciplined intelligence" was grounded in the traditional academic disciplines and was intended to create people of good character. There was an optimistic spirit that pervaded policy-making for schools; educational leaders assumed that graduates of good character would contribute to the task of building the new province. They would preserve the harmony and orderliness that characterized the young community; they would contribute to the economic and political progress of the region. The message of the curriculum was that Canadian citizens should be defined by their country's role within the British Empire.

After World War I, a more conscious attempt was made to address the social aims of education. From 1920 to 1935, the aim of schooling in Alberta was to create good citizens. Good citizens were defined by their virtues, their character. The experience of the war taught educational leaders that it was not enough for these virtues to be encouraged or modeled; they should be taught directly. Social harmony could only be demonstrated by students who were taught skills of cooperation. Material and political progress were not inevitable; students must be prepared to take on their vocational and political responsibilities through appropriate schooling. Schooling was still seen as a mark of cultivation and useful for an individual's future prosperity, but increasingly, it was primarily viewed as the tool by which a large number of young people could be molded for their role as future citizens.

The purpose of schooling in the progressive era of 1935 to 1945 was to effect social change. The dramatic political and economic events of the 1930s, combined with the desire of a new generation of educationalists to demonstrate their professionalism, led to the progressive revisions of the period. The hallmark of the progressive curriculum was its abandonment of tradition. Progressive educators sought to create a new world; they wanted to use the tools of science to solve social problems and reconstruct society according to more rigorous standards of social justice. Despite the preoccupation of educationalists with social and economic problems, they were optimists. Their reconstructionist message demonstrated an incredible confidence in the ability of people to build a better world. The themes embedded in the curriculum reflected that confidence. Students learned about the efficacy of state planning, of the infinite benefits of technology, and they were called to create a peaceful world in which all forms of government are tolerated. Progressive educationalists believed not only in social planning, they believed that the lives and futures of individual students could be efficiently directed. They sought to create citizens who would participate in the task of social reconstruction and find their proper roles through the guidance of psychological tests and trained counselors.

World War II and the Cold War demonstrated that democracy could not be defended simply as a good way of life; politicians and educators now understood that democracy must be actively nurtured. Schools must prepare students for the practical exercise of their rights and responsibilities. The school curriculum of the 1950s and 1960s was intended to demonstrate the superiority of democracy by providing students with a better life. The task of schools was to prepare students for building and sharing the province's prosperity. The war effort had demonstrated the possibility of social and economic planning; the same attitude and effort, if not financial support, was brought to the task of educational planning. School facilities grew tremendously. New programs were introduced. But all subjects in the school program were assessed in terms of the marketable skills they taught.

The 1950s and 1960s were decades of technological and ideological competitiveness, so there was a new seriousness of purpose in schools. The vocational emphasis of the curriculum was intended to demonstrate to students the material benefits of democracy. It was intended to give all students, not just those bound for postsecondary education, an opportunity to share in the province's prosperity. Schooling was still emphasized as preparation for citizenship, even training in virtue, but increasingly the citizen it fostered was defined as a hard worker. An attempt to define the Canadian identity was included in the curriculum. Schools introduced students to the uniqueness of Canada, historically tied to Britain but defined by its geographical proximity to and cooperative relationship with the United States. The story of Canada's growth from colony to nation was intended to foster pride in the country's growth. But any sense of political identity was undermined by the curriculum's emphasis on material success. It was difficult to define an enduring sense of national identity or citizenship in a curriculum that celebrated affluence. By tying a defence of democracy and an understanding of citizenship to prosperity, educators failed to define a common civic culture. They encouraged individualism by celebrating the potential of every student to find material success and to get a share of Alberta's wealth.

This sense of individualism was further cultivated by the neoprogressive curriculum of the 1970s that encouraged a desire for self-fulfillment and defined good citizenship as a process of self-actualization. Faced with an exhausting list of global and national problems, and armed with only the skills of clarifying alternative value systems, students were ill-prepared for active civic engagement. Rather than finding a sense of community in the social studies curriculum, they found only fragmentation and despair.

School curriculum has embodied the vision of citizenship, history and identity that educators have had for the province. Generally, that vision has been exclusionary or restrictive. While there has often been considerable public interest about the purpose of schooling and the content of school curriculum, there really have never been effective channels through which the public could contribute to the development of curriculum policy. Instead, an academic or professional elite determined the curriculum based on what they felt would be most useful for Alberta's students. In the early part of the century, useful knowledge was knowledge that would serve students well in a professional career or help them gain entrance to the university. After World War I, useful knowledge was that knowledge that would help students fit into society. For the progressive educationalists who formalized their control of the curriculum building process before World War II, knowledge and skills were useful to the extent to which they would help citizens solve the pressing social problems facing Alberta. In the post-war period, schools transmitted the knowledge they felt would be useful for students in taking advantage of the opportunities for prosperity. In the 1970s, neoprogressive educators celebrated knowledge that would increase students' appreciation for other belief systems and other cultures. In a world of crises and seemingly insurmountable problems, educators believed that only citizens with appropriate values could adapt to a rapidly changing society and plan the future to ensure justice for all.

The enduring commitment to "useful" education has not served the teaching of history well. In the early history of the province, an ethnocentric, narrative history that celebrated Canada's ties to Great Britain and denigrated or ignored others was most "useful." With the adoption of social studies, units of historical study were included only when they could assist students in solving current problems. The study of history was simply not seen as useful in a world dominated by rapid technological and social change. No coherent treatment of the country's past was ever included in social studies curriculum. The past was fragmented and obscure. This lack of sustained inquiry into the nature of the past meant that students were left with little historical consciousness. They had few opportunities to examine change in any society, let alone Canadian society over time. They were left with a limited understanding of their place in a changing community; they were left with an inadequate sense of themselves.

## APPENDIX 1: CURRICULUM OVERVIEW

**1905–1911**

Standard II:
*Biography*: Lives of distinguished men described, e.g., Columbus, the Cabots, Jacques Cartier, Champlain, Bishop Laval, Frontenac, La Salle, Montcalm, Wolfe, Sir Guy Carleton, Lyon Mackenzie, Papineau, Joseph Howe, Alexander Mackenzie, Sir John Macdonald, etc. Discussion of the chief excellences and defects in their character to teach moral discrimination and ultimately to derive principles of conduct. Reading and reciting patriotic poems.

Standard III:
*Canadian History*: Outline study from leading features, e.g., discovery, exploration, struggle between the French and English colonists; Treaty of Paris; Quebec Act; Constitutional Act; War of 1812; Rebellion of 1837; Union Act; Clergy Reserves; Land Tenures – feudal, freehold, leasehold, seigniorial; Reciprocity Treaty; British North America Act, etc.
*British History*: Biography of persons honoured as types of state or individual life, e.g., Caractacus, Julius Caesar, Arthur, Alfred, Canute, William I, Simon de Montfort, Edward I, Wolsey, Elizabeth, Charles I, John Hampden, Oliver Cromwell, Marlborough, Pitt, Nelson, Wellington, Lord John Russell, Victoria, etc. Discussion of their deeds to train moral judgment and incidentally to teach patriotism and civic duty. Reading and reciting patriotic selections.

Standard IV:
*Canadian History*: The text book studied as a review and expansion of the topics discussed in the previous standards.

*British History*: Outline study of each people or period to exhibit its chief characteristics, e.g., Saxons – a farmer people; brought with them the germs of our political institutions – a limited monarchy, parliament, courts of justice, personal holdings of lands; gave us the body of our English tongue; became Christians from choice.

Standard v:
*Canadian History*: The leading events of Canadian history with particular attention to events subsequent to 1840.
*British History*: The outlines of British History.

Standard vi:
The leading events of Canadian and British History. Examinations in history will be so framed as to require comparison and the use of judgement on the student's part rather than the mere use of memory.

Standard vii:
Myers' *General History* – to the close of the Mediaeval period (p. 485); Bourinot's *How Canada is Governed*.

Standard viii:
Bagehot's *The English Constitution*; Cunningham's *Outline of English Industrial History*; and Myers (p. 486 on).

## 1912–1922

"The right teaching of history takes account of it ultimately as a study of the institutional life of a people or of the progress of whole social organizations rather than as a chronicle of the doings of individuals; but as movements can best be understood in relation to those who are connected with their progress, history resolves itself into a study of the institutional life of the race concretely set forth in the ideas and actions of its men and women." (Alberta Education, Annual Report [Edmonton: King's Printer, 1912], 99.)

Grades Two to Four:
Historical stories (fables, myths, tales of Greece, Rome and the North, adventures, great heroes, Bible stories) should be incorporated into reading lessons.

Grade Five:
*Local history*: origin and settlement of the community; development of the social life of the community; comparison of lives of boys and girls today and in the past.
*Regional history*: development of the Canadian West; pioneer life; Indian life; fur trade; heroes of exploration; cowboy experiences; North-West Mounted Police.

Grade Six:
*Canadian West*: history of the development of the west from its earliest days to the establishment of Alberta and Saskatchewan as provinces. Particular attention should be given to the Red River and Northwest Rebellions, the CPR.
*Romantic Side of Canadian History*: discovery and exploration; the native races; story of French Canada from the founding of New France to the Conquest.

Grade Seven:
*Story of British Canada*: political development of Canada from the Conquest to the present day.
*Romantic Period of British History*: Early Britons; Roman Britain; Anglo-Saxons; Norman period; the Plantagenet kings; the Houses of Lancaster and York to the War of the Roses.

Grade Eight:
*Canadian history*: with reference to events after 1760.
*British history*: with reference to events and political developments after 1485; the Tudor period to the present empire.

Grade Nine:
*Canadian history*: the leading events after 1763.
*British history*: to the year 1485.

Grade Ten:
Leading events of British history after 1485; outline of general history of Greece and Rome as outlined in the prescribed text.

Grade Eleven:
General [European] history to the close of the Mediaeval period (p. 485); constitutional history of Canada.

Grade Twelve:
Bagehot's *The English Constitution*; Myers' *General History* on the modern age.

## 1922–1936

Grades One and Two:
*Citizenship*: lessons in personal discipline and the formation of right habits in connection with school expectations. Stories and talks emphasizing character building in: cleanliness, manners, kindness, gratitude, fairness, truthfulness and courage, as recommended by the Special Committee of the Moral Education League of Great Britain.

Grades Three and Four:
*Citizenship*: development of community pride and appreciation of the obligations of citizenship. A sense of responsibility, appreciation and self-discipline should be encouraged. In Grade Four, specific history talks should be introduced on the theme of the Indians of Alberta.

Grade Five:
*Citizenship*: Stories and discussions in this grade should be about admirable people, as this is the beginning of a period of hero worship. Qualities that should be emphasized include: self-respect, a sense of personal honour, a sense of justice, courage, forethought and right use of leisure time.
*History*: Readings and oral discussions should awake the imagination and interest. Material should be related to the winning of our Canadian West for civilization, from Indian life before settlement to the stories of the Royal North-West Mounted Police.

Grade Six:
*History*: the formal study of history should begin in this grade. The chief aim is still to arouse curiosity about the past. Content should be drawn from the Mediaeval and Tudor period of British history and from the exploration of eastern and western North America.
*Civics*: consideration of the organization of social life in relation to institutions such as the family, the school and the church.

Grade Seven:
*History*: the course is based upon the prescribed text, Wallace's *A New History of Great Britain and Canada*, Part I, pp. 18–150, covering England from the feudal period to the age of colonization, and Part II, pp. 3–91, covering the history of North America from the early discoverers to settlement of the Canadian West.
*Civics*: social relationships based on making a living. Specific attention should be given to wants and needs in rural and urban homes; private and public property; the nature of trade; needs of transportation; and, evolution of means of communication.

Grade Eight:
*History*: the text is continued, covering Part I, pp. 89–235, covering the Hanoverians to the growth of the British Empire in the twentieth century, and Part II, pp. 101–180, from the achievement of responsible government in Canada to the country's achievements in the Great War.
*Civics*: the structure and function of all levels of government.

Grade Nine (History 1):
Ancient and Mediaeval History

Grade Ten (History 2):
British History from 1485 to the Present Day

Grade Eleven (History 3):
Canadian History: New France to the Conquest, British North American colonies
Canadian Civics: structure and function of the imperial government, and levels of the dominion government
Elementary Economics: current Canadian economic institutions and discussion of current problems

Grade Twelve (History 4):
General History of the Modern Age (from the close of the Middle Ages to the present day)
English Constitutional History

**1936–1963**

Enterprise (Divisions I and II, or Grades I through VI):[1]
The enterprise was "a series of purposeful activities arising out of the pupils' needs and interests and revolving around one central theme." Out of the chosen theme, students would undertake activities in the subject areas of social studies, science, health, language and possibly several of the fine arts. While very specific guidelines were still provided for "tool" subjects such as reading, handwriting and arithmetic, specific content or skill requirements in the other subjects disappeared from the course of studies.

"Themes of Social Living" were identified in 1940 to guide teachers' selection of Enterprise topics in the elementary grades. Food; Clothing; Shelter; Work; Transportation and Communication; Recreation; Expression; Education; and, Government, Health and Protection. Grade I, II and III teachers were directed to address these themes within a context familiar to young children, i.e., home, school and community. Teachers in Grades IV, V and VI were encouraged to examine the same themes in times and places more remote from students, i.e., in history and in other countries.

Grade VII
Social Studies: Our Country and its People, examination of Canadian history and development with an emphasis on studies of immigrant groups and their countries of origin.

Grade VIII
Social Studies: Canada and the Commonwealth, a study of Canadian regions and economic development and the countries of the modern Commonwealth.

Grade IX
Social Studies: The World of Today, emphasizing industrial and technological developments in the western world.

Social Studies 1 (Grade X): Story of Man to 1500 within the context of many different civilizations: Egypt, Babylonia, Phoenicia, Greece, Rome, the Arab Empire and China.

Social Studies 2 (Grade XI): History of Western Civilization to 1914.

Social Studies 3 (Grade XII): International history since 1914.[2]

**1963–1971**

The integrated Enterprise program was now specifically identified as an Enterprise/Social Studies program for elementary school. Four Enterprise/Social Studies themes were required every year for Grades III to VI: one historical, one economic, one geographical, and one that examined the impact of science and technology on social life.

Grade One: Our School and Homes.

Grade Two: Our Community.

Grade Three: Primitive Cultures; Life in our Community; Geographical study of Japan, the Netherlands, the Nile or Indus Valley, and Christmas Around the World; Using and Conserving Natural Wealth.

Grade Four: Pioneer Life in our Community; Occupations in Europe; Life in Mountain Regions (Switzerland, Norway, Mexico, Ceylon, or the Himalayas); Contributions of Scientists and Inventors to Travel and Communication.

Grade Five: Discovery and Exploration of Canada; Alberta Industries; Life on the Plains (in Argentina, Russia, China or Australia); Contributions of Scientists to Health.

Grade Six: Life in the Past (the ancient World and the Middle Ages); Canadian Industries; Life in Coastal Regions (West Indies or Fiji, Indonesia, New Zealand, or Portugal); Contributions of Science to Social Progress in Canada and the United States (case studies in the United States, the St. Lawrence River, or Columbia River Project).

Grade Seven
Social Studies: Developing Canadian Culture: Canadian geography; primary and secondary industries in Canada; Canadian history from New France to the early nineteenth century; the development of Western Canada; and, local government.

Grade Eight
Social Studies: Canada's and the Commonwealth: economic development in Europe from the Middle Ages to the Industrial Revolution; the geography and political development of all Commonwealth members; the constitutional development of Great Britain from feudal times to the interwar period.

Grade Nine
Social Studies: Canada in the Western Hemisphere: physical geography of the western hemisphere; examination of the impact of the industrial revolution on businesses, homes and community living; examination of the settlement and development of Latin America and the United States from the time of the first European settlers; machinery of Canadian government and constitutional development; a study of various cultural organizations and institutions.

Social Studies 10: the beginnings of human civilization to the fall of Rome; citizenship and local government; consumer education.

Social Studies 20: the Renaissance, Reformation, Scientific Revolution, Enlightenment, Rise of Nation-States and the Development of Parliamentary Democracy.

Social Studies 30: Canada in the Modern World: geography, the nature of Canadian trade, participation in twentieth-century conflicts, the growth of Canadian nationalism from Confederation through the creation of the modern Commonwealth, and an outline of the responsibilities of citizenship.

**1971–1981**

Grade One: families, their own and case studies of other cultures and other countries.

Grade Two: neighbourhoods, including rural and urban neighbourhoods and case studies from other cultures.

Grade Three: comparison and contrast of students' own communities with unique communities in Canada (Eskimo and Hutterites), and case studies from other cultures around the world.

Grade Four: Alberta was contrasted with similar areas around the world (Australia, Argentina, the U.S.S.R., the oil-producing regions of the Middle East and the western U.S.A.).

Grade Five: life in Canadian regions through case studies.

Grade Six: Roots of Man: case studies of ancient civilizations in the Mediterranean, the Far East, the Americas and Africa.

Grade Seven: Man, Technology and Culture through case studies of primitive, pre-industrial societies.

Grade Eight: Man, Technology and Culture in Afro-Asian societies using case studies selected from Africa, Asia, the Middle East and the Pacific Islands.

Grade Nine: Man, Technology and Culture in western societies chosen from the Americas (not including Canada), Europe, the U.S.S.R., Australia and New Zealand.

Social Studies 10: Canadian Studies

Social Studies 20: World Problems, including "Population and Production" and "Tradition and Change." Tradition and Change involved an examination of the history of western civilization from the Middle Ages to the twentieth century.

Social Studies 30:[3] World Problems, including "Political and Economic Systems" and "Conflict and Cooperation." Conflict and Cooperation was an examination of twentieth-century history.

## APPENDIX 2: NOTE ON SOURCES

I have approached this examination of the history of Alberta's school curriculum with an understanding of curriculum borrowed from American historian Herbert Kliebard: "A curriculum is the ambiguous outcome of a complex interplay between certain social conditions and prevailing conceptions of how schools are supposed to function."[1] Curriculum historians recognize that determining what was taught in schools is difficult because not all teachers taught the official curriculum and because, of course, not all students learned what was intended. Despite this dilemma, examining the official curriculum is important, because "[a] proclaimed curriculum is a potent way to validate certain forms of knowledge and belief and, whether or not it is implemented in any substantial way, it can be extraordinarily revealing about the values a given society or some segment thereof cherishes.... The curriculum thus becomes one of those arenas in which various interest groups struggle for dominance and control."[2] Because I sought to examine the aims of those who wrote the curriculum, the process by which the curriculum was developed and implemented, as well as the official content of curriculum in history, civics and social studies, many different sources were consulted.

I attempted in this study to establish the intellectual milieu in which public discussions about curriculum were undertaken. What did "the public" value about education? About curriculum? Public discussions regarding schools and school curriculum were drawn from regional newspapers. I surveyed stories, editorials, and letters to the editor in daily newspapers in Edmonton, Calgary, Lethbridge, and Red Deer, as well as widely circulated rural papers like the UFA. I also examined articles about schools and education published in popular magazines like *Maclean's*. In order to understand politicians' views about school content, I turned to the debates of the Alberta Legislature. Because no official Hansard was kept in the period under study, I consulted the "Scrapbook Hansard," which records legislative debates as reported by the *Edmonton*

*Bulletin* and *Edmonton Journal* and is available at the Legislative Library in Edmonton as well as the University of Alberta library. The Premiers' Papers and the official papers of various Ministers of Education were helpful in clarifying the government's position on school curriculum and the relationship between the government and its bureaucrats in the Department of Education.

In order to determine the views of stakeholders in education, I turned to specific articles regarding history, civics and social studies curriculum and curriculum revision published in the *ATA Magazine*, Home and School Association newsletters and files, and in *The Alberta School Trustee*. The newsletter of the Social Studies Council of the Alberta Teachers' Association, *One World*, was also consulted for the period after 1963. The records of various local school boards were also consulted to gather information about how boards interpreted curriculum revisions and helped teachers in their implementation of new programs. Particularly useful were the excellent records of the Edmonton Public School Board.

Many different sources were consulted to determine the official curriculum in history, civics and social studies: government policy statements; programs of study; and, curriculum guides which were the Department of Education's official statement of required school content. In order to get a better sense of what teachers actually taught, I also consulted departmental examinations for the relevant periods. Until 1935, the program of studies and departmental examinations were included in the *Annual Reports* of the Department of Education. In the years following, they were published separately. I located most of them in the files of the Edmonton Public School Board Archives. Programs of study were written by officials in the Department of Education and members of curriculum committees. The minutes and papers of these committees were consulted. They are housed with the Papers of the Department of Education at the Provincial Archives. Official school knowledge was largely communicated via textbooks. The textbooks and other teaching resources examined in great detail in this study were all officially authorized by the Department of Education and used in classrooms in Alberta. In order to identify relevant titles, I made use of the Historical Bibliography of Alberta School Resources, 1885 to 1985, at the University of Alberta. This is an invaluable resource for the curriculum historian and I thank the librarians at the H.T. Coutts Library at the University of Alberta for their extraordinary assistance.

In order to better understand the aim and philosophy of the school curriculum, I needed to know about the people who wrote the programs of study and the approved teaching resources. Who were they? What were their educational and professional backgrounds? To what extent were their views representative of a "public" view of education? I consulted the autobiographies and memoirs of relevant figures. Where primary sources were not available, I made use of published interviews and biographies and several helpful, unpublished dissertations and theses. In some cases, the papers of specific educational leaders were available: a small collection of H.C. Newland's papers is at the Alberta Teachers' Association archives; the papers of the men who became professors and/or deans of Education at Alberta universities, such as W.D.

McDougall, A. Doucette, M. LaZerte, and H.T. Coutts, were available at the relevant university archives.

Discovering how teachers translated the official curriculum into the lived curriculum of the classroom was much more challenging. In order to find out how teachers taught in the period before World War II, I examined inspectors' reports from the Department of Education. During these years, these reports were included in the Annual Reports of the Department. I also sought out teachers' memoirs. Some published memoirs, listed in the Bibliography, were very helpful. Other, unpublished memoirs are housed at the Provincial Archives. I found the Carr/McCormick Papers, the Anette Christofferson Papers and the Muriel Clipsham Papers at the Glenbow Archives very useful. For the later period, a lot of information about teaching strategies was included with text resources. Professional magazines like the *A.T.A. Magazine* and *One World* also contained helpful advice for teachers regarding practical teaching strategies.

Insights into teacher practice were also provided by information about teacher education. It was helpful to know what exactly pre-service teachers were being taught about history and social studies teaching. Textbooks used in Normal Schools, and later in faculties of Education, were helpful in this regard. All the texts listed in the Bibliography were identified for use in Normal Schools, or were required reading for teachers upgrading their certificates. Texts for the later period were identified in course outlines for courses in the teaching of elementary and secondary social studies in the faculties of Education. The papers of the Calgary Normal School and the Faculty of Education at the University of Alberta gave important insights into the aims of teacher education generally and the educational philosophies of those in positions of educational leadership.

The central problem in any curriculum history is in determining what students learned. In order to go some way to determining the students' view of history and social studies curriculum, I examined samples of student work in archives. The Alan Bell Papers, the Betty Horton Files, the Roger McKee Papers, and the William Tomyn Papers at the Edmonton Public School Board Archives were very helpful, as were the Glengarry School Papers at the Glenbow Archives. Student yearbooks often contained interesting insights into the classroom and extracurricular experiences of students. The School Yearbook Collection at the Glenbow Library was consulted for the relevant years. As tainted as they are by the passage of time, Albertans' memoirs and reminiscences about life in schools were also useful when used in conjunction with official programs of study.

# NOTES

## INTRODUCTION

1  Daniel Francis, *National Dreams: Myth, Memory and Canadian History* (Vancouver: Arsenal Pulp Press, 1997), 13.
2  Michael Bliss, "Privatizing the Mind: the Sundering of Canadian History, the Sundering of Canada," *Journal of Canadian Studies* 26, 4 (1991–92): 5–17.
3  Bob Davis, *Whatever Happened to High School History?* (Toronto: James Lorimer & Company, 1995).
4  J.L. Granatstein, *Who Killed Canadian History?* (Toronto: Harper Collins, 1998).
5  Keith Spicer, "Canada: Values in Search of a Vision," in *Identities in North America: the Search for Community*, ed., Robert L. Earle and John D. Wirth (Stanford, CA: Stanford University Press, 1995), 18.
6  Association for Canadian Studies. *Bulletin de l'AEC*, 13 (Summer 1992): 13.
7  The Dominion Institute, 'Polls and Publications,' http://www.dominion.ca/English/polls.html (accessed on 26 May 2004).
8  Historica Foundation, 'Historica,' http://www.histori.ca/default.do (accessed on 26 May 2004).
9  Mark Starowicz, *Making History: The Remarkable Story Behind Canada: A People's History* (Toronto: McClelland & Stewart, 2003), 267.
10 The American history wars are summarized in Gary B. Nash, Charlotte Crabtree and Ross E. Dunn, *History on Trial: Culture Wars and the Teaching of the Past* (New York: Alfred A. Knopf, 1997).
11 The particularly contentious and politicized debate surrounding the creation and implementation of the National Curriculum in History is described in Chapter Six of Duncan Graham and David Tytler, *A Lesson for Us All: The Making of the National Curriculum* (London: Routledge, 1993). Graham was the chairman and chief executive of the National Curriculum Council.

12  For a brief summary of these international cases, see Chapter Six in Nash, Crabtree and Dunn.
13  Nash, Crabtree and Dunn, 7.
14  Granatstein, xviii.
15  Spicer, 18.
16  Benedict Anderson, *Imagined Communities: Reflections on the Origin and Spread of Nationalism*, rev. ed. (London: Verso, 1991), 6.
17  Anthony D. Smith, *National Identity* (Reno: University of Nevada Press, 1991), 3–15.
18  Brian S. Osborne, "Landscapes, Memory, Monuments, and Commemoration: Putting Identity in its Place," *Canadian Ethnic Studies* 33, 3 (2001), 41.
19  For a succinct historical summary of the search for Canadian identity, see Jack Bumsted, "Visions of Canada: A Brief History of Writing on the Canadian Character and the Canadian Identity," in *A Passion for Identity: Canadian Studies for the 21st Century*, 4th ed., ed. David Taras and Beverly Rasporich (Scarborough, ON: Nelson Thomson Learning, 2001), 17–35.
20  See for example *Far and Wide: Essays from Canada*, ed. Sean Armstrong (Toronto: Nelson Canada, 1995); *The Thinking Heart*, ed. George Galt (Kingston: Quarry Press, 1991); *Belonging: The Meaning and Future of Canadian Citizenship*, ed. William Kaplan (Montreal and Kingston: McGill-Queen's University Press, 1993); Philip Resnick, "English Canada: the Nation that Dares Not Speak its Name," in *Beyond Quebec: Taking Stock of Canada*, ed. Kenneth McRoberts (Montreal and Kingston: McGill-Queen's University Press, 1995), 81–92.
21  For analyses of Canada as the world's first postmodern state, see Richard Gwyn, *Nationalism Without Walls: The Unbearable Lightness of Being Canadian* (Toronto: McClelland and Stewart, 1995), and John Ralston Saul, *Reflections of a Siamese Twin: Canada at the End of the Twentieth Century* (Toronto: Viking, 1997).
22  Ken Osborne, "'Our History Syllabus Has us Gasping': History in Canadian Schools – Past, Present, and Future," *Canadian Historical Review* 81, 3 (September 2000), 404–35.
23  Marcel Trudel and Genevieve Jain, *Canadian History Textbooks: a Comparative Study*, Studies of the Royal Commission on Bilingualism and Biculturalism, 5 (Ottawa: Queen's Printer, 1970).
24  See for example Grant McDiarmid and David Pratt, *Teaching Prejudice: A Content Analysis of Social Studies Textbooks Authorized For Use in Ontario* (Toronto: OISE Press, 1971); Kenneth Osborne, *"Hard-working, Temperate and Peaceable" – the Portrayal of Workers in Canadian History Textbooks*, Monographs in Education Series, edited by Alexander Gregor and Keith Wilson (Winnipeg: University of Manitoba, 1980); and, Penney Clark, "Between the Covers: Exposing Images in Social Studies Textbooks," in *The Canadian Anthology of Social Studies: Issues and Strategies for Teachers*, edited by Roland Case and Penney Clark (Vancouver: Pacific Educational Press, 1999), 339–48.
25  Beth Light, Pat Staton and Paula Bourne, "Sex Equity Content in History Textbooks," *The History and Social Science Teacher* 25, 1 (Fall 1989), 18–20; Patricia Baldwin and Douglas Baldwin, "The Portrayal of Women in Classroom Textbooks," *Canadian Social Studies* 26, 3 (Spring 1992), 110–14.

26 Amy von Heyking, "Talking About Americans: the Image of the United States in Canadian Schools, 1900 to 1970 (paper presented at the annual meeting of the Canadian Historical Association, Winnipeg, MB, June 2004).
27 Ian Grosvenor, "'There's No Place Like Home': Education and the Making of National Identity," *History of Education* 28, 3 (1999), 246. In his analysis, Grosvenor draws on the work of cultural theorist Homi Bhabha, best represented in his edited book, *Nation and Narration* (London: Routledge, 1990).
28 Michael Apple and Linda K. Christian-Smith, "The Politics of the Textbook," in *The Politics of the Textbook*, ed. Michael Apple and Linda K. Christian-Smith (New York: Routledge, 1991), 2.
29 Ibid., 4.
30 Robert M. Stamp, "Canadian education and the national identity," in *Canadian Schools and the Canadian Identity*, ed. Alf Chaiton and Neil McDonald (Toronto: Gage Educational Publishing, 1977), 29–37.

## CHAPTER 1

1 Howard Palmer and Tamara Palmer, *Alberta, A New History* (Edmonton: Hurtig Publishers, 1990), 78.
2 George S. Tomkins, *A Common Countenance* (Scarborough, Ontario: Prentice-Hall Canada, 1986), 110.
3 For a thorough examination of the Report and its significance for Canadian schools as well as a general treatment of the impact of the ideas of the New Education on Canada, see Neil Sutherland, *Children in English-Canadian Society: Framing the Twentieth Century Consensus* (Toronto: University of Toronto Press, 1976).
4 Royal Commission on Industrial Training and Technical Education, *Report*, Part IV, 1913, 2290.
5 John M. MacEachran, "History of Education in Alberta," in *Canada and its Provinces*, Vol. 20, edited by Adam Shortt and Arthur G. Doughty (Toronto: Glasgow, Brook & Co., 1914), 494–97.
6 Paul Voisey, *Vulcan: the Making of a Prairie Community* (Toronto: University of Toronto Press, 1988), 180.
7 H.T. Coutts and B.E. Walker, *G. Fred: The Story of G. Fred McNally* (Don Mills: J.M. Dent & Sons, 1964), 60–61.
8 Ibid., 61.
9 "Report of the Committee on School Curriculum," 1911–12, File 26, Box 1, Legislative Papers, Provincial Archives of Alberta, n.p.
10 Voisey, 182.
11 Department of Education, *Annual Report of the Alberta Department of Education* (Edmonton: King's Printer, 1907), 43, hereafter referred to as *Annual Report*.
12 Department of Education, *Annual Report*, 1915, 107.
13 M.I. McKenzie, "School Memories," *Alberta Historical Review* 7, 1 (Winter 1959): 15.
14 George F.G. Stanley, "School Days! School Days!," in *Citymakers*, edited by Max Foran and Sheila S. Jameson (Calgary: Historical Society of Alberta, Chinook Country Chapter, 1987), 11.

15 Examinations in this period are contained in the Department of Education's Annual Reports for the years noted.
16 J.J. Tilley, ed., *Methods in Teaching* (Toronto: George N. Morang & Co., 1899), 243–44.
17 James L. Hughes, et al., eds., *Public School Methods*, vol. 5 (Toronto: School Methods Co., 1908), 165.
18 J.B. Calkin, *Notes on Education* (Truro, Nova Scotia: D.H. Smith & Co., 1888), 265.
19 Ibid., 262.
20 "Report of the Committee on School Curriculum," 1911–12, File 26, Box 1, Legislative Papers, Provincial Archives of Alberta, n.p.
21 James McCaig, "Superintendent's Report," *Annual Report of the Edmonton Public School Board*, 1919, 54–55, Edmonton Public School Board Archives.
22 Quoted in Beverly A. Drake, "Edison School District," *Alberta Historical Review* 19, 4 (Autumn 1971): 23.
23 Maisie Emery Clark, *Memories of a Pioneer Schoolteacher* (n.p., 1968), 10.
24 George F.G. Stanley, 4, 17.
25 Inez B. Hosie, "Little White School House," *Alberta Historical Review* 15, 4 (Autumn 1967): 28.
26 Hugh Garth Teskey, "Memoirs and Musings" (unpublished manuscript, 1993), 15.
27 Charles H. McKenzie, "Growing Up in Alberta, Part Two," *Alberta History* 37, 4 (Autumn 1989): 19.
28 For more on the theme of harmony in nature, see David C. Jones, "The Zeitgeist of Western Settlement: Education and the Myth of the Land," in J. Donald Wilson and David C. Jones, eds., *Schooling and Society in Twentieth Century British Columbia* (Calgary: Detselig Enterprises, 1980), 71–89.
29 W.A. McIntyre, John Dearness and John C. Saul, *Third Book*, Alexandra Readers (Toronto: Morang Educational Co., 1908), 228–31.
30 W.A. McIntyre, John Dearness and John C. Saul, *Second Book*, Alexandra Readers (Toronto: Morang Educational Co., 1908), 86.
31 "The Golden Window," *Third Book*, 32–35; "Country Mouse and City Mouse," *First Book*, Alexandra Readers (Toronto: Morang Educational Co., 1908), 43–47.
32 *Third Book*, 269.
33 W.A. McIntyre, John Dearness and John C. Saul, *Fourth Book*, Alexandra Readers (Toronto: Morang Educational Co., 1908), 261.
34 W.A. McIntyre and John C. Saul, *Primer*, Alexandra Readers (Great Britain: Morang Educational Co., 1908), 71.
35 *Second Book*, 61.
36 E.S. Symes and G.M. Wrong, *An English History* (Toronto: Copp Clark, 1905), 31.
37 W.H.P. Clement, *The History of the Dominion of Canada* (Toronto: W. Briggs, 1897), 122.
38 Arabella B. Buckley and W.J. Robertson, *High School History of England and Canada* (Toronto: Copp Clark, 1891), 259.
39 D.M. Duncan, *The Story of the Canadian People* (Toronto: The MacMillan Co. of Canada, 1913), 219.
40 Ibid., 301.
41 Buckley and Robertson, 400.
42 Duncan, 375.

43 William Swinton, *Outlines of the World's History*, rev. Canadian edition (Halifax: A & W MacKinlay, 1883), iii–iv.
44 Buckley and Robertson, 372.
45 Philip Van Ness Myers, *General History*, revised edition (Boston: Ginn & Co., 1906), 116–17.
46 Duncan, v.
47 Herbert Butterfield, *The Whig Interpretation of History* (London: G. Bell and Sons, 1950), 5. Originally published in 1931.
48 Myers, 11.
49 Ibid., 335.
50 Ibid., 69.
51 W.H.P. Clement, 12–13.
52 Edith L. Marsh, *Where the Buffalo Roamed: The Story of Western Canada Told for the Young* (Toronto: William Briggs, 1908), 175.
53 Duncan, 80.
54 Clement, 39.
55 Duncan, 205.
56 Clement, 99–100.
57 Myers, 269.
58 Ibid., 601.
59 Ibid., 611.
60 *Third Book*, 184.
61 Ibid., 244–48.
62 *Fourth Book*, 314–15.
63 Duncan, 60.
64 For more information about this understanding of English-Canadian identity as defined by its role within the British Empire and its promoters within education, the press and politics, see Carl Berger, *The Sense of Power* (Toronto: University of Toronto Press, 1970).
65 Michael A. Kostek, *A Century and Ten: A History of Edmonton Public Schools* (Edmonton: Edmonton Public Schools, 1992), 192.
66 George F.G. Stanley, 4–5.
67 *Fourth Book*, p. 202.
68 R.S. Jenkins, *Canadian Civics*, Alberta edition (Toronto: Copp Clark, 1912), 7.
69 Marsh, 146.
70 Duncan, 202.
71 Ibid., 172.
72 Clement, 192.
73 *Highroads of British History*, Highroads of History Series, Book VII (London: Thomas Nelson & Sons, n.d.), 259.
74 Symes and Wrong, 155.
75 *Stories from British History*, Highroads of History Series, Book II (London: Thomas Nelson & Sons, 1908), 130.
76 Duncan, 40.
77 Steven P. Boddington, "Education from the Top Down: a Biography of W.H. Swift" (Ph.D. diss., University of Alberta, 1998), 39–40.
78 Marsh, 242.

79 *Primer*, 87.
80 Symes and Wrong, 206.
81 *Stories from British History*, 61.
82 Ibid., 141.
83 Quoted in Michael Kostek, "The Archivist's Corner," *Staff Bulletin* (8 February 1993): 13, Edmonton Public School Board Archives.
84 Hughes et al., eds., 167.
85 Tilley, 8.
86 For more on this theme see, Nancy Sheehan, "Character Training and the Cultural Heritage: An Historical Comparison of Canadian Elementary Readers," in *The Curriculum in Canada in Historical Perspective*, George Tomkins, ed. (Vancouver: Canadian Society for the Study of Education, University of British Columbia, 1979), 77–84.
87 *Second Book*, p. 11.
88 Jenkins, 169.
89 National Conference on Character Education in Relation to Canadian Citizenship, *Report of the Proceedings*. (Winnipeg: Council on Character Education, 1919), 94.
90 *Fourth Book*, 291.
91 *Primer*, 67.
92 *A Handbook to the Alexandra Readers* (Toronto: Macmillan Co. of Canada, 1914), 29.

## CHAPTER 2

1 John W. Chalmers, *Schools of the Foothills Province* (Toronto: University of Toronto Press, 1967), 88.
2 "Women's Institute Doing Splendid Service Toward Betterment of Education," *Calgary Herald* 14 June 1922.
3 "Value of Education: an Editorial for Young People," *Calgary Herald* 1 September 1922.
4 "Report of the Education Committee," File 170A, Premier Papers, Provincial Archives of Alberta.
5 Department of Education, *Annual Report* (Edmonton: Department of Education, 1926), 14.
6 "Today's Young Girls," *Calgary Herald* 12 March 1923.
7 "Crescent Heights P.-T. Association Held Last Meeting," *Calgary Herald* 5 June 1922.
8 Rachel Horner, "Valedictory," *The Yearbook, South Calgary High School, 1924–5*, School Yearbook Collection, Glenbow Library.
9 Charles H. McKenzie, "Growing Up in Alberta, Part Three," *Alberta History* 38, 1 (Winter 1990), 27–28.
10 H.T. Coutts and B.E. Walker, *G. Fred: The Story of G. Fred McNally* (Don Mills: J.M. Dent & Sons, 1964), 40–43.
11 John W. Chalmers, *Gladly Would He Teach* (Edmonton: ATA Educational Trust, 1978), 30.

12 See Chapters Four through Nine in R.J.W. Selleck, *The New Education: The English Background 1870–1914* (Melbourne: Sir Isaac Pitman & Sons, 1968).
13 For an examination of these reforms in Ontario, see Chapter Three in Robert M. Stamp, *The Schools of Ontario, 1876–1976* (Toronto: University of Toronto Press, 1982).
14 Ibid., 312.
15 Department of Education, *Annual Report*, 1921, 42.
16 Department of Education, *Part I of the Programme of Studies for the Elementary Schools of Alberta, English, Citizenship and Arithmetic* (Edmonton: King's Printer, 1929), 127. For the sake of clarification, it should be noted that the revised course of studies for elementary schools was developed in 1921, introduced in 1922, and underwent minor revisions again in 1929, at which point it was renamed the "programme" of studies.
17 Department of Education, *Part I of the Course of Studies for the Elementary Schools of Alberta, English and Citizenship* (Edmonton: King's Printer, 1922), 128.
18 Ibid., 130, 135, 138, 141.
19 "Report of Calgary Teachers," Curriculum History File #3, H.C. Newland Papers, Alberta Teachers' Association Archives.
20 A. Jordan, "Citizenship in Grades Six, Seven and Eight," A.T.A. *Magazine* 4, 9 (February 1924): 15–18.
21 Phyllis M.E. La Fleur, "Three Alberta Teachers: Lives and Thoughts" (master's thesis, University of Alberta, 1977), 66.
22 *Annual Report*, 1931, 49.
23 Ibid., 54.
24 *Annual Report*, 1934, 63.
25 Ibid., 55.
26 See, for example, Roger McKee Papers and William Tomyn Papers in the Edmonton Public School Board Archives and the Anette Christofferson Papers in the Glenbow Archives.
27 La Fleur, 30.
28 Ibid., 50.
29 Quoted in Boddington, 67.
30 *Annual Report*, 1924, 20–21.
31 *Annual Report*, 1925, 21.
32 See the reports of Chief Inspector of Schools G.W. Gorman and Inspector MacGregor in *Annual Report*, 1924, 63, 65.
33 *Annual Report*, 1928, 44.
34 *Annual Report*, 1925, 61.
35 Annual General Meeting Minutes, 1925, 9, AGM Records, Alberta Teachers' Association Archives.
36 Annual General Meeting Minutes, 1927, 57–58, AGM Records, Alberta Teachers' Association Archives.
37 David Tyack and Larry Cuban, *Tinkering Toward Utopia: A Century of Public School Reform* (Cambridge, MA: Harvard University Press, 1995).

38 Department of Education, *Handbook of Secondary Schools* (Edmonton: Department of Education, 1927), 83.
39 W.L. Grant, *History of Canada*, new and revised edition (London: William Heinemann, 1923), 84.
40 *The Canadian Readers, Book IV* (Toronto: W.J. Gage & Co., 1922), 123–24.
41 *Annual Report*, 1917, 96.
42 *Annual Report*, 1919, 80.
43 *Annual Report*, 1920, 106.
44 Neil Sutherland, *Children in English-Canadian Society: Framing the Twentieth-Century Consensus* (Toronto: University of Toronto Press, 1976), 203.
45 For more information see N. Kach, "Education and Ethnic Acculturation: a Case Study," *Essays on Canadian Education*, ed. Nick Kach, et al. (Calgary: Detselig Enterprises, 1986): 41–60; and, Manoly R. Lupul, "The Schools and French- and Ukrainian-Language Claims in Alberta to 1918," *Exploring Our Educational Past*, ed. Nick Kach and Kas Mazurek (Calgary: Detselig Enterprises, 1992): 73–91.
46 For a discussion of the impact of these policies on Alberta minority groups, see Manfred Prokop, "Canadianization of Immigrant Children," *Alberta History* 37, 2 (Spring 1989): 1–10.
47 Rosa Bruno-Jofre, "Citizenship and Schooling in Manitoba, 1918–1945," *Manitoba History* 36 (Winter 1998), 28. For more within a general Canadian context, see Ken Osborne, "Education is the Best National Insurance: Citizenship Education in Canadian Schools, Past and Present," *Canadian and International Education* 25, 2 (December 1996): 40–43.
48 Osborne, 44–45.
49 See for example Chapter 34 on "Literature and Art" in Grant, *History of Canada*, new and revised edition.
50 *Ryerson Canadian History Readers* (Toronto: Ryerson, 1926–32) and D.J. Dickie, *Dent's Canadian History Readers*, 8 vols. (Toronto: Dent, 1925–28).
51 D.J. Dickie, *Canadian Geography Readers*, 5 vols. (Toronto: Dent, 1928–32).
52 M.H. Long, *Knights Errant of the Wilderness* (Toronto: The Macmillan Company, 1919).
53 See letters to the I.O.D.E. chapters in Correspondence File, 1930–1939, Department of Education, Provincial Archives of Alberta.
54 Annual General Meeting, 1925, 12, AGM Records, Alberta Teachers' Association Archives.
55 *Handbook for Secondary Schools*, 86, 87.
56 H. Napier Moore, "Why United States Textbooks in Canadian Schools?" *MacLean's*, 1 July 1929, 3.
57 Report to Premier Brownlee from the Edmonton Chamber of Commerce Special Committee on Textbooks in Alberta, dated 24 September 1930, File 138A, Premier's Papers, Provincial Archives of Alberta.
58 "1931 U.F.A. Annual Conference Resolutions," File 170C, Premier's Papers, Provincial Archives of Alberta.
59 James McCaig, *Studies in Citizenship* (Toronto: Educational Book Co., 1927), 55.
60 *Part I of the Course of Studies for the Elementary Schools of Alberta*, 134.
61 *Handbook for Secondary Schools*, 98.

62  H.J. Keith, National Secretary of the League of Nations Society in Canada to G.F. McNally, 30 May 1934, Correspondence Files, Department of Education Papers, Provincial Archives of Alberta.
63  *Handbook for Secondary Schools*, p. 90.
64  Grant, *History of Canada*, new and revised edition, 16–17.
65  Ibid., 283. It was statements such as these that resulted in complaints being made about the textbook in British Columbia. Under pressure from the Orange Lodge, the Department of Education in B.C. banned the book. See Charles W. Humphries, "The Banning of a Book in British Columbia," *BC Studies* 1 (Winter 1968–69): 1–12. Alberta authorized a revised version of this text.
66  Department of Education, *Part I of the Programme of Studies for the Elementary Schools of Alberta* (Edmonton: King's Printer, 1929), 127.
67  *South Calgary High School Yearbook, 1925–6*, 2, School Yearbook Collection, Glenbow Library.
68  "Report of the Committee on Physical Education," Curriculum History File #1, H.C. Newland Papers, Alberta Teachers' Association Archives.
69  W.A. McIntyre, *Talks and Discussions With Young Teachers* (Toronto: Copp Clark, 1915), 100.
70  Henry S. Curtis, *Education Through Play* (New York: The Macmillan Co., 1915), 75.
71  *Annual Report*, 1920, 98.
72  Herbert T. Coutts, "The Unfinished Journey of Herbert T. 'Pete' Coutts," unpublished manuscript, 1982, 35–36.
73  W.B. Poaps, "The Teacher," *A.T.A. Magazine* 2, 7 (December 1921), 34.
74  W.E. Hay, "The Canadian Consciousness," *A.T.A. Magazine* 8, 1 (July 1927), 15.
75  "Report of Calgary Local on Curriculum Revision," Curriculum History File #3, H.C. Newland Papers, Alberta Teachers' Association Archives.
76  "Report of the General Committee on the Revision of the Elementary School Curriculum," 1921, Legislative Papers, Provincial Archives of Alberta.
77  *The Canadian Reader*, Book II (Toronto: W.J. Gage & Co., 1931), 10–14 and 31–32.
78  Alice M. Chesterton, *The Garden of Childhood* (London: Thomas Nelson & Sons, 1905), 16.
79  McCaig, 54.
80  Ibid., 4.
81  Osborne, 43.
82  "High Schools Fails to Meet Needs of Modern Students," *Albertan*, 7 November 1934.
83  "Report of the Educational Committee," *The U.F.A.* 10, 3 (February 2, 1931), 22.
84  "Are Our Objectives in Education Valid?" *A.T.A. Magazine* 10, 11 (July 1930), 18.
85  W. Cameron, "School History and Culture," *A.T.A. Magazine* 6, 11 (November 1926), 30.
86  "Is our Education on the Right Track?" *A.T.A. Magazine* 9, 3 (November 1928), 28.
87  H.R. Leaver, "History – Record or Opinion?" *A.T.A. Magazine* 13, 11 (July 1933), 2.
88  "1934 Resolutions of the Annual Convention of the United Farmers of Alberta," File 170D, Premier's Papers, Provincial Archives of Alberta.
89  Annual General Meeting, 1934, 9, AGM Records, Alberta Teachers' Association Archives.

## CHAPTER 3

1. Palmer and Palmer, 244.
2. "Humanization of Education Imperative Need Premier Aberhart Tells H.S.A. Federation," *Calgary Herald*, 7 November 1936.
3. Osborne, "Education is the Best National Insurance," 42.
4. David Elliott and Iris Miller, *Bible Bill* (Edmonton: Reidmore Books, 1987), 44.
5. The fact that progressive curriculum reform was initiated by the U.F.A. government and continued by the Social Credit government is clarified in J. Donald Wilson, Robert M. Stamp and Louis-Philippe Audet, eds., *Canadian Education: A History* (Scarborough, ON: Prentice-Hall, 1970), 375.
6. T.C. Byrne, *Alberta's Revolutionary Leaders* (Calgary: Detselig Enterprises, 1991), 127. McNally led Bible study classes for many years. His students, who called themselves "The Knights of the Cross," included education professors such as K.F. Argue, at least one Minister of Education in Anders Aalborg, and others such as educational historian John Chalmers and teacher Earl Buxton. There is strong evidence that McNally, like Aberhart, supported progressive education reforms because he felt they encouraged Christian virtues like honesty, cooperation, sharing and compassion for others. See H.T. Coutts and B.E. Walker, G. Fred, Chapter Eleven.
7. G.W. Congo to Aberhart, 20 March 1939, File 740B, Premiers' Papers, Provincial Archives of Alberta.
8. "The Theory of Evolution: Can it Be Proven?", 6, File 703B, Premier's Papers, Provincial Archives of Alberta.
9. Memorandum from McNally to Aberhart, 14 July 1942, File 703B, Premier's Papers, Provincial Archives of Alberta.
10. Aberhart to Mabel Giles, 25 July 1942, File 703B, Premier's Papers, Provincial Archives of Alberta.
11. R.S. Patterson, "The Canadian Response to Progressive Education," *Essays on Canadian Education*, ed. N. Kach, et al. (Calgary: Detselig Enterprises, 1986), 62.
12. Ibid., 67.
13. Ibid., 68–69.
14. Quoted in Stamp, *The Schools of Ontario*, 167.
15. Patterson, 71.
16. Ibid., 72–73.
17. Ibid., 73.
18. Ibid., 73–74.
19. Stamp, 178–82.
20. Quoted in La Fleur, 15.
21. For a complete analysis of this movement within American progressivism, see Chapter Seven in Herbert M. Kliebard, *The Struggle for an American Curriculum, 1893–1958*, 2nd ed. (New York: Routledge, 1995).
22. Chalmers, 464.
23. Quoted in Boddington, 161.
24. Ibid., 156–59.
25. "Who's Who Among Educationalists," *Edmonton Bulletin*, 8 July 1936.

26  Donalda Dickie, *The Enterprise in Theory and Practice* (Toronto: W.J. Gage & Co., 1941), 43.
27  Ibid., 57.
28  Harold Rugg and Ann Shumaker, *The Child-Centered School* (New York: World Book Co., 1928), 36.
29  K.F. Argue, "These New Methods," *Alberta School Trustee* 13, 3 (March 1943), 13.
30  Ibid., 14.
31  Ibid., 15.
32  Department of Education, *Programme of Studies for the Elementary School* (Edmonton: Department of Education, 1942), 57.
33  Department of Education, *Programme of Studies for the Intermediate School* (Edmonton: Department of Education, 1935), 28.
34  For a thorough discussion of the lively debates about history teaching in the 1920s in Canada, see Ken Osborne, "'New Teaching' or 'Idealistic Twaddle'? A 1920s Model of History Teaching," *Canadian Social Studies* 35, 3 (Spring 2001), http://www.quasar.ualberta.ca/css/Css_35_3/CLvoices_from_the_past.htm (accessed on 18 August 2004).
35  See Peter Novick, *That Noble Dream: The "Objectivity Question" and the American Historical Profession* (Cambridge: Cambridge University Press, 1988).
36  Rugg's social studies program, called *Man and His Changing Society*, was organized around critical social problems facing the United States and openly advocated left-leaning solutions that he argued would lead to greater social justice. The program was initially popular in many school districts, but was eventually abandoned when it was widely criticized as anti-capitalist and even anti-American. For more information about this program, see Kliebard, *The Struggle for the American Curriculum, 1893–1958*, 171–8.
37  See W.D. McDougall, *In and Out of the Classroom, 1914–1964*, unpublished manuscript in McDougall Papers, Provincial Archives of Alberta.
38  Ibid., 69.
39  Department of Education, *Programme of Studies for the High School, Bulletin III* (Edmonton: Department of Education, 1939), 3.
40  For more information about how the curriculum was communicated to teachers and the public, see Amy von Heyking, "Selling Progressive Education to Albertans," *Historical Studies in Education/Revue d'histoire de l'éducation* 10, 1 & 2 (Spring and Fall 1998): 67–84.
41  "The Chronicle, 1941–2," Calgary Normal School Papers, University of Calgary Archives.
42  G. Derwood Baker, "When Parents Ask," *A.T.A. Magazine* 22, 6 (February 1942): 6–8.
43  J.F. Watkin, "Classroom Procedure in High School Social Studies," *A.T.A. Magazine* 20, 5 (January 1940), 13.
44  Gulbrand Loken, "Scrapbook Work and Topics for Social Studies in Grade IX," *A.T.A. Magazine* 19, 2 (October 1938), 27.
45  *Annual Report*, 1936, 53.
46  *Annual Report*, 1941, 71.
47  *Annual Report*, 1945, 24.

48  Stanley Clarke, "Evaluation in Social Studies I and II," *A.T.A. Magazine* 20, 1 (September 1939).
49  *Annual Report*, 1937, 62.
50  "Book Review," *A.T.A. Magazine* 27, 2 (October 1937), 12.
51  Grade VIII Social Studies Notebook, Alan Bell Papers, Edmonton Public School Board Archives.
52  W.D. McDougall and Gilbert Paterson, *Our Country and its People* (Toronto: Ryerson Press, 1938), 18.
53  J.S. Schapiro, R.B. Morris and F.H. Soward, *Civilisation in Europe and the World* (Toronto: Copp Clark, 1938), 19 and 43.
54  W.D. McDougall and Gilbert Paterson, *Our Empire and its Neighbours* (Toronto: Ryerson Press, 1937), 236–37.
55  *Our Country and its People*, 142 and 155.
56  For more information about the committee appointed by the Canadian and Newfoundland Education Association to survey history texts used in Canadian schools, and about the 1944 Senate debates surrounding history instruction in schools, see Ken Osborne, "Canadian Historians and National History: a 1950 Survey," *Canadian Social Studies* 36, 3 (Spring 2002) http://www.quasar.ualberta.ca/css/Css_36_3/CLvoices_from_the_past.htm (accessed on 18 August 2004), and Ken Osborne, "The Senate Textbook Debate of 1944," *Canadian Social Studies* 37, 1 (Fall 2002) http://www.quasar.ualberta.ca/css/Css_37_1/CLvoices_from_the_past.htm (accessed on 18 August 2004).
57  G. Fred McNally, "The Place of the School," *The Alberta School Trustee* 14, 6 (June 1944), 8.
58  W. Stewart Wallace, *A Reader in Canadian Civics* (Toronto: MacMillan Co. of Canada, 1935), 105.
59  George W. Brown, *Building the Canadian Nation* (Toronto: J.M. Dent & Sons, 1942), 435.
60  V.P. Seary and Gilbert Paterson, *The Story of Civilization* (Toronto: Ryerson Press, 1934), 691.
61  F.R. Scott, *Canada Today* (London: Oxford University Press, 1938). See 34–35 and 47–52. Scott's support of government activism was also demonstrated by the leading role he played in the establishment of the C.C.F.
62  George Brown, *Canadian Democracy in Action* (Toronto: J.M. Dent & Sons, 1945), 4.
63  James A. Quinn and Arthur Repke, *Living in the Social World*, revised edition, (Chicago: J.B. Lippincott Co., 1948), 526–27 and 529.
64  "General Science in the Intermediate School," 1940s, Addresses to the A.T.A., Doucette Papers, File 2: Public Addresses, University of Calgary Archives. Doucette was a school inspector, Normal School instructor, and later head of the Calgary Branch of the University of Alberta.
65  *Programme of Studies for the Elementary School* (1936), 144.
66  Ibid., 57–58.
67  Department of Education, *Programme of Studies for the High School, Bulletin IV* (Edmonton: A. Shnitka, 1939), 27.
68  *Programme of Studies for the Intermediate School* (1935), 48 and 52.

69   Schapiro et al., 335.
70   Seary and Paterson, 698.
71   Hanson Hart Webster, *The World's Messengers* (Boston: Houghton Mifflin Co., 1938), 3.
72   Scott, 83.
73   Ibid., 52.
74   W.D. McDougall and Gilbert Paterson, *The World of To-day* (Toronto: The Ryerson Press, 1937), 237.
75   McDougall and Paterson, *Our Country and its People*, 33.
76   *Programme of Studies for the Elementary School* (1936), 113.
77   *Our Country and its People*, 179 and 183.
78   *Programme of Studies for the Intermediate School*, 41.
79   *Our Empire and its Neighbors*, pp. 9–10.
80   *Programme of Studies for the Elementary School* (1936), 116.
81   See *Our Country and its People*, 194.
82   W.R. McAuliffe, *Modern Europe Explained: A Guide to Present-Day History*, revised edition (London: Blackie & Son, 1938), 1.
83   R.O. Hughes, *The Making of Today's World*, revised edition, (Boston: Allyn & Bacon, 1950), 736.
84   "School Book Nazi Tinted Voters Told," *Calgary Albertan*, 15 November 1939. See also "Nazi Propaganda in Alberta School Book?" *Calgary Herald*, 15 November 1939.
85   Quoted in "About a Textbook," *Calgary Albertan*, 20 November 1939.
86   Newland to Mr. J.H. Jackson, 4 November 1939, File 740B, Premier's Papers, Provincial Archives of Alberta.
87   "Committee on Social Studies," dated 2 December 1939, File 740B, Premier's Papers, Provincial Archives of Alberta.
88   W.D. McDougall, *In and Out of the Classroom*, 73. It should be noted that the candidate who raised the issue, E.H. Starr, was defeated in the municipal election. However, the controversy surrounding the text did not disappear. In May 1941 the Liberal M.P. from Athabasca, Mr. Dechene, read the same passages from *The World of To-day* in the House of Commons to illustrate the "bunk" the Social Credit government in Alberta was teaching children. Mr. Dechene argued that the text taught children that democracy had failed and demonstrated the lack of patriotism of the Social Credit party. Lethbridge Social Credit M.P. Mr. Blackmore ended the debate by reading a letter from Aberhart explaining that the book in question had been revised. House of Commons, *Debates*, 8 May 1941, 2655–7, and 12 May 1941, 2754–8.
89   Stanley Rand, "Social Studies in Grade Nine," *A.T.A. Magazine* 17, 5 (January 1937): 24–25.
90   C. Sansom, "Progressive Curriculum," *A.T.A. Magazine* 22, 5 (January 1942): 40.
91   Quoted in "Teachers Told to Preach Democracy," *Edmonton Bulletin*, 16 October 1941.
92   Lucy A. Bagnall, *Contemporary Problems, National, Imperial and International* (Calgary: Western Canada Institute, 1939), 101.
93   *Annual Report*, 1942, 14.

180 NOTES

94 Quoted in "History and Objectives of the Junior High School in Alberta," 5, Correspondence with M. Watts, Faculty of Education Papers, University of Alberta Archives.
95 "A Guide for Evaluating Growth in Citizenship," (1947), 1–2, Bayly Papers, Edmonton Public School Board Archives.
96 "The Ethical Content of Alberta School Programme," File 703A, Premier's Papers, Provincial Archives of Alberta.
97 "Address by Honorable R.E. Ansley," *The Alberta School Trustee* 17, 1 (December 1947), 24.
98 Letter from Ivan Casey to John Gereluk, dated 3 March 1952, File 1578, Premier's Papers, Provincial Archives of Alberta.
99 Stamp, *The Schools of Ontario, 1876–1976*, 175.
100 Frances L. Ormond, *Highroads to Reading, Book Two* (Toronto: Ryerson Press, 1934), 117–23 and 164–67.
101 "Complete Change in School Subjects Suggested," *The Albertan*, 9 February 1934.
102 Donalda Dickie, "New Lamps for Old," *The Alberta School Trustee* 9, 10 (December 1939), 13.
103 "Convention Address, Hon. Solon Low," *The Alberta School Trustee* 13, 11 (December 1943), 7.
104 H.E. Smith, "Is Education a Failure?" *The Alberta School Trustee* 18, 5 (May 1948), 14.
105 "Canadian Education at the Junction," Speech to the Women's University Club, 3 April 1950, Box 2: Public Addresses, Doucette Papers, University of Calgary Archives.
106 "Education in the Modern World," Speech to the Women's Canadian Club, 1947, Box 2: Public Addresses, Doucette Papers, University of Calgary Archives.
107 "Canadian Education at the Junction," Doucette Papers, University of Calgary Archives.
108 "Complete Change in School Subjects Suggested," *The Albertan*, 9 February 1934.
109 Alberta Department of Education, *Foundations of Education* (Edmonton: King's Printer, 1949), 9.

## CHAPTER 4

1 In 1947, Manning purged the party of its older Social Credit hardliners. The anti-Semitism of the Social Credit Board and several members of the provincial and federal parties increasingly embarrassed him. By disbanding the Board and expelling the radicals from the party, Manning created a party that appealed to mainstream, conservative voters. Among the party members expelled in the purge was R.E. Ansley, then Minister of Education.
2 Palmer and Palmer, 303.
3 Alvin Finkel, *The Social Credit Phenomenon in Alberta* (Toronto: University of Toronto Press, 1989), 100–101.
4 Ibid., 124.
5 Dr. W.G. Hardy, *Education in Alberta* (Calgary: Calgary Herald, n.d.). The articles originally appeared in February 1954 in the *Calgary Herald*, the *Edmonton Journal*,

the *Lethbridge Herald* and the *Medicine Hat News*. The *Calgary Herald* published the articles together in a pamphlet.
6   Department of Education, *Annual Report* (1945), 24.
7   "The Three R's," *Lethbridge Herald*, reprinted in *The Alberta School Trustee* 16, 9 (September 1946), 28.
8   Hardy, Education in Alberta, 17.
9   Ibid., 13.
10  Betty Horton, "Memories of Inglewood School," unpublished manuscript in Edmonton Public School Board Archives.
11  "Education Commission Urged to Suggest Annual Revisions," *Edmonton Journal*, 28 February 1953, Scrapbook Hansard.
12  "Page Regrets Low Standard for High School Diplomas," *Edmonton Journal*, 26 February 1953, Scrapbook Hansard.
13  *Calgary Herald*, 24 March 1954, Scrapbook Hansard.
14  *Calgary Herald*, 28 March 1952, Scrapbook Hansard.
15  "6-Week Training for Teachers Far 'Short of Need'," *Calgary Herald*, 23 March 1955, Scrapbook Hansard.
16  Ibid.
17  "Progressive Education 'Uniform Mediocrity'," *Alberta School Trustee* 17, 9 (October 1947), 24.
18  Hardy, Education in Alberta, 31–33.
19  "MLA Would Boost Salary For Teachers," *Edmonton Journal*, 4 March 1958, Scrapbook Hansard.
20  "MLA Raps Neglect of 3-Rs in Schools," *Edmonton Journal*, 18 March 1958, Scrapbook Hansard.
21  Hardy, Education in Alberta, 23.
22  Citizens' Committee on Education, "Submission on the Problems of Education," and University Women's Clubs, "A Brief on Education," Cornelia Wood Papers, Box 4: Submissions to the Standing Committee of the Legislature on Agriculture, Colonization, Immigration and Education, Provincial Archives of Alberta.
23  Hilda Neatby, *So Little for the Mind* (Toronto: Clarke, Irwin & Co., 1953), 17.
24  Hardy, Education in Alberta, 19.
25  Ibid.
26  "The Three R's," *The Alberta School Trustee* 16, 9 (September 1946), 28, reprinted from the *Lethbridge Herald*.
27  *Calgary Herald*, 24 November 1947.
28  Angus MacQueen, "The Failure of Education," *Alberta School Trustee* 18, 3 (March 1948), 6–10.
29  Edmonton Diocesan Board of Religious Education of the Church of England in Canada, "Submission on Christian Education in Alberta Schools," Box 15: Correspondence regarding religious education, Department of Education Papers, Provincial Archives of Alberta.
30  Teachers' Catechetics Class Notes, 28 November 1937, Bishop Carroll Papers, Calgary Roman Catholic Diocese Archives.
31  Talk Number One to the Catholic Education Association, 10 April 1947, Bishop Carroll Papers, Calgary Roman Catholic Diocese Archives.

32 "Report of the Education and Finance Committee," Minutes of the Ratepayers' Meeting, 29 October 1943, Annual Reports, Calgary Roman Catholic School District #1, Calgary Roman Catholic Diocese Archives.
33 "Report of the Education and Finance Committee," Minutes of the Ratepayers' Meeting, 3 November 1944, Annual Reports, Calgary Roman Catholic School District #1, Calgary Roman Catholic Diocese Archives.
34 "Report of the Board of Trustees," Minutes of the Ratepayers' Meeting, 23 September 1952, Annual Reports, Calgary Roman Catholic School District #1, Calgary Roman Catholic Diocese Archives.
35 *Calgary Herald*, 28 March 1952, Scrapbook Hansard.
36 Jennie Elliott, "Discipline and the 3 R's," *Alberta School Trustee* 16, 12 (December 1946), 17.
37 Alberta Federation of Home and School Associations, "A Brief Concerning Education in Alberta," March 1954, Box 4: Submissions to the Standing Committee of the Legislature on Agriculture, Colonization, Immigration and Education, Cornelia Wood Papers, Provincial Archives of Alberta.
38 "Radio, Telephone Called School 'Fifth Columns'," *Calgary Herald*, 19 April 1950.
39 "Students Must Obtain Sense of Direction," *Calgary Herald*, 7 March 1951.
40 M.E. LaZerte, "Fifty Years of Education in Alberta," *A.T.A. Magazine* 35, 10 (June 1955), 7.
41 F.G. Buchanan, "Revision of the School Curriculum," in Programme for Alberta's Child Welfare Week, April 12 to 18, 1936, in File 1263B, Premier's Papers, Provincial Archives of Alberta.
42 "Educational Problems," a booklet published by the Alberta Education Council, 1952, in Box 15: Pamphlets, Clippings, Doucette Papers, University of Calgary Archives.
43 H.E. Smith, "Can Schools Improve Society?" *A.T.A. Magazine* 31, 6 (February 1951), 11.
44 "Low Standards in Education," *Calgary Herald*, 18 March 1955, Scrapbook Hansard.
45 "Aalborg Defends Education System," *Calgary Herald*, 1 April 1955, Scrapbook Hansard.
46 L.H. Bussard, "School Board Review of Progress," *Hamilton Highlights, Hamilton Junior High School Yearbook*, 1955–56, 3, School Yearbook Collection, Glenbow Library.
47 S.R. Hrynewich, "Principal's Message," *The Cornerstone, Bassano High School Yearbook*, 1959, n.p., School Yearbook Collection, Glenbow Library.
48 F. Betton, "Principal's Message," *Footprints, Yearbook of Bow Valley Central High School*, 1954–55, 6, School Yearbook Collection, Glenbow Library.
49 T.C. Byrne, "On Curriculum Building," *Occasional Speeches and Writings, Vol. 2* (Athabasca: Athabasca University, 1971), 595.
50 For a discussion of Royal Commissions on Education across Canada and resulting curriculum policy revisions in this era, see George S. Tomkins, *A Common Countenance* (Scarborough, ON: Prentice-Hall, 1986), 278–83, 291–94.
51 Senate, *Debates*, 19 February 1959, 193–94.
52 "Low Standards in Education," *Calgary Herald*, 18 March 1955, Scrapbook Hansard.
53 Department of Education, *Annual Report* (1952), 58.

54 Dr. A.G. McCalla, "A Parent's View," *Alberta Home and School News* 10, 6 (March 1955), 3.
55 "Facing the Problem of Curriculum Organization," radio script aired 22 February 1956, Box 3, Doucette Papers, University of Calgary Archives.
56 "Watkins Motion Stirs Clash Over Curricula in Schools," *Calgary Herald*, 21 March 1958, Scrapbook Hansard.
57 H.L. Campbell, *Curriculum Trends in Canadian Education* (Toronto: W.J. Gage & Co., 1952), 106.
58 "Education and the Child," Box 2: Public Addresses, Doucette Papers, University of Calgary Archives.
59 Department of Education, *Senior High School Handbooks, 1957–8* (Edmonton: Curriculum Branch, 1957), in Box 2 (uncatalogued), Curriculum Branch Papers, Provincial Archives of Alberta.
60 Ibid., 5–6.
61 Department of Education, *Elementary Curriculum Guide for Social Studies-Enterprise (Interim)* (Edmonton: Curriculum Branch, 1964), 6.
62 Department of Education, *Program of Studies for the Elementary Schools of Alberta* (Edmonton: Curriculum Branch, 1963), 17.
63 Department of Education, *Senior High School Curriculum Guide for Social Studies 10, 20 and 30* (Edmonton: Curriculum Branch, 1955), 16.
64 Department of Education, *Program of Studies for Junior High Schools* (Edmonton: Curriculum Branch, 1963).
65 Department of Education, *Program of Studies for Senior High Schools of Alberta* (Edmonton: Curriculum Branch, 1965).
66 Lewis Hertzman, "The Sad Demise of History: Social Studies in the Alberta Schools," *Dalhousie Review* 43, 4 (Winter 1963–4), 516.
67 "A Look at Social Studies," Curriculum Newsletter, March 1962, 3, Box 2 (uncatalogued), Department of Education Papers, Education Publications, Provincial Archives of Alberta.
68 Department of Education, *Junior High School Curriculum Guide for Social Studies-Language* (Edmonton: Curriculum Branch, 1963), 19.
69 Department of Education, *Annual Report* (1957), 32.
70 Department of Education, *Annual Report* (1958), 42.
71 Department of Education, *Annual Report* (1959), 64.
72 Department of Education, *Annual Report* (1960), 33.
73 See for example, *Program of Studies for Junior High Schools of Alberta* (1963), p. 24.
74 A.F. Olsen, "Teaching Procedures in Social Studies," *Alberta Journal of Educational Research* 11, 2 (June 1965): 116–24.
75 D.W. Ray, "An Experimental Comparison of the Relative Effectiveness of Two Methods of Teaching the Social Studies in Grade Eleven," *Alberta Journal of Educational Research* 11, 1 (March 1965), 52.
76 Quoted in *One World* VII, 2 (January 1969): n.p. More information about the impact of Hodgetts' report, *What Culture? What Heritage?*, will be provided in Chapter Five.
77 Ibid.
78 Griffith Taylor, Dorothy J. Seivereight and Trevor Lloyd, *Canada and Her Neighbours*, rev. ed. (Toronto: Ginn & Co., 1958), p. 3.

79 "6-Week Training For Teachers Far 'Short of Need'," *Calgary Herald*, 23 March 1955, Scrapbook Hansard.
80 A Froebel, "What Subjects Should be Taught in Our Schools?" *The Alberta School Trustee* 27, 4 (April 1957), 19.
81 Reprinted as, Robert Warren, "Are We Raising a Generation of Failures?" *The Alberta School Trustee* 31, 4 (April 1961), 15.
82 Department of Education, *Program of Studies for Elementary Schools of Alberta* (1963), 7.
83 M.L. Watts, "Change Factors and Trends in the High School Program," in *Educational Change: Problems and Prospects*, edited by R. Wardhaugh and J.W.G. Ivany (Edmonton: Department of Secondary Education, University of Alberta, 1964), 54–55.
84 Department of Education, *Program of Studies for Junior High Schools of Alberta* (1963), 28–29.
85 Chester W. New and Charles E. Phillips, *Ancient and Medieval History* (Toronto: Clarke, Irwin & Co., 1941), 1.
86 Lester B. Rogers, Fay Adams and Walker Brown, *The Ancient and Medieval World* (Toronto: Clarke, Irwin & Co., 1949), 128.
87 W.G. Hardy, *Our Heritage from the Past* (Toronto: McClelland & Stewart, 1964), 42. Hardy's text was unusual for the period, however, in that it was one of the few written solely by a university professor. Generally textbooks used in the history sections of social studies courses were coauthored by university professors and classroom teachers or authors of children's literature. For example, *The Story of Canada*, used in Grade VII, was written by George Brown, a professor of history at the University of Toronto. Eleanor Harman and Marsh Jeanneret, who were editors specializing in works for children, were given credit for coauthoring the text. Likewise, Queen's history professor Arthur Lower coauthored the high school textbook *Canada – A Nation and How it Came To Be*, with J.W. Chafe, a Winnipeg high school teacher. The text was based on Prof. Lower's *Colony to Nation* (Toronto: Longman, Green & Company, 1946). Edmonton high school teachers Bertha Lawrence, L.C. Mix and C.S. Wilkie modified University of Toronto history professor Edgar McInnis's *North America and the Modern World* to create *Canada and the Modern World*, the required text for Grade XII social studies for fifteen years. Because of the unique demands of the Alberta social studies program, Alberta educators continued to write many of the textbooks used in the province. Lawrence, Mix and Wilkie, who also served on the secondary social studies curriculum committee for the Department of Education, collaborated to write the Grade XI textbook, *Our European Heritage*. W.D. McDougall wrote the civics text used in this period, the Grade VIII text on the Commonwealth, and with T.G. Finn, another professor of education, wrote the Grade IX text, *Canada in the Western World*.
88 J.W. Chafe and A.R.M. Lower, *Canada – A Nation and How It Came To Be* (Toronto: Longman, Green & Co., 1948), xi.
89 George W. Brown, Eleanor Harman, Marsh Jeanneret, *The Story of Canada* (Toronto: Copp Clark, 1950), 261.
90 *Senior High School Curriculum Guide for Social Studies 10, 20 and 30* (1955), 80.

91 W.D. McDougall, *The Commonwealth of Nations* (Toronto: Ryerson Press, 1952), 406.
92 For more on the treatment of the United States in Canadian schools, see Amy von Heyking, "Talking About Americans: The Image of the United States in English-Canadian Schools, 1900 to 1970" (paper presented at the annual meeting of the Canadian Historical Association, Winnipeg, MB, June 2004).
93 Brown, et al., vii–viii.
94 Lucy Bagnall and Douglas Norton, *Contemporary Problems, National, Imperial and International*, rev. ed. (Calgary: Western Canada Institute, 1946), 169.
95 W.D. McDougall and T.G. Finn, *Canada in the Western World* (Toronto: W.J. Gage & Co., 1955), 428–29.
96 Brown, et al., 399; and, Chafe and Lower, xi.
97 "Social Credit Attitude to UN Questioned by PC Member," *Edmonton Journal*, 24 March 1954, Scrapbook Hansard.
98 "Premier Declares SC Party Supports Principle of UN," *Edmonton Journal*, 26 March 1954, Scrapbook Hansard.
99 *Senior High School Curriculum Guide for Social Studies 10, 20 and 30*, p. 123.
100 Chafe and Lower, 486.
101 Bertha Lawrence, L.C. Mix, C.S. Wilkie and Edgar McInnis, *Canada in the Modern World* (Toronto: J.M. Dent & Sons, 1955), 259.
102 Frank Baer, "Do We Educate for Democracy?" A.T.A. *Magazine* 36, 8 (April 1956), 44.
103 Edmonton Public School Board, *Annual Report*, 1955, Edmonton Public School Board Archives.
104 V. Gable, "New Social Studies Courses for Survival," A.T.A. *Magazine* 38, 3 (November 1957), 26.
105 *Elementary Curriculum Guide for Social Studies-Enterprise* (1964), 6.
106 *Edmonton Public School Board, Policy Handbook, 1939–60*, Box 3, File 11: Superintendent's Bulletins, Edmonton Public School Board Archives.
107 *Program of Studies for Elementary Schools of Alberta* (1963), 7.
108 *Program of Studies for Junior High Schools of Alberta* (1963), 30.
109 *Senior High School Curriculum Guide for Social Studies 10, 20 and 30* (1955), 53.
110 Rogers, Adams and Brown, *The Ancient and Medieval World*, 224.
111 Royal Commission on Education in Alberta, *Report*, 45.

## CHAPTER 5

1 Paul Bunner, ed., *The Sixties Revolution and the Fall of Social Credit*. Alberta in the 20th Century, Vol. X (Edmonton: United Western Communications, 2002), 6.
2 Palmer and Palmer, 327.
3 Robert M. Stamp, *School Days: A Century of Memories* (Calgary: Calgary Board of Education and McClelland & Stewart West, 1975), 123.
4 Tomkins, *A Common Countenance*, 278–83.
5 Alberta Commission on Educational Planning, *A Future of Choices, a Choice of Futures: Report of the Commission on Educational Planning* (Edmonton: Queen's Printer, 1972), 31–32.

6   Tomkins, *A Common Countenance*, 291.
7   Ibid., 293.
8   Ibid., 292.
9   Edwin Fenton, *The New Social Studies* (New York: Holt, Rinehart & Winston, 1967), 7.
10  Ibid., 12.
11  See Edwin Fenton, ed., *Introduction to the Study of History. The Shaping of Western Society: An Inductive Approach*, vol. 2 (New York: Holt, Rinehart & Winston, 1966).
12  Evelyn Moore and Edward E. Owen, *Teaching the Subjects in the Social Studies: A Handbook for Teachers* (Toronto: Macmillan Co. of Canada, 1966), i.
13  Byron G. Massialas and C. Benjamin Cox, *Inquiry in Social Studies* (New York: McGraw-Hill Book Co., 1966), 8–21.
14  Ibid., i.
15  Frank Simon, "Can History Teach Students How To Think?" *One World* 5, 3 (February 1967), 3–4.
16  G.L. Berry, *Problems and Values* (Toronto: J.M. Dent & Sons (Canada), 1967), 3–4.
17  Laurens Korteweg, "A Decade of Social Studies Curriculum Development in Alberta" (PH.D. diss., University of Alberta, 1972), 94–97.
18  "A Breakthrough in Social Studies? Department of Education Conference June 19–29, 1967," *One World* 6, 1 (December 1967), 4.
19  Ibid., 2–3.
20  The committee consisted of four teachers and school administers and was led by C.D. (Doug) Ledgerwood, a consultant for the Department of Education working out of Grande Prairie.
21  Korteweg, 124.
22  Louis Raths, Merrill Harman and Sidney B. Simon, *Values and Teaching: Working With Values in the Classroom* (Columbus, OH: Charles E. Merrill Books, 1966).
23  Korteweg, 111–12.
24  Ibid., 140–41.
25  Alberta Education, *Program of Studies for Elementary Schools* (Edmonton: Alberta Education, 1975), 36–37.
26  Alberta Commission on Educational Planning, 190.
27  C.D. Ledgerwood, "Education in an Age of Internationalism," *One World* 7, 4 (June 1969), 6.
28  A popular case study of "modern Stone Age people" was the Tasaday of the Philippines, a group of 26 people discovered in 1971. They were exposed as a fraud perpetrated by Ferdinand Marcos and Manuel Elizalde in 1986.
29  Department of Education, *Program of Studies for Junior High Schools* (Edmonton: Department of Education, 1971), 14.
30  The national Canada Studies Foundation and its impact on Alberta will be examined later in the chapter.
31  Department of Education, *Program of Studies for Senior High Schools* (Edmonton: Department of Education, 1975), 220–24. The units on "Population and Production" and "Political and Economic Systems" were originally designed for the revision of Social Studies 30 in 1967. The program revision of 1971 moved the unit on "Population and Production" to Social Studies 20.

32 Department of Education, *Responding to Change: A Handbook for Teachers of Secondary Social Studies* (Edmonton: Curriculum Branch, 1975), 21.
33 *Program of Studies for Senior High Schools*, 221.
34 Ibid.
35 Ibid., 224.
36 See, for example, Nicholas Wickenden, "What is History," *One World* 7, 1 (October 1968): n.p.; Moira Hegarty, "Possibilities for Inquiry Within the Present High School Curriculum," *One World* 8, 3 (March 1969): n.p.; Frank Simon, "Inquiry Skills – What For?" *One World* 8, 3 (March 1969): n.p.; Melvin Ezer, "Don't Transmit – TEACH – Values," *One World* 9, 1 (November 1970): n.p.
37 See *One World* 9, 2 (January 1971) and 10, 2 (February 1972) for excellent examples.
38 Gary De Leeuw, *Holt Sample Studies: An Inductive Approach Teacher's Manual*, ed. Evelyn Moore (Toronto: Holt, Rinehart & Winston of Canada, 1968).
39 Virginia F. Allen et al., *People and Culture, Teacher's Edition*, Man and His World (New York: Noble & Noble, 1974), TE6.
40 Ibid., 54.
41 Maureen Farrell Moran, *Response Book: Families Live Everywhere*. Ginn Social Science Series, ed. Leonard S. Kenworthy (Boston, MA: Ginn & Co., 1972), 64–65.
42 Evelyn Berger, *Response Book: Everyone Lives in Communities*. Ginn Social Science Series, ed. Leonard S. Kenworthy (Boston, MA: Ginn & Co., 1972), 71.
43 Ibid., 20.
44 Leon E. Clark, ed., *Teacher Lesson Plans, Vol. 1: Coming of Age in Africa: Continuing and Changing. Through African Eyes: Cultures in Change* (New York: Praeger, 1969), 24.
45 *Teacher's Manual, Ginn Studies in Canadian History* (Toronto: Ginn & Co., 1972), 11.
46 Neil Sutherland, *When Grandma and Grandpa Were Kids*, A Gage World Community Study (Toronto: W.J. Gage, 1970).
47 Bernard Feder, *Feudalism: Political Disaster or Stabilizing Force? Viewpoints in World History*, Vol. 21 (New York: American Book Co., 1968), 30.
48 Don C. Barnett and R. Pat Mogen, *Alberta: A People and a Province* (Vancouver: Fitzhenry & Whiteside, 1975), 41.
49 See, for example, Virginia F. Allen et al., *People and the Land*, Man and His World Series (New York: Noble & Noble, 1974). The student readers on the Inca and on Ancient Egypt contained only about twenty pages each of very brief text about the history of these civilizations. This was probably an appropriate beginning for the American Grade Four students for whom the series was designed, but would certainly have been insufficient for the Grade Six students for whom the volumes were approved in Alberta.
50 T.L. Powrie, ed., *Political and Economic Systems* (Toronto: J.M. Dent & Sons (Canada), 1967), 5.
51 Cottie Burland, *Men Without Machines: The Story of Primitive Peoples* (Garden City, NY: Natural History Press, 1969), 14–15.
52 Seymour Fersh, ed., *Culture Regions of the World Series: A Guide for Teachers* (New York: Macmillan, 1973), 3.

53 See John Ricker and John Saywell, *Europe and the Modern World* (Toronto: Clarke, Irwin & Co., 1969, 1976) and Daniel Roselle and Anne P. Young, *Our Western Heritage* (Lexington, Mass: Ginn & Co., 1972).
54 Roselle and Young, iii.
55 Ibid., 189–92.
56 Ibid., 403–6.
57 Ibid., 75.
58 Ricker and Saywell, 241–42.
59 Roselle and Young, 232.
60 Ricker and Saywell, 254.
61 Roselle and Young, 459.
62 Ledgerwood, 6.
63 Korteweg, 65.
64 Bernard Feder, *Can the Earth Support its Growing Population, Viewpoints in World History, Vol. 17* (New York: American Book Co., 1968), 10.
65 Ibid., 17–18.
66 Ibid., 18–22.
67 Ricker and Saywell, 110.
68 Derald C. Willows and Stewart Richmond, *Canada: Colony to Centennial* (Toronto: McGraw-Hill Co. of Canada, 1970), 177–84.
69 Ibid., 191.
70 Ibid., 165.
71 Ibid., 241.
72 Paul Cornell et al., *Canada: Unity in Diversity* (Toronto: Holt, Rinehart & Winston of Canada, 1967), xii.
73 Alberta Commission on Educational Planning, 190.
74 Willows and Richmond, 374.
75 H.H. Herstein et al., *Challenge and Survival: The History of Canada* (Scarborough, ON: Prentice-Hall of Canada, 1970), 112.
76 Cornell et al., 484.
77 Ibid., 483.
78 Herstein et al., 420–26.
79 Willows and Richmond, 381.
80 Ibid., 372.
81 Herstein et al., 416.
82 Cornell et al., 485.
83 Herstein et al., 419.
84 For a summary of the Canadian experience with the values clarification, see Kathleen M. Gow, *Yes Virginia, There is Right and Wrong!* (Toronto: J. Wiley & Sons, 1980).
85 Department of Education, *Responding to Change: A Handbook for Teachers of Secondary Social Studies* (Edmonton: Curriculum Branch, 1975), 48.
86 The magazine *Alberta Report* became one of the most vocal and consistent critics of the values-clarification approach in the curriculum. For an example of their reporting, see "Under the Carpet," *Alberta Report* 8, 13 (6 March 1981): 45–49.
87 Donald L. Massey, "Social Studies for the Seventies – Sense and Nonsense," *One World* 12, 2 (Spring 1974): 25.

88  Hugh Lytton, "A Critique of the New Social Studies," *One World* 10, 2 (May 1972), 3
89  Ibid., 5–6.
90  For an examination of the impact of the report across the country, see Osborne, "Education is the Best National Insurance," 49–51.
91  For a detailed description of the history and work of the Canada Studies Foundation, see John N. Grant et al., eds., *The Canada Studies Foundation* (Toronto: Canada Studies Foundation, 1986).
92  Alberta Commission on Educational Planning, 190.
93  Ken Osborne, "'Our History Syllabus Has Us Gasping': History in Canadian Schools – Past, Present and Future," *Canadian Historical Review* 31, 3 (September 2000).
94  L.W. Downey Research Associates, *The Social Studies in Alberta, 1975: A Report of An Assessment* (Edmonton: Department of Education, 1975). Downey had been one of the architects of the new program and was a professor in the Faculty of Education at the University of Alberta.
95  Alberta Education, *Annual Report* (Edmonton: 1977–78), 24.
96  Evelyn Moore, "But is it History?" *One World* 19, 2 (Fall 1981), 22.
97  See, for example, McDiarmid and Pratt; and Osborne, *"Hard-working, Temperate and Peaceable" – the Portrayal of Workers in Canadian History Textbooks*
98  Committee on Tolerance and Understanding, *Final Report* (Edmonton: Committee on Tolerance and Understanding, 1984).
99  See Penney Clark; and Light, Staton and Bourne.
100 See, for example, Jennifer Tupper, "The Gendering of Citizenship in Social Studies," *Canadian Social Studies* 36, 3 (Spring 2002), http://www.quasar.ualberta.ca/css/Css_36_3/ARgendering_of_citizenship.html (accessed on 8 May 2003).

## CONCLUSION

1  Douglas John Hall, "Man and Nature in the Modern West: A Revolution of Images," in *Man and Nature on the Prairies*, ed. Richard Allen (Regina: Canadian Plains Research Center, 1976), 80.

## APPENDIX 1

1  The original Enterprise curriculum was entirely skill-based and extremely vague in terms of subject-specific content. An attempt was made to provide more specific guidelines for thematic studies in 1940, and then theme headings were replaced with focus questions for inquiry in 1947.
2  In response to pressure to provide greater Canadian content in the social studies program after 1945, senior high school courses were renamed: Ancient Origins of Canadian Society; Modern Background of Canadian Civilization; and, Problems of Canadian Citizenship for Grades 10, 11 and 12 respectively. Changes in course titles signaled no great change in course content.

3 A new Social Studies 30 course was introduced in the 1967 that included units on "Population and Production" and "Political and Economic Systems." The 1971 revision moved the first unit into Social Studies 20 (Grade 11).

## APPENDIX 2

1 Herbert M. Kliebard, *Forging the American Curriculum: Essays in Curriculum History and Theory* (New York: Routledge, 1992), xiv.
2 Ibid., xiv–xv.

# BIBLIOGRAPHY

## PRIMARY SOURCES

**ALBERTA TEACHERS' ASSOCIATION ARCHIVES**
Annual General Meetings Records
General Curriculum Committee Files
H.C. Newland Papers
Provincial Executive Council Minutes

**CALGARY ROMAN CATHOLIC DIOCESE ARCHIVES**
Annual Reports of the Calgary Roman Catholic School District #1
Bishop Carroll Papers
Papers of the Faithful Companions of Jesus
St. Mary's High School Files

**EDMONTON PUBLIC SCHOOL BOARD ARCHIVES**
Annual Reports of the Edmonton Public School Board
A.G. Bayly Papers
Alan Bell Papers
Examinations File
Betty Horton Files
Roger McKee Papers
School Management Committee Files
Staff Bulletins
William Tomyn Papers

**GLENBOW ARCHIVES**
Alberta Federation of Home and School Associations Papers
Perren Baker Papers

Calgary School Board Files
Carr/McCormick Papers
Central High School Papers
Anette Christofferson Papers
Muriel Clipsham Papers
E.W. Coffin Papers
A.M. Curtis Papers
Glengarry School Papers

GLENBOW LIBRARY
School Yearbook Collection

PROVINCIAL ARCHIVES OF ALBERTA
Anders O. Aalborg Papers
Department of Education Papers
Downes Papers
Legislative Papers
W.D. McDougall Papers
Premier's Papers
Cornelia Wood Papers

UNIVERSITY OF ALBERTA ARCHIVES
Education Society of Edmonton Papers
Faculty of Education Papers
M.E. LaZerte Papers

UNIVERSITY OF CALGARY ARCHIVES
A.L. Doucette Papers
Calgary Normal School Papers
Faculty of Education Papers

*Alberta Report*
*Calgary Albertan*
*Calgary Herald*
*Edmonton Bulletin*
*Edmonton Journal*
*Lethbridge Daily Herald*
*Lethbridge News*
*Red Deer Advocate*
*The UFA*

*The Alberta Home and School News*
*The Alberta School Trustee*
*The A.T.A. Magazine*
*One World, the Newsletter of the Alberta Social Studies Council*

Alberta Scrapbook Hansard
Sessional Papers

Annual Reports of the Department of Education, Alberta
Department of Education, Programmes of Studies
Department of Education, Curriculum Guides

Coutts, Herbert T. "The Unfinished Journey of Herbert T. 'Pete' Coutts." Unpublished manuscript, 1982.
Newland, H.C. "Collected Papers." Compiled by B.E. Walker. Unpublished manuscript, n.d.
Teskey, Hugh Garth. "Memoirs and Musing." Unpublished manuscript, 1993.

STUDENT TEXTBOOKS, 1905 TO 1920

Bagehot, Walter. *The English Constitution and Other Political Essays*. Latest revised ed. New York: D. Appleton, 1902.
Bourinot, J.G. *How Canada is Governed*. Toronto: Copp Clark, 1895.
Buckley, Arabella B., and W.J. Robertson. *High School History of England and Canada*. Toronto: Copp Clark, 1891.
Clement, W.H.P. *The History of the Dominion of Canada*. Toronto: W. Briggs, 1897.
Cunningham, W. and Ellen A. McArthur. *Outlines of English Industrial History*. 2nd ed. Cambridge, UK: Cambridge University Press, 1898.
Duncan, D.M. *The Story of the Canadian People*. Toronto: MacMillan Co. of Canada, 1913.
*Highroads of History*. 11 volumes. London: Thomas Nelson & Sons, 1908.
Jenkins, R.S. *Canadian Civics*. Alberta ed. Toronto: Copp Clark, 1912.
Marsh, Edith L. *Where the Buffalo Roamed: The Story of Western Canada Told For the Young*. Toronto: William Briggs, 1908.
McIntyre, W.A., John Dearness and John C. Saul. *Alexandra Readers*. 5 volumes. Toronto: Morang Educational Co., 1908.
Myers, Philip Van Ness. *General History*. Revised ed. Boston: Ginn & Company, 1906.
Swinton, William. *Outlines of the World's History*. Revised Canadian ed. Halifax: A & W MacKinlay, 1883.
Symes, E.S. and G.M. Wrong. *An English History*. Toronto: Copp Clark, 1905.

TEACHER TRAINING TEXTBOOKS AND TEACHER RESOURCES, 1905 TO 1920

Anderson, J.T.M. *The Education of the New Canadian*. London: J.M. Dent & Sons, 1918.
Calkin, J.B. *Notes on Education*. Truro, NS: D.H. Smith & Co., 1888.
*A Handbook to the Alexandra Readers*. Toronto: Macmillan Co. of Canada, 1914.
Hartwell, Ernest C. *The Teaching of History in the High School*. Boston: Houghton Mifflin Co., 1913.
Hughes, James L., ed. *Public School Methods*. 5 volumes. Toronto: School Methods Co., 1908.
McIntyre, W.A. *Talks and Discussions With Young Teachers*. Toronto: Copp Clark Co., 1915.
Swett, John. *Methods of Teaching*. New York: Harper & Brothers, 1886.
Tilley, J.J., ed. *Methods in Teaching*. Toronto: George N. Morang & Co., 1899.

## STUDENT TEXTBOOKS, 1920 TO 1935

Burt, A.L. *High School Civics*. Edmonton: School Book Branch, Department of Education, 1933.
*The Canadian Readers*. 5 volumes. Toronto: W.J. Gage & Co., 1922.
*The Canadian Readers*. 5 volumes. Toronto: W.J. Gage & Co., 1931–2.
Chesterton, Alice. M. *The Garden of Childhood*. London: Thomas Nelson & Sons, 1905.
Dickie, D.J. *Dent's Canadian History Readers*. 8 volumes. Toronto: J.M. Dent, 1925–8.
Eastman, Mack. *A Short History of Early Peoples*. Boston: Allyn & Bacon, 1923.
Grant, W.L. *History of Canada*. New and revised ed. London: William Heinemann, 1923.
Long, M.H. *Knights Errant of the Wilderness*. Toronto: MacMillan Co., 1919.
*Makers of Canada Series*. 20 volumes. Toronto: Morang & Co., 1903 to 1908.
Marriott, J.A.R. *English Political Institutions*. Oxford: Clarendon Press, 1925.
McCaig, James. *Studies in Citizenship*. Toronto: Educational Book Co., 1927.
Mowat, R.B. *A New History of Great Britain*. Toronto: Oxford University Press, 1924.
Robinson, James H. *Medieval and Modern Times*. Boston: Ginn & Co., 1916.
*Ryerson Canadian History Readers*. Toronto: Ryerson Press, 1926–1932.
Wallace, W. Stewart. *By Star and Compass*. Toronto: Oxford University Press, 1922.
–––. *A New History of Great Britain and Canada*. Toronto: MacMillan Co. of Canada, 1925.

## TEACHER TRAINING TEXTBOOKS AND TEACHER RESOURCES, 1920 TO 1935

Curtis, Henry S. *Education Through Play*. New York: MacMillan Co., 1915.
Gesell, Arnold L., and Beatrice Chandler Gesell. *The Normal Child and Primary Education*. Boston: Ginn & Co., 1912.
Hardy, E.A. *Talks on Education*. Toronto: MacMillan Co. of Canada, 1923.
McIntyre, W.A. *Talks and Discussions With Young Teachers*. Toronto: Copp Clark, 1915.
*Principles of Method*. Toronto: Copp Clark, 1930.
Smith, William Hawley. *All the Children of All the People*. New York: Macmillan Co., 1912.

## STUDENT TEXTBOOKS, 1935 TO 1945

Bagnall, Lucy A. *Contemporary Problems: National, Imperial and International*. Calgary: Western Canada Institute, 1939.
Beresford, M.A. *Highroads to Reading, Book 3*. Toronto: Ryerson Press, 1934.
Brown, George W. *Building the Canadian Nation*. Toronto: J.M. Dent & Sons, Canada, 1942.
–––. *Canadian Democracy in Action*. Toronto: J.M. Dent & Sons, Canada, 1945.
Jeffreys, C.W. *The Picture Gallery of Canadian History*. 3 volumes. Toronto: Ryerson Press, 1942, 1945, 1950.
McAuliffe, W.R. *Modern Europe Explained: A Guide to Present-Day History*. Revised ed. London: Blackie & Son, 1938.
McDougall, W.D., and Gilbert Paterson. *Our Country and its People*. Toronto: Ryerson Press, 1938.
–––. *Our Empire and its Neighbors*. Toronto: Ryerson Press, 1937.
–––. *The World of To-day*. Toronto: Ryerson Press, 1937.
Ormond, Frances L. *Highroads to Reading, Book Two*. Toronto: Ryerson Press, 1934.
Quinn, James A., and Arthur Repke. *Living in the Social World*. Revised ed. Chicago: J.B. Lippincott Co., 1948.

Schapiro, J.S., R.B. Morris, and F.H. Soward. *Civilisation in Europe and the World*. Toronto: Copp Clark, 1938.
Scott, F.R. *Canada Today*. London: Oxford University Press, 1938.
Seary, V.P., and Gilbert Paterson. *The Story of Civilization*. Toronto: Ryerson Press, 1934.
Tenen, I. *The Ancient World*. London: MacMillan & Co., 1936.
Wallace, W. Stewart. *A Reader in Canadian Civics*. Toronto: MacMillan Co. of Canada Limited, 1935.
Webster, Hanson Hart. *The World's Messengers*. Boston: Houghton Mifflin Co., 1938.
West, Willis M., and S. Mack Eastman. *Story of World Progress*. Canadian ed. Boston: Allyn & Bacon, 1936.

TEACHER TRAINING TEXTS AND TEACHER RESOURCES, 1935 TO 1945

Branom, Frederick K. *The Teaching of Social Studies in a Changing World*. New York: W.H. Sadlier, 1942.
Dickie, Donalda. *The Enterprise in Theory and Practice*. Toronto: W.J. Gage & Co., 1941.
Melvin, A. Gordon. *The Technique of Progressive Teaching*. New York: John Day Co., 1932.
Rugg, Harold, and Ann Shumaker. *The Child-Centered School*. New York: World Book Co., 1928.
Strayer, George Drayton, et al. *Principles of Teaching*. New York: American Book Co., 1936.

STUDENT TEXTBOOKS, 1945 TO 1970

Alberta Department of Education, *Tales of the Red River*. Edmonton: Author, 1948.
Baker, L.D., and J.M. Brown. *Civics and Citizenship: A Sourcebook for Schools*. Alberta ed. Regina: School Aids & Text Book Publishing Co., 1961.
Brown, George W., Eleanor Harmon and Marsh Jeanneret. *The Story of Canada*. Toronto: Copp Clark, 1950.
Chafe, J.W., and A.R.M. Lower. *Canada – A Nation and How It Came To Be*. Toronto: Longman, Green & Co., 1948.
Dickie, Donalda. *The Great Adventure*. Toronto: J.M. Dent & Sons, 1950.
Hardy, W.G. *Our Heritage from the Past*. Toronto: McClelland & Stewart, 1964.
Hughes, R.O. *The Making of Today's World*. Revised ed. Boston: Allyn & Bacon, 1950.
Lawrence, Bertha, et al. *Canada in the Modern World*. Toronto: J.M. Dent & Sons (Canada), 1955.
———. *Our European Heritage*. Toronto: J.M. Dent & Sons (Canada), 1962.
McDougall, W.D. *The Commonwealth of Nations*. Toronto: Ryerson Press, 1952.
———. *Our Provincial Government*. Edmonton: Department of Education, 1946.
McDougall, W.D., and T.G. Finn. *Canada in the Western World*. Toronto: W.J. Gage & Co., 1955.
New, Chester W. and Charles E. Phillips. *Ancient and Medieval History*. Toronto: Clarke, Irwin & Co., 1941.
Rogers, Lester B., Fay Adams, and Walker Brown. *The Ancient and Medieval World*. Toronto: Clarke, Irwin & Co., 1949.
———. *Story of Nations*. Toronto: Clarke, Irwin & Co., 1947.
Taylor, Griffith, Dorothy J. Seivereight, and Trevor Lloyd. *Canada and Her Neighbours*. Rev. ed. Toronto: Ginn & Co., 1958.

TEACHING TRAINING TEXTS AND TEACHER RESOURCES, 1945 TO 1970

Bining, Arthur C., and David H. Bining. *Teaching the Social Studies in Secondary Schools*. 3rd ed. New York: McGraw-Hill Book Co., 1952.

Cantor, Nathaniel. *The Teaching–Learning Process*. New York: Dryden Press, 1953.

Frasier, George Willard. *An Introduction to the Study of Education*. Rev. ed. New York: Harper & Brothers, 1956.

Ingram, E.J. *Action Research: A Guide to Curriculum Improvement*. Edmonton: Alberta Teachers' Association, 1959.

Moffatt, Maurice P. *Social Studies Instruction*. 2nd ed. New York: Prentice-Hall, 1954.

Oliver, R.A. *Effective Teaching: A Guide to General Methods*. Toronto: J.M. Dent & Sons (Canada), 1956.

Spears, Harold. *Principles of Teaching*. New York: Prentice-Hall, 1951.

Wesley, Edgar B., and Stanley P. Wronski. *Teaching Social Studies in High Schools*. 4th ed. Boston: D.C. Heath & Co., 1958.

STUDENT TEXTBOOKS AND LEARNING RESOURCES, 1971 TO 1980

Allen, Virginia F., et al. *Man And His World Series*. New York: Noble & Noble, 1974.

Barnett, Don C., and R. Pat Mogen. *Alberta: A People and a Province*. Vancouver: Fitzhenry & Whiteside, 1975.

Burland, Cottie A. *Men Without Machines: The Story of Primitive Peoples*. Garden City, NY: Natural History Press, 1965.

*Canadian Series of Jackdaws*. Toronto: Clarke, Irwin, 1968.

Clark, Leon E. *Through African Eyes: Cultures in Change*. New York, NY: Frederick A. Praeger, 1969.

Cornell, Paul, et al. *Canada: Unity in Diversity*. Toronto: Holt, Rinehart & Winston of Canada, 1967.

Feder, Bernard. *Viewpoints in World History Series*. 21 vols. New York, NY: American Book Co., 1968.

Fenton, Edwin, ed. *The Shaping of Western Society: An Inductive Approach*. 3 vols. New York, NY: Holt, Rinehart & Winston, 1966.

Fersh, Seymour, ed. *Culture Regions of the World Series: A Guide for Teachers*. New York: Macmillan Publishing Co., 1973.

*Ginn Studies in Canadian History*. Toronto: Ginn, 1969–74.

*Ginn World Studies Series*. Toronto: Ginn, 1975.

*Heath Social Studies Series*. Lexington, MA: D.C. Heath, 1969.

Herstein, H.H., et al. *Challenge and Survival: The History of Canada*. Scarborough, ON: Prentice-Hall of Canada, 1970.

*In Your Community Series*. Don Mills, ON: J.M. Dent & Sons (Canada), 1974.

Kenworthy, Leonard S., ed. *Ginn Social Science Series*. Boston, MA: Ginn, 1972.

Kirman, Joseph M. *World Discovery Program*, 6 vols. Don Mills, ON: Dent, 1971.

Moir, John S., and Farr, D.M.L. *The Canadian Experience*. Toronto: Ryerson Press, 1969.

Moore, Evelyn, ed. *Holt Sample Studies: An Inductive Approach*. Toronto: Holt, Rinehart & Winston of Canada, 1968.

———. *People and Places in Canada Series*, 10 vols. Toronto: Holt, Rinehart & Winston of Canada, 1968–73.

*One World Series*. Toronto: Fitzhenry & Whiteside, 1971.

Powrie, T.L., ed. *Political and Economic Systems.* Toronto: J.M. Dent & Sons (Canada), 1967.
Ricker, John, and John Saywell. *Europe and the Modern World.* Toronto: Clarke, Irwin & Co., 1969, 1976.
Roselle, Daniel, and Anne P. Young. *Our Western Heritage.* Lexington, Mass: Ginn & Co., 1972.
Smith, P.J. *Population and Production.* Toronto: J.M. Dent & Sons (Canada), 1967.
*Story of Canada Series.* Toronto: McGraw-Hill, 1966.
Sutherland, Neil, ed. *Gage World Community Studies Series.* Toronto: Gage Educational, 1972.
*The Taba Program in Social Science.* Don Mills, ON: Addison-Wesley (Canada), 1972.
Tomkins, Doreen M., et al. *Discovering Our Land.* Toronto: W.J. Gage, 1966.
Tomkins, Doreen M., et al. *Regional Studies of Canada Series.* Toronto: W.J. Gage, 1970.
Wiley, William et al. *Canada: This Land of Ours.* Toronto: Ginn & Co., 1970.
Willows, Derald C., and Stewart Richmond. *Canada: Colony to Centennial.* Toronto, ON: McGraw-Hill Co. of Canada, 1970.

### TEACHER RESOURCES, 1971 TO 1980

Berry, G.L. *Problems and Values.* Toronto: J.M. Dent & Sons (Canada), 1967.
De Leeuw, Gary, *Holt Sample Studies: An Inductive Approach Teacher's Manual,* ed. Evelyn Moore. Toronto: Holt, Rinehart & Winston of Canada, 1968.
Fenton, Edwin. *The New Social Studies.* New York: Holt, Rinehart & Winston, 1967.
Kenworthy, Leonard S. *Social Studies for the Seventies.* Waltham, MA: Blaisdell Publishing Co., 1969.
Logan, Lillian M., and Gerald T. Rimmington. *Social Studies: A Creative Direction.* Scarborough, ON: McGraw-Hill Co. of Canada, 1970.
Massialas, Byron G., and C. Benjamin Cox. *Inquiry in Social Studies.* New York: McGraw-Hill Book Co., 1966.
Massialas, Byron G., and Jack Zevin. *Creative Encounters in the Classroom – Teaching and Learning Through Discovery.* New York: John Wiley & Sons, 1967.
Moore, Evelyn, and Edward E. Owen. *Teaching the Subjects in the Social Studies: A Handbook for Teachers.* Toronto: Macmillan Co. of Canada, 1966.
Raths, Louis, Merrill Harman and Sidney B. Simon. *Values and Teaching: Working with Values in the Classroom.* Columbus, OH: Charles E. Merrill Books, 1966.

### PUBLISHED PRIMARY SOURCES

Alberta Commission on Educational Planning. *A Future of Choices, a Choice of Futures: Report of the Commission on Educational Planning.* Edmonton: Queen's Printer, 1972.
Alberta Department of Education. *Foundations of Education.* Edmonton: King's Printer, 1949.
"A Breakthrough in Social Studies? Department of Education Conference June 19–29, 1967." *One World* 6, 1 (December 1967): 1–4.
Byrne, T.C. *Occasional Speeches and Writings.* 2 vols. Athabasca: Athabasca University, 1971.

Campbell, H.L. *Curriculum Trends in Canadian Education*. Toronto: W.J. Gage & Co., 1952.
Canada and Newfoundland Education Association. *Report of the Survey Committee*. Toronto: The Association, 1943.
Clark, Maisie Emery. *Memories of a Pioneer Schoolteacher*. No publisher given, 1968.
Ezer, Melvin. "Don't Transmit – TEACH – Values," *One World* 9, 1 (November 1970): n.p.
Hardy, W.G. *Education in Alberta*. Calgary: The Calgary Herald, n.d.
Hegarty, Moira. "Possibilities for Inquiry Within the Present High School Curriculum." *One World* 8, 3 (March 1969): n.p
Hertzman, Lewis. "The Sad Demise of History: Social Studies in the Alberta Schools." *Dalhousie Review* 43, 4 (Winter 1963–4): 512–21.
Hodgetts, A.B. *What Culture? What Heritage?: A Study of Civic Education in Canada*. Toronto: Ontario Institute for Studies in Education, 1968.
Hosie, Inez. B. "Little White School House." *Alberta Historical Review* 15, 4 (Autumn 1967): 26–8.
Jordan, A. "Citizenship in Grades Six, Seven and Eight." *A.T.A. Magazine* 4, 9 (February 1924): 15–18.
Ledgerwood, C.D. "Education in an Age of Internationalism." *One World* 7, 4 (June 1969): 1–8.
L.W. Downey Research Associates. *The Social Studies in Alberta, 1975: A Report of an Assessment*. Edmonton: Department of Education, 1975.
Lytton, Hugh. "A Critique of the New Social Studies." *One World* 10, 2 (May 1972): 1–6.
MacEachran, John M. "History of Education in Alberta." In *Canada and its Provinces*. Vol. 20, edited by Adam Shortt and Arthur G. Doughty, 477–506. Toronto: Glasgow, Brook & Co., 1914.
Massey, Donald L. "Social Studies for the Seventies – Sense and Nonsense." *One World* 12, 2 (Spring 1974): 18–29.
McKenzie, Charles H. "Growing Up in Alberta, Part One." *Alberta History* 37, 3 (Summer 1989): 14–23.
———. "Growing Up in Alberta, Part Two." *Alberta History* 37, 4 (Autumn 1989): 17–24.
———. "Growing Up in Alberta, Part Three." *Alberta History* 38, 1 (Winter 1990): 25–32.
McKenzie, M.I. "School Memories." *Alberta Historical Review* 7, 1 (Winter 1959): 14–17.
Moore, Evelyn. "But is it History?" *One World* 19, 2 (Fall 1981): 18–25.
Moore, H. Napier. "Why United States Textbooks in Canadian Schools?" *Maclean's* 1 July 1929, 3, 57–58, 61, 65.
National Conference on Character Education in Relation to Canadian Citizenship. *Report of the Proceedings*. Winnipeg: Council on Character Education, 1919.
Neatby, Hilda. *So Little For the Mind*. Toronto: Clarke, Irwin & Co., 1953.
Olsen, A.F. "Teaching Procedures in Social Studies." *Alberta Journal of Educational Research* 11, 2 (June 1965): 116–24.
Pylypow, Henry. "Two First Days." *Alberta History* 27, 3 (Summer 1979): 31–34.
Ray, D.W. "An Experimental Comparison of the Relative Effectiveness of Two Methods of Teaching the Social Studies in Grade Eleven." *Alberta Journal of Educational Research* 11, 1 (March 1965): 45–53.
Royal Commission on Education in Alberta. *Report*. Edmonton: Queen's Printer, 1959.

Royal Commission on Industrial Training and Technical Education. *Report of the Commissioners*. Ottawa: King's Printer, 1913.
Simon, Frank. "Can History Teach Students How To Think?" *One World* 5, 3 (February 1967): 3–4.
Simon, Frank. "Inquiry Skills – What For?" *One World* 8, 3 (March 1969): n.p.
Stanley, George F.G. "School Days! School Days!" In *Citymakers*, edited by Max Foran and Sheilagh S. Jameson, 1–31. Calgary: Historical Society of Alberta, Chinook Country Chapter, 1987.
Swift, William H. *Memoirs of a Frontier School Inspector in Alberta*. Ed. John W. Chalmers. Edmonton: Education Society of Edmonton, 1986.
Wickenden, Nicholas. "What is History." *One World* 7, 1 (October 1968): n.p..
Underhill, Frank H. "So Little for the Mind: Comments and Queries." *Transactions of the Royal Society of Canada* 48, Series III (June 1954): 15–23.

## SECONDARY SOURCES

Alberta Committee on Tolerance and Understanding. *Final Report*. Edmonton: Committee on Tolerance and Understanding, 1984.
Anderson, Benedict. *Imagined Communities*. Rev. ed. London: Verso, 1991.
Apple, Michael W., and Linda K. Christian-Smith, eds. *The Politics of the Textbook*. New York: Routledge, 1991.
Armstrong, Sean, ed. *Far and Wide: Essays from Canada*. Toronto: Nelson Canada, 1995.
Association for Canadian Studies. *Bulletin de l'AEC* 13 (Summer 1992): 13.
Baldwin, Patricia, and Douglas Baldwin. "The Portrayal of Women in Classroom Textbooks." *Canadian Social Studies* 26, 3 (Spring 1992): 110–4.
Berger, Carl. *The Sense of Power*. Toronto: University of Toronto Press, 1970.
Bhabha, Homi K., ed. *Nation and Narration*. London: Routledge, 1990.
Bliss, Michael. "Privatizing the Mind: the Sundering of Canadian History, the Sundering of Canada." *Journal of Canadian Studies* 26, 4 (1991–2): 5–17.
Boddington, Steven P. "Education From the Top Down: A Biography of W.H. Swift." PH.D. diss., University of Alberta, 1998.
Bruno-Jofre, Rosa. "Citizenship and Schooling in Manitoba, 1918–1945." *Manitoba History* 36 (Winter 1998): 26–36.
Bumsted, Jack. "Visions of Canada: a Brief History of Writing on the Canadian Character and the Canadian Identity." In *A Passion for Identity: Canadian Studies for the 21st Century*, 4th ed., edited by David Taras and Beverly Rasporich, 17–35. Scarborough, ON: Nelson Thomson Learning, 2001.
Bunner, Paul, ed. *The Sixties Revolution and the Fall of Social Credit*. Alberta in the 20th Century, Vol. X. Edmonton: United Western Communications, 2002.
Butterfield, Herbert. *The Whig Interpretation of History*. London: G. Bell & Sons, 1950. Originally published in 1931.
Byrne, T.C. *Alberta's Revolutionary Leaders*. Calgary: Detselig Enterprises, 1991.
Chalmers, John W. *Gladly Would He Teach*. Edmonton: A.T.A. Educational Trust, 1978.
———. *Schools of the Foothills Province*. Toronto: University of Toronto Press, 1967.
Clark, Penney. "Between the Covers: Exposing Images in Social Studies Textbooks." In *The Canadian Anthology of Social Studies: Issues and Strategies for Teachers*, edited

by Roland Case and Penney Clark, 339–48. Vancouver: Pacific Educational Press, 1999.

Coutts, H.T., and B.E. Walker. G. *Fred: The Story of G. Fred McNally*. Don Mills, ON: J.M. Dent & Sons, 1964.

Davis, Bob. *Whatever Happened to High School History?* Toronto: James Lorimer & Co., 1995.

Elliott, David, and Iris Miller. *Bible Bill*. Edmonton: Reidmore Books, 1987.

Finkel, Alvin. *The Social Credit Phenomenon in Alberta*. Toronto: University of Toronto Press, 1989.

Francis, Daniel. *National Dreams: Myth, Memory and Canadian History*. Vancouver: Arsenal Pulp Press, 1997.

Galt, George, ed. *The Thinking Heart*. Kingston: Quarry Press, 1991.

Gow, Kathleen M. *Yes Virginia, There is Right and Wrong!* Toronto: J. Wiley & Sons, 1980.

Graham, Duncan and Tytler, David. *A Lesson for Us All: The Making of the National Curriculum*. London: Routledge, 1993.

Granatstein, J.L. *Who Killed Canadian History?* Toronto: HarperCollins, 1998.

Grosvenor, Ian. "'There's No Place Like Home': Education and the Making of National Identity." *History of Education* 28, 3 (1999): 235–50.

Gwyn, Richard. *Nationalism Without Walls: The Unbearable Lightness of Being Canadian*. Toronto: McClelland & Stewart, 1995.

Hall, Douglas John. "Man and Nature in the Modern West: A Revolution of Images." In *Man and Nature on the Prairies*, edited by Richard Allen, 77–92. Regina: Canadian Plains Research Center, 1976.

Humphries, Charles W. "The Banning of a Book in British Columbia." *B.C. Studies* 1 (Winter 1968–9): 1–12.

Jones, David C. "The Zeitgeist of Western Settlement: Education and the Myth of the Land." In *Schooling and Society in Twentieth Century British Columbia*, edited by J. Donald Wilson and David C. Jones, 71–89. Calgary: Detselig Enterprises, 1980.

Kach, N. "Education and Ethnic Acculturation: A Case Study." In *Essays on Canadian Education*, edited by Nick Kach et al., 41–60. Calgary: Detselig Enterprises, 1986.

Kaplan, William, ed. *Belonging: The Meaning and Future of Canadian Citizenship*. Montreal and Kingston: McGill-Queen's University Press, 1993.

Kliebard, Herbert M. *Forging the American Curriculum: Essays in Curriculum History and Theory*. New York: Routledge, 1992.

———. *The Struggle for an American Curriculum, 1893–1958*. 2nd ed. New York: Routledge, 1995.

Korteweg, Laurens. "A Decade of Social Studies Curriculum Development in Alberta." Ph.D. diss., University of Alberta, 1972.

Kostek, Michael A. *A Century and Ten: A History of Edmonton Public Schools*. Edmonton: Edmonton Public Schools, 1992.

La Fleur, Phyllis M.E. "Three Alberta Teachers: Lives and Thoughts." Master's thesis, University of Alberta, 1977.

Light, Beth, Pat Staton, and Paula Bourne. "Sex Equity Content in History Textbooks." *The History and Social Science Teacher* 25, no.1 (Fall 1989): 18–20.

Lupul, Manoly R. "The Schools and French- and Ukrainian-Language Claims in Alberta to 1918." In *Exploring Our Educational Past*, edited by Nick Kach and Kas Mazurek, 73–91. Calgary: Detselig Enterprises, 1992.

McDiarmid, Grant, and David Pratt. *Teaching Prejudice: A Content Analysis of Social Studies Textbooks Authorized for Use in Ontario.* Toronto: OISE Press, 1971.

Nash, Garry B., Charlotte Crabtree, and Ross E. Dunn. *History on Trial: Culture Wars and the Teaching of the Past.* New York: Alfred A. Knopf, 1997.

Novick, Peter. *That Noble Dream: The "Objectivity Question" and the American Historical Profession.* Cambridge: Cambridge University Press, 1988.

Osborne, Brian S. "Landscape, Memory, Monuments, and Commemoration: Putting Identity in its Place." *Canadian Ethnic Studies* 33, 3 (2001): 39–77.

Osborne, Ken. "Canadian Historians and National History: a 1950 Survey." *Canadian Social Studies* 36, 3 (Spring 2002) http://www.quasar.ualberta.ca./css/Css_36_3/CLvoices_from_the_past.htm Accessed on 18 August 2004.

———. "Education is the Best National Insurance: Citizenship Education in Canadian Schools, Past and Present." *Canadian and International Education* 25, 2 (December 1996): 31–58.

———. *"Hard-working, Temperate and Peaceable" – the Portrayal of Workers in Canadian History Textbooks.* Monographs in Education Series, edited by Alexander Gregor and Keith Wilson. Winnipeg: University of Manitoba, 1980.

———. "'New Teaching' or 'Idealistic Twaddle'? A 1920s Model of History Teaching." *Canadian Social Studies* 35, 3 (Spring 2001) http://www.quasar.ualberta.ca/css/Css_35_3/CLvoices_from_the_past.htm Accessed on 18 August 2004.

———. "'Our History Syllabus has Us Gasping': History in Canadian Schools – Past, Present and Future." *Canadian Historical Review* 81, 3 (September 2000): 404–35.

———. "Public Schooling and Citizenship Education in Canada." *Canadian Ethnic Studies* 32, 1 (2000): 8–37.

———. "The Senate Textbook Debate of 1944." *Canadian Social Studies* 37, 1 (Fall 2002) http://www.quasar.ualberta.ca./css/Css_37_1/CLvoices_from_the_past.htm Accessed on 18 August 2004.

Palmer, Howard, and Tamara Palmer. *Alberta: A New History.* Edmonton: Hurtig Publishers, 1990.

Patterson, R.S. "The Canadian Response to Progressive Education." In *Essays on Canadian Education,* edited by N. Kach et al., 61–77. Calgary: Detselig Enterprises, 1986.

Prokop, Manfred. "Canadianization of Immigrant Children." *Alberta History* 37, 2 (Spring 1989): 1–10.

Resnick, Philip. "English Canada: The Nation that Dares Not Speak its Name." In *Beyond Quebec: Taking Stock of Canada,* edited by Kenneth McRoberts, 81–92. Montreal and Kingston: McGill-Queen's University Press, 1995.

Saul, John Ralston. *Reflections of a Siamese Twin: Canada at the End of the Twentieth Century.* Toronto: Viking, 1997.

Selleck, R.J.W. *The New Education: The English Background 1870–1914.* Melbourne: Sir Isaac Pitman & Sons, 1968.

Sheehan, Nancy J. "Character Training and the Cultural Heritage: An Historical Comparison of Canadian Elementary Readers." In *The Curriculum in Canada in Historical Perspective,* edited by George Tomkins, 77–84. Vancouver: Canadian Society for the Study of Education, University of British Columbia, 1979.

Smith, Anthony D. *National Identity.* Reno: University of Nevada Press, 1991.

Spicer, Keith. "Canada: Values in Search of a Vision." In *Identities in North America: The Search for Community*, edited by Robert L. Earle and John D. Wirth, 13–28. Stanford, CA: Stanford University Press, 1995.
Stamp, Robert M. "Canadian education and the national identity." In *Canadian Schools and the Canadian Identity*, edited by Alf Chaiton and Neil McDonald, 29–37. Toronto: Gage Educational Publishing, 1977.
———. *School Days: A Century of Memories*. Calgary: Calgary Board of Education and McClelland & Stewart West, 1975.
———. *The Schools of Ontario, 1876–1976*. Toronto: University of Toronto Press, 1982.
Starowicz, Mark. *Making History: The Remarkable Story Behind Canada: A People's History*. Toronto: McClelland & Stewart, 2003.
Sutherland, Neil. *Children in English-Canadian Society: Framing the Twentieth Century Consensus*. Toronto: University of Toronto Press, 1976.
Tomkins, George S. *A Common Countenance*. Scarborough, ON: Prentice-Hall Canada Inc., 1986.
Trudel, Marcel, and Jain, Genevieve. *Canadian History Textbooks: A Comparative Study*. Studies of the Royal Commission on Bilingualism and Biculturalism, Vol. 5. Ottawa: Queen's Printer, 1970.
Tupper, Jennifer. "The Gendering of Citizenship in Social Studies Curriculum," *Canadian Social Studies* 36, 3 (Spring 2002) http://www.quasar.ualberta.ca/css/Css_36_3/ARgendering_of_citizenship.html Accessed on 8 May 2003.
Tyack, David, and Cuban, Larry. *Tinkering Toward Utopia: A Century of Public School Reform*. Cambridge, MA: Harvard University Press, 1995.
Voisey, Paul. *Vulcan: The Making of a Prairie Community*. Toronto: University of Toronto Press, 1988.
von Heyking, Amy. "Selling Progressive Education to Albertans." *Historical Studies in Education/Revue d'histoire de l'éducation* 10, 1 & 2 (Spring and Fall 1998): 67–84.
———. "Talking About Americans: The Image of the United States in Canadian Schools." Paper presented at the annual meeting of the Canadian Historical Association, Winnipeg, MB, June 2004.
Wilson, J. Donald, Robert M. Stamp, and Louis-Philippe Audet, eds. *Canadian Education: a History*. Scarborough, ON: Prentice-Hall of Canada, 1970.

# INDEX

## A
Aalborg, Anders, 104
Aberhart, William, 5, 56, 59, 91
   "Theory of Evolution, The," 58
   understanding of progressive education, 57
Aboriginal people, 35
   challenges to racism, 124
   omission in Canadian history, 115
   treatment in textbooks, 4, 18–19, 23, 46, 82, 140, 144–45, 150
academic skills, 8, 99, 106–7, 127, 130
   declining academic standards, 98–99
   under progressive education, 93–95
Acadians, 23
"activity" programs. *See* progressive education
Adler, Felix, 34
agricultural education, 8, 34, 44
agriculture, 29, 55, 91
Alberta
   economic boom, 124
   identity, 4, 6
   multicultural and multiracial, 124
   oil boom, 91
   political culture, 5, 40
   population, 7, 91, 129
   regional boosters, 7
   regional grievances, 6, 76–77
   western alienation, 124
*Alberta: A People and a Province*, 138
Alberta Department of Education. *See* Department of Education
Alberta Federation of Agriculture, 103
Alberta Federation of Home and School Associations, 51, 98, 101–3
Alberta Federation of Labour, 103
Alberta Heritage Learning Resources Project, 149
Alberta Heritage Savings Trust Fund, 149
Alberta Human Rights Act, 123
*Alberta School Trustee*, 66, 95–96
Alberta School Trustees' Association, 102
Alberta Teachers' Association, 36, 56, 103
   Annual General Meetings, 38, 42
   *A.T.A. Magazine*, 36, 52, 62, 72–73, 118
   Bureau of Education, 62
   Easter Convention, 70
   request for social sciences in curriculum, 53
   Social Studies Council, 130, 134
Alberta Wheat Pool, 44
*Alexandra Readers*, 16
   British content, 21–22
   Canadian heroes in, 20
   duty to serve others, 28
   ethnocentricity, 24
   "gems of wisdom," 26
   historical characters, 26
   romantic view of nature, 15
American content. *See* American ideas; American textbooks
American expansionism, 146–47. *See also* United States
American graduate programs, 52
American ideas in "New Social Studies," 127, 129, 131

American ideas of democracy, 40
American investment, 123
American oil companies, 91
American Progressive Education Association, 62
American Progressives, 56, 60, 66, 71, 78, 107
American Revolutionary War, 145
American settlers, 40, 91
American-style pleasures, 31
American textbooks in Alberta and Canada, 42–44, 136
Andersen, Hans Christian, 26
Anderson, Benedict, 3
Ansley, R.E., 87
Apple, Michael, 4–5
Argue, K.F., 66–67
assimilationist policies and programs for schools, 41. *See also* ethnocentrism
Associated Chambers of Commerce, 103
A.T.A. *See* Alberta Teachers' Association

## B

Baer, Frank, 118
Barnett, J.W., 62
Baxter, Tompsie, 72
Beard, Charles, 69
Becker, Carl, 69
behavioural psychology, 66, 87
Berry, G.L., 110, 129
  *Problems and Values*, 130
Bible stories and teaching, 26, 58, 96
Bliss, Michael, 1
Bode, Boyd H., 71–72
Bond, L.A., 96
Bracken, Paul, 95, 117
Britain, 16, 18–19, 28, 82, 147
  Canada's close relationship with, 13, 21–22, 115, 152–53
  educational reforms, 2, 33
Britain's Moral Instruction League, 50
British Empire, 11, 13, 24, 43, 152
  Canadian pride in, 42
  pure motives, 23
  symbols of, 21
British-style parliamentary democracy, 22, 30, 43, 115
Broadus, E.K., 10, 22
Brock, Isaac, 20
Bronfman, Charles, 2
Brown, George, 78–79, 116
Brownlee, John, 43, 55
Bruner, Jerome, 128, 130–31
  *Process of Education, The*, 127

Buchanan, F.G., 99
Burt, A.L., 39, 46–47
Burt, Cyril, 34
business and philanthropic associations, 31
Buxton, Earl, 37
Byrne, T.C., 58, 63, 101, 111
  on New Social Studies, 130–31

## C

Cain, W.E., 117
Calgary, 31
  Citizens' Committee on Education, 96
  growth, 91, 123
*Calgary Herald*, 30–31, 95–96
Calgary Public School Board, 99, 113
Calgary's Educational Progress Club, 56
Cameron Commission, 101, 107, 120
Campbell, H.L., 103
Camrose Normal School, 33–34, 37
*Can the Earth Support its Growing Population?* (Feder), 143
Canada
  cooperative relationship with U.S., 115–16, 153
  growth from colony to nation, 153
  historic disagreements with United States, 116
  historical relationship with Great Britain, 13, 21, 115, 153
  major study of education systems (1960-1970), 125
  national identity (*See* Canadian identity)
  national unity, 77, 134
  regional and cultural division, 134, 145–46
  role as mediator between U.S. and Great Britain, 116
  role in Commonwealth, 115
  role in global affairs, 117, 146–47
  self-government, 18, 21, 47
  tolerance of dual nationalities, 47
*Canada: a People's History* (TV series), 2
*Canada: Colony to Centennial*, 144–45
*Canada: Unity and Diversity*, 147
*Canada and Her Neighbours*, 112
Canada and Newfoundland Education Association, 77
*Canada in the Modern World*, 118
"Canada in the Modern World" (course), 109
Canada Studies Foundation, 148
*Canada Today* (Scott), 78
*Canadian Civics* (Jenkins), 22
Canadian content, 40, 70, 148–49
  in elementary school readers, 20, 41

New Social Studies, 133
Canadian Content Project, 149
Canadian Geography Readers, 42
*Canadian Historical Review*, 39
Canadian history, 23
   celebration of Canadian accomplishments in World War I, 42–44
   emphasis on tolerance and cooperation, 115
   mix of problem-centred and traditional, 144
   in New Social Studies, 133
   omission of conflicts, 115
Canadian history readers, 42
Canadian identity, 2, 5, 29, 39, 41–42, 153
   defined by Britain, 22, 152
   and provincial jurisdiction over education, 6
   role of schools in creating and sustaining, 3–4
*Canadian Readers*, 40
   Canadian content, 41
   stories glorifying war, 46
   traditional virtues, 50
*Canadian Series of Jackdaws*, 137
Canadian studies, 149
Canadian Studies Association, 1
"Canadian Studies" (course), 133
Canadian Teachers' Federation, 62
*Canadian Unity in Diversity*, 145
Canadian "value issues," 134
Carleton, Sir Guy, 23
Carnegie Institute of Technology, 127
Carpenter, W.G., 33
Cartier, Jacques, 20, 40, 115
Casey, Ivan, 87, 95, 98
Catholic Church
   criticism of progressive education, 97
   overpopulation and, 143
Catholic Education Association, 97
Catholic school board, 98
Cavell, Edith, 40, 50
Chafe, J.W., 115–17
*Challenge and Survival*, 145–47
Chalmers, John, 63, 110
Champlain, Samuel de, 20
Chaput, Marcel, 145
character education, 51, 57, 86
   good character, 13, 25–28, 51, 81, 151–52
"Charge of the Light Brigade" (Tennyson), 46
child-centred education, 8, 34, 60, 65–66. *See also* progressive education

Chinese, 82. *See also* People's Republic of China
Chinese civilization, 18
Christian-Smith, Linda K., 4–5
Christianity, 16, 120
   Christian ethos in curriculum, 119
   Christian service concept, 50
Citizens' Committee on Education, Calgary, 96
citizenship, 5, 28, 39, 42, 86, 109
   depoliticizing, 51
   ideology of Anglo-conformity, etc., 41
   as matter of personality and character, 51, 57
   responsibilities of, 119
   self-actualization, 153
   service ideal of, 27–28, 41, 50
   sportsmanlike behaviour, 48, 50
citizenship education, 29, 34–35, 37, 45, 50
   accomplishments of great men in history, 40
   cooperation, 45, 47
   criticisms of, 36, 52
   developing consumer competence, 106
   displaying democratic attitudes, 106
   Enterprise curriculum, 107
   importance of history in, 11
   marginalization of women, 150
   preventing the spread of political radicalism, 51
   protection of children from Communism, 118
   in social studies, 107
   virtues, 35
citizenship textbooks, 44, 51
civics, 22–23, 38, 78, 109, 119
Clark, Maisie, 14
Clarke, Stanley, 73–74
Clement, W.H.P., 18–19, 23
Cold War, 101, 115, 152
Commager, Henry Steele, 129
Commission on Educational Planning. *See* Worth Commission
Committee for the Study of Canadian History Textbooks, 77
"Committee of Five," 131
Committee on Tolerance and Understanding, 150
Commonwealth, 115, 147
Communism
   Cold War rhetoric, 101–2
   textbooks on, 117–18

composite high schools, 92, 125
conformity, 113, 121
Connor, Ralph, 41
consumer education, 86–87, 114
*Contemporary Problems* (Bagnall), 85
"Continuous Progress Plan," 121
cooperation, 44–45, 116–17, 152
    Canada's close relationship with U.S., 116
    between French and English, 47, 115
    global, 44, 117
    North Atlantic alliance, 116
    with peers, 86
    social studies curriculum, 114–15, 117
Cooperative Commonwealth Federation, 55
Cornell, Paul, 145–46
"Country Mouse," 15
Counts, George, 63, 78
Coutts, Herbert T. "Pete," 49
Cox, C. Benjamin, 129
crime and delinquency, 129
"Crisis in Education, The" (Katz), 93
critical thinking, 86, 110, 119, 135–36, 149
Cuban, Larry, 38
Cubberly, E.P., 33
curriculum, 9–11, 22, 29, 52, 148. *See also* citizenship; history; social studies
    British content, 40
    calls for Canadian perspective in, 40, 77
    character (*See* character education)
    Christian ethos, 70 (*See also* religion in schools)
    creators of (*See* curriculum building; curriculum committees; curriculum revision)
    enriched program for gifted students, 95–96
    Enterprise, 80, 94, 107
    gender roles and, 125
    harmony and order, 15, 17
    important element of public thought, 151
    inquiry-based, process-oriented, 127, 130
    link to cultural heritage, 9
    neoprogressive, 126, 131–32, 134–35, 153
    to nurture national unity, 77
    reflection of dominant values of privileged groups, 5
    for social activism, 78, 85
    theme of utility, 120
    useful curriculum, 100–102, 113–14
curriculum building, 5, 59, 69–70, 103, 105, 135, 151, 154. *See also* educationalists
    as "scientific" task, 29, 104

    teachers involvement, 102, 104
curriculum committees, 10, 14, 32, 50, 63, 68, 70, 84, 131, 161
    General Curriculum Committee, 102–5
curriculum implementation, 5
curriculum overview, 155–62
curriculum revision, 32, 34, 39, 43, 50, 52, 56–57, 63, 68, 70, 101, 105, 109, 131
    made-in-Alberta course of study, 10
    modified physical training program, 48
    "New Education," 33
    progressive education, 56, 65, 152
    revision (1971), 149
    revision (1981), 149
Curriculum Revision Committee (1912), 14
Currie, Arthur, 42

**D**

Davis, Bob, 1
declining academic and moral standards, 98–99
democracy, 18, 71, 86, 106, 153
    democratic classrooms, 60, 67
    education for, 85, 95, 118
    as "good" of public education, 84
    need for active nurture, 119, 152
    as "state of mind," 118
    uncritical promotion of, 85
Department of Education, 7, 33, 35, 39, 89, 94
    on aims of education, 106
    *Annual Report* (1942), 85
    Conference (June 1967), 130–31
    Curriculum Branch, 98, 102, 106, 110 (*See also* curriculum committees)
    "Ethical Content of Alberta School Programme, The," 86
    Examination Branch, 102
    General Curriculum Committee, 102–5
    prominent role in setting curriculum, 9, 56–57, 59, 103–5
    Social Studies Committees, 131
    summer sessions on progressive education, 71
    survey of public opinion (1921), 32
    "These Make History" program, 72
Department of Education Manual, 38
departmental examinations, 9–10, 22
Dewey, John, 57, 78
Dickie, Donalda, 39, 63, 65–66, 68, 71, 88
    *Great Adventure, The*, 64
Diefenbaker, John, 146
"discovery learning," 127, 131

domestic science, 8–9, 34–35
Dominion Education Association, 4
Dominion Institute, 1–2
Donald, Melvin, 58
Doucette, A.L., 80, 88, 105
Douglas, C.H., 55–56
drug education, 121, 131
Duncan, D.M., 20, 23
  *Story of the Canadian People*, 17–19

**E**

Eastman, Mack, 39
Edmonton, 9, 94
  growth, 91, 123
*Edmonton Bulletin*, 7, 63
Edmonton Chamber of Commerce
  on Americanization of textbooks in Alberta schools, 43–44
Edmonton Normal School, 61, 71
Edmonton Public School Board, 21, 86, 118
  Bylaws and Rules of Order, 25
  "Continous Progress Plan," 121
  religious instruction, 120
  social studies-enterprise units, 107
  standardized tests, 107
education
  for democracy, 84–85, 95, 118
  experimentation and flexibility (late 1960s), 121
  for "good character" (*See* character education)
  graduate training in, 32–33, 60
  per capita spending, 92
  as personal growth, 57
  public education debate, 7–8, 92, 94
  relation to business success, 30
  social aims of, 152
"education for disciplined intelligence," 151
Education Society of Edmonton, 33, 62–63, 70
*Education Through Play* (Curtis), 48
Educational Committee of the United Farmers of Alberta, 30, 52
educational "experts," 11, 32, 59. *See also* educationalists
  commitment to progressive aims, 105
Educational Progress Club in Calgary, 33
educationalists, 29, 33–34, 39, 65, 85, 87, 94. *See also* educational "experts"
  curriculum building, 59
  defense of progressive education, 98–99
  "Education for democracy," 85
  influenced by American progressives, 64
  introduction of social studies, 53
  on relationship between schools and society, 99–100
  separation from teaching force, 36
Elizabeth I, Queen, 24
Elliott, David, 57
Elliott, Jennie, 98
Empire Day, 21, 42
English-Canadian identity, 28
*English History* (Symes), 16
English Moral Instruction League, 34
Enterprise, 60, 64, 68, 71, 81, 90, 132
  democracy through cooperative learning, 118
  purpose of, 73
  scientific method in action, 80
Enterprise curriculum, 80
  citizenship education, 107
  creativity and initiative, 86
  parental concern about, 94
Ericsson, Leif, 20
"Ethical Content of Alberta School Programme, The," 86
Ethical Culture movement, 34
ethnocentrism, 41, 140, 150. *See also* racial hierarchy
  *Alexandra Readers*, 24
  history textbooks, 4, 16
Evolution, 58
Ewing, John M., 93
extra-curricular activities, 32

**F**

"Facing the Problems of Curriculum Organization," 104
family, 35, 45, 129
  external social forces and, 99
Family Compact, 23
Family Life courses, 121
Fathers of Confederation, 21
Feder, Bernard, 138
  *Can the Earth Support its Growing Population?*, 143
feminist scholars, 124, 150
Fenton, Edwin, 127, 131
  curriculum materials for inquiry-based teaching, 127
  experimental teaching units, 128
  *New Social Studies, The*, 127
Fisher, Olive, 68
France, 2, 24
Frederick the Great, 15, 20
free enterprise, 91, 123

free market of ideas, 119
freedom, 18, 23, 46
    new freedom for girls, 31
    student freedom, 67
French Canadians, 146. *See also* Quebec
    textbooks, 4, 77
    treatment in English language textbooks, 18–19, 46–47, 81–82, 115
Froebel, A., 113
Froebel, Friedrich, 33
Frye, Northrop, 127
fur-trading era, 36

## G

Gable, V., 118
*Gage World Community* series, 137
Galton, Francis, 33
*Garden of Childhood, The*, 50
Garrison, D., 14
gender roles
    boy-girl relationships, 87
    curricular paths and, 125
General Curriculum Committee, 102–5
*General History* (Myers), 11, 18, 43
geography, 135, 149
    inquiry approach, 128
    in social studies courses, 69, 109
George I, King, 25
George II, King, 24
German schools, 96
Germans, 82
Germany, 2, 83, 142
Gestalt school of psychology, 66
Ghitter, Ron, 150
Gilbert, Humphrey, 24, 40
Giles, Mabel, 59
Ginger Group, 55
*Ginn Studies in Canadian History*, 137
Goggin, D.G., 61
"Golden Window, The," 15
Goldsmith, Oliver, 21
    "Moses Goes to the Fair," 16
good character, 13, 25–28, 151–52
    hallmark of good citizenship, 51
    new understanding of, 87
good citizenship. *See* citizenship
Gordon, Walter, 146
Gorman, G.W., 41
government intervention in economy, 78–79
government intervention in social affairs, 129
grade system, 9, 67–68
Granatstein, Jack, 1, 3

Grant, W.L., 39
    *History of Canada*, 38, 40
    treatment of aboriginal groups and French, 46–47
Gray, Lillian, 72
*Great Adventure, The* (Dickie), 64
Great Britain. *See* Britain; British Empire
Great Depression, 29, 55–56
great men and women of history, 26, 39, 141
    accomplishments of, 40
    examples of virtues, 24, 51
Great War. *See* World War I
Grimms' fairytales, 26
Grosvenor, Ian, 4
group living, 36
    skills necessary for, 35, 46, 67
Guidance, 86–87
"Guide for Evaluating Growth in Citizenship," 86

## H

Hall, Douglas John, 151
Hall, G. Stanley, 34
Hall, Richard, 95, 100
Hall-Dennis Report, 125
Hamelin, Jean, 145
Hanna, Lavone, 107
Hardy, W.G., 93–96, 114
harmony and order, 15, 17, 44–45, 152
Hay, W.E., 50
Hay, William, 68
health, and physical training. *See* physical education
Health and Personal Development (course), 87
Henry, Alexander, 20
Herbart, Johann, 33
heroes in Canadian history, 20. *See also* great men and women
Hertzman, Lewis, 109
high school curricula. *See also* secondary education
    British content, 22
    compulsory subjects, 10
    university preparation as dominant, 52
    vocational preparation, 52
high school entrance examinations, 9
*High School History of England and Canada*, 17
*Highroads of History*, 23, 25
*Highroads to Reading*, 87
Historica, 2

historical "facts"
  problematic nature of, 69–70, 129
historical figures. *See* great men and women of history
historical thinking, 150
  objectivity in, 69, 79
  skills of, 138
history, 13, 88
  in 1981 program, 149
  biographical approach to, 142, 144
  Canadian, 23, 42, 115, 122, 133, 144
  elementary school, 35–36
  examinations, 12, 18, 22, 25
  inquiry approach, 128, 137–38, 140–41
  new philosophy of, 69, 71
  required to be useful, 52, 71, 89, 119
  in social studies courses, 69–71, 109, 114, 128–29, 133, 154
history curriculum, 10, 16–17, 35, 46, 52
  British and Canadian history, 23, 35–36
  British emphasis, 22, 43
  French regime in, 46
"History Laboratory," 138
*History of Canada* (Grant), 38, 40
*History of England and Canada* (Mowat), 37
history teaching, 1, 5, 11–13, 36–39
  criticisms of, 3, 52
  Hodgett's national survey, 4, 148
  national standards of, 2
  replacement with social studies, 53
history textbooks, 23, 47, 137. *See also* textbooks
  different versions (English and French), 4, 77
  ethnocentrism, 4, 16
  growth of Canadian art and literature, 42
  harmony and order, 16–17
  heroes of progress, 20–21
  for inquiry-based investigation, 137–38, 140–41
  neglect of ordinary people, 142
history *vs.* social sciences in social studies, 129
Hitler, Adolf, 142
Hodgetts, A.B., 112
  national survey of history teaching (1968), 4, 148
  *What Culture? What Heritage*, 148
Home and School Associations, 31, 51, 57, 98, 101–3. *See also* parent-teacher organizations
home economics, 30, 69

Horner, Rachel, 32
Horowitz, Gad, 146
Horton, Betty, 94
Hosie, Inez, 15
*How Canada is Governed* (Bourinot), 11
"How Parents Fail," 31
Hrabi, J.S.T., 130
Hudson Bay Company, 23
*Hungry Planet* (Borgstrom), 143

**I**
identity
  Albertan, 4, 6
  Canadian, 3–4, 6, 22, 29, 39, 41, 153
  English-Canadian, 28
  as global problem-solvers, 133
  national, 2–5
*Imperial Oil Review*, 113
*In Flanders Fields* (McCrae), 42
Indians. *See* Aboriginal people
individualism, 153
industrial education, 9. *See also* technical education
inquiry-based, process-oriented curriculum, 130
inquiry-based programs, 127–28, 140. *See also* "discovery learning"
  American models of, 127
inquiry-based teaching, 134, 136
  curriculum materials for, 127
*Inquiry in Social Studies* (Massialas), 129
Institute of Applied Arts, 37
International Bank for Reconstruction and Development, 143
internationalism, 46, 133
I.O.D.E., 31, 42, 103
I.Q. measurement, 31, 34, 65
Irvine, William, 55

**J**
J. M. Dent, 42
James Fowler (vocational high school), 125
Japanese internment, 115
Johnson, Pauline, 41
Jonason, J.C., 110
"Junior-Academic Vocational Program," 125
Junior Civic League, 36
Junior Red Cross, 36

**K**
Katz, Sidney, "Crisis in Education, The," 93
Kenny, Fred, 98

210 INDEX

Kilpatrick, William H., 33
Kirby, W. (Cam), 94, 100–101
Kliebard, Herbert, 63
*Knights Errant of the Wilderness* (Long), 42

**L**

L. W. Downey Research Associates, 149
"Land Where There Are No Punishments, The," 51
Latin, 30, 95
Laurier, Wilfrid, 115
lay groups (on curriculum committees), 103–5
LaZerte, M.E., 33, 99
League of Nations, 47
League of Nations Society, 46
learning process, 66–67
   direct experiential learning, 71
   "discovery learning," 127
   learning as total experience, 66
   "learning by doing," 60
   mental discipline theory of, 35 (See also memorization and memory training)
   motivation as key factor in, 71
   "open learning," 124
   program on independent and cooperative learning, 71
Leavitt, Lee, 95, 112
Ledgerwood, C.D., 133
Ledgerwood, Doug, 142
Leduc oil strike, 91
leisure time, 31
Lenin, Vladimir, 141
Lethbridge, 9
*Lethbridge Daily Herald*, 8
*Lethbridge Herald*, 93, 96
*Lethbridge News*, 8
liberal arts education, 95
Life Raft (self-awareness exercise), 147
local issues, 109
   importance in progressive education, 76–77
Lord's Prayer, 120
Lougheed, Peter, 6, 124
Low, Solon, 88
Lower, Arthur, 93, 115–17
Lytton, Hugh, 148

**M**

Macdonald, Hugh, 94
Macdonald, John A., 21, 23, 115
Mackenzie, Alexander, 20, 23
Mackenzie, William Lyon, 17
*Maclean's*, 93
   on American texts in Canadian school system, 43
   "women's" section, 31
MacQueen, Angus, 96
*Making of Today's World* (Hughes), 83
*Man and His World* series, 136
Manning, Ernest, 91–92, 119, 123
manual training, 8–9, 30, 33–35
Marsh, Edith, 19, 24
   *Where the Buffalo Roamed*, 23
Massey, Donald, 148
Massialas, Byron G., 130–31
   *Inquiry in Social Studies*, 129
materialism, 56, 97, 153
mathematics, 101
   American models, 127
McAuliffe, W.R., 83
McCaig, James, 14, 27, 51
McCalla, A.G., 103
McCrae, John, *In Flanders Fields*, 42
McDougall, W.D., 71–72, 74–75, 77, 81–84, 115
   social studies program, 70
   sympathetic treatment of Germany, 83
   *World of To-day*, 83
McGee, Thomas D'Arcy, 20
McInnis, Edgar, 118
McIntyre, W.A., 48
McKenzie, Charles H., 15, 32
McKenzie, M.I., 12
McKinney, Louise, 27
McLeod, Alan, 42, 46
McNally, G. Fred, 10, 46, 58, 63, 77
   on Aberhart's "Theory of Evolution," 59
   graduate training in education, 32–33
memorization and memory training, 12–13, 35–36, 69, 110
*Men Without Machines*, 140
minority groups. See Aboriginal people; ethnocentrism; French Canadians
*Modern Progress* (West), 43
Montgomery, L.M., 41
Moore, Evelyn, 132
   *Teaching the Subjects in the Social Studies*, 128
moral educationalists, 34–35
moral relativism. See relativism
moral standards, 98–99
"Moses Goes to the Fair" (Goldsmith), 16
motivation as centre of learning process, 66
Mounted Police, heroic men of, 40

"Mouse's Troubles, The," 16
movies, radio, comics. *See* social forces (external)
Mowat, R.B., 11, 39
   *History of England and Canada*, 37
multi-media teaching resources, 149
Myers, Philip, 18–19
   *General History*, 11, 18, 43

# N

narrative history, 140
National Conference on Character Education, 27, 41
National Council of the Social Studies, 131
National History Project in Alberta Classrooms, 112
national identity, 2–3, 5
   as contingent and relational, 4
National Policy, 79
national unity, 77, 134
native groups. *See* Aboriginal people
NATO, 147
naturalists, 33
nature study, 8–9
Neatby, Hilda, *So Little for the Mind*, 93, 96
neoprogressive curriculum, 126, 131–32, 153
   resources for, 134–35
New Brunswick, 60
"New Education," 8, 33–34, 39
   moral educationalists, 35
New France, 19, 47. *See also* French Canadians; Quebec
"New Social Studies," 126–27
   American leaders in, 129
   discovery-oriented, 131
   textbooks, 131
*New Social Studies, The* (Fenton), 127
Newbolt, Henry, "Torch of Life, The," 49
Newland, H.C., 60–63, 70, 84–85, 88–89, 93
   curriculum reform, 63
   resignation, 102
Nightingale, Florence, 50
Noble and Noble, 136
Normal Schools, 29, 33
   adolescent psychology, 34
   Calgary, 63–64, 84
   Camrose, 33–34, 37
   Edmonton, 61, 71
   Regina Normal School, 61, 63
   teaching methods, 39
   textbooks, 13, 25, 48
North-West Mounted Police, 145

nuclear arms race, 129, 147

# O

occupational preparation. *See under* vocational education
oil industry, 29, 91
*On Christian Education of Youth* (encyclical letter), 97
*One World*, 134
Ontario, 9
   activity approach (based on Alberta program), 60
   Hall-Dennis Report, 125
"open learning," 124
"open-mindedness," 86
optimism, 79–80, 152
Osborne, Brian, 3
Osborne, Ken, 4, 51, 57
Ouellet, Fernand, 145
*Our Empire and its Neighbours*, 75
*Our Western Heritage*, 140
*Outlines of the World's History* (Swinton), 17
overpopulation. *See under* world problems
Owen, Edward E., 128

# P

Page, Percy, 94
"Page and King, The," 26
pan-Canadian curriculum, 77
Panabaker, H.E, 99
parent-teacher organizations, 31–32. *See also* Home and School Associations
Paris Peace Conference, 42
Paterson, Gilbert, 75, 77–78, 81–84
Patrick, Russell, 95
patriotism, 10, 41, 43
Patterson, R.S., 59–60
Payne, John Howard, 15
Pearson, Lester B., 146
*People and Places in Canada, The*, 135
People's Republic of China
   superiority of technical education, 101
"Person-Centred Society," 126
personal development, 87, 105–6
personality growth, 65
pessimism, 117
Pestalozzi, Johann, 33
physical education, 33, 35, 68
   organized games and supervised play, 48–49
Pius XI, Pope, *On Christian Education of Youth* (encyclical letter), 97

Poaps, W.B., 50
political action, 86
"Political and Economic Systems" (course), 133
*Political and Economic Systems* (Powrie), 142
political radicalism, 41, 51
  American settlers, 40
Powrie, T.L., *Political and Economic Systems*, 142
practical ducation, 8, 33. *See also* technical education; vocational education
  parental demands for, 35
practical ethics, 34
printed materials. *See also* textbooks
  effect on vitality of teaching, 37
problem-solving, 69–71, 80, 90, 132–33, 137, 142–47
*Problems and Values* (Berry), 130
process, 132
  as basic ingredient of social studies curriculum, 129
*Process of Education, The* (Bruner), 127
professionalism, 33, 36, 56, 152
progress, 7–8, 17–19, 39–40, 152
  under British rule, 17, 36
  heroes of, 20
  scientific and technological, 80–82
  Whiggish belief in, 13
Progressive Conservative government, 6, 124
progressive education, 5–6, 59–76, 80, 88. *See also* Enterprise
  abandonment of courses in history and civics, 69
  Aberhart's understanding of, 57
  American roots, 56–57, 60
  as central to democracy, 67
  criticism, 72, 93, 95–98, 101, 118
  Dickie, Donalda, 63–66, 68
  difficulties of translating into classroom practice, 72–74, 93
  emphasis on fun in the classroom, 96
  emphasis on materialism, 56
  evaluating students' progress, 73
  Fisher, Olive, 68
  grade system, 67–68
  Hay, William, 68
  local issues, 76–77
  moral relativism, 56, 96
  new technology for, 72
  Newland, H.C., 61–63
  rejection of historical understanding, 88–89
  rejection of tradition in pedagogy, 88
  on role of schools, 67
  Social Credit support for, 94–95
  teacher training for, 71–72
Progressive Education Association, 73
*Progressive Education* (journal), 72
Project Canada West, 148
psychohistory, 141
psychology, 65–66, 86
public education debate, 7–8, 92
  Alberta's politicians, 94
public health initiatives, 34
*Public School Methods* (Normal school text), 25
public service. *See* service ideal of citizenship

Q

Quance Lectures, 104
Quebec, 60, 125
  nationalism, 145, 147
Quebec Act, 19, 82
"Quest, The," 15
Quillen, James, 107
Quinn, James, 79

R

racial conflict, 129
racial hierarchy, 25. *See also* Aboriginal people; French Canadians
  persistence of, 82
  in textbooks, 18
radicalism. *See* political radicalism
Radio Sunday School, 58
Rand, Stanley, 84
readers
  *Alexandra Readers*, 15–16, 20–22, 24, 26, 28
  Canadian content, 41
  *Canadian Geography Readers*, 42
  Canadian history readers, 42
  *Canadian Readers*, 40, 46, 50
  *Canadian Series of Jackdaws*, 137
  *Highroads to Reading*, 87
Reed, Edna, 72
Regina Normal School, 61, 63
relativism, 56, 85, 147
religion in schools, 26–27, 34, 50, 59, 96, 120
  Catholic Church, 97–98
  Christian ethos in curriculum, 119
  secularization, 58, 125
Repke, Arthur, 79
"Responsibility of Parents in the Moral Education of the Teen Age Boy and Girl, The," 32
responsible government, 47, 82, 115

Rhodes, Cecil, 115
Ricker, Belle, 71, 141–42, 144
"Riders of the Plains, The," 40
Riel, Louis, 17, 46–47
Rio Pact nations, 118
Robertson, J.W., 8
Robinson, James Harvey, 69
Roman Catholic Church. See Catholic Church
Ross, John T., 8, 12
Royal Commission on Bilingualism and Biculturalism, 4
Royal Commission on Education. See Cameron Commission
Royal Commission on Industrial Training And Technical Education, 8
Rugg, Harold, 66, 70–71
"Rule Britannia" (Tennyson), 46
rural school district consolidation, 56
rural students, 29–30, 35, 92
Russia, 2, 83
Rutherford, A.C., 7
Ryerson Press, 42

S

Sanson, Clarence, 85
*Saturday Night*, 93
school gardening, 8, 34
school inspectors, 7, 10, 12, 15, 38, 40–41
  call for supervised, healthy play, 48
  criticism of ready-made enterprise units, 74
  on progressive education, 72–73, 93
  on "Teacher Helps," 37
School Ordinance (1901), 7
school taxes, 7, 125
schools. *See also* education
  purpose of, 57, 60, 100–101, 113
  as reflection of public opinion, 99
  responsibilities from family, church, community, 99
science, 79, 152
  American models, 127
  eugenics, 81
  infallibility myth, 118
  "scientific" approach, 29, 31, 34, 39, 83
  "scientific attitude," 80, 86
  scientific educationalists, 33
  scientific farmers, 30
  "scientific" skills, 35
scientific and technological progress, 80–82
Scott, A.M., 33
Scott, Duncan Campbell, 41
Scott, Frederick George, 81

*Canada Today*, 78
  support for government intervention, 79
Scott, Thomas, 17
Seary, V.P., 78, 81
second language education, 114
"Second-Phase Industrial Society," 125
secondary education, 9, 68
  departmental examinations (provincial), 10
  expansion, 29–30
  progressive education, 68
  rural students, 29–30, 92
Secord, Laura, 20
secularization of schools, 58, 125
*Seigneury of Longueuil, The* (painting), 137
self-fulfillment, 153
Selleck, R.J.W., 33–34
"Sentinel's Pouch, The," 15
service ideal of citizenship, 27–28, 41
sex adjustment, 86
Shaughnessy (junior high school), 124
shop courses, 69
*Short History of Early Peoples, A*, 38
Simon, Frank, 129
Sims, A.L., 95
situation ethics, 87
Smith, Anthony D., 3
Smith, H.E., 88, 99
Smith, J.A., 31
*So Little for the Mind* (Neatby), 93, 96
"social activism"
  new curriculum for, 78, 85
social and industrial history, 35
social change, 31, 76, 152
Social Credit government, 5–6, 56–57, 92
  appointment of Worth Commission, 125
  defense of progressive education, 94–95
  on religious instruction, 120
Social Credit League, 92
Social Credit Party
  anti-United Nations statements, 117
  rural representation and attitudes, 123
  transformation from radical movement to free enterprise, 91, 123
social forces (external)
  problems in schools, 98–99
social gospel, 50
social harmony. *See* harmony and order
social improvement, 28, 34
social justice, 33, 63, 76, 152
social reconstruction, 57
social responsibility, 86
social sciences, 79, 129–30

thinking patterns of, 128
social stability, 41, 45
social studies, 53, 60, 68, 70, 77, 83, 90, 111, 130
  American content, 116
  Anglocentric emphasis, 115
  Canadian content, 70, 133, 149
  celebratory attitude toward technological innovation, 80
  citizenship education, 107
  coverage of conflicts and problems, 143
  criticisms, 94–98, 147–50
  "expanding horizons" approach, 132
  factual knowledge in, 110
  hallmark of progressive education, 69
  possibility of human triumph, 88
  purpose of, 73
  and teaching history, 69–71, 109, 114, 128–29, 133, 140–42, 149–50, 154
social studies curriculum, 70–71, 80, 107–10, 114–21, 129, 131–33, 149–50
  "appreciation for the beautiful and the good," 119
  cooperation, 114–15, 117
  coverage of conflicts and problems, 143
  creators of, 69–70
  local government in, 109
  "usefulness" of knowledge, 114
  world security issues, 117
social studies teaching
  criticisms, 94–98, 147–50
social studies textbooks, 73–75, 110–12, 114–18, 134–47, 150
  Alberta's regional grievances, 76–77
  return to national focus (World War II), 77
social utility. *See* "utility"
solving global problems. *See* problem-solving
sovereignty, 134
Soviet Union, 146
  superiority of technical education, 101
Spicer, Keith, 1, 3
Spicer Task Force on National Unity, 1
Sputnik I, 101
Stamp, Robert, 87
Standards system, 9
Stanford University, 60
Stanley, George, 12, 15, 21
Stanley, T.E.A., 48
Starr, E.H., 83–84
*Story of Canada, The*, 115
*Story of Civilization, The*, 78
*Story of the Canadian People* (Duncan), 17
"story telling" lessons in civics and history, 38

Strayer, G.D., 33
streaming students by I.Q. scores, 34
structure of knowledge or discipline, 127–28
structure (or thinking patterns) of the social sciences, 128
student councils, 118
student dropout, 124
student enrolment, 7, 29–30
student freedom, 67
subject disciplines
  skills associated with, 149
suffrage, 31
supranationalism, 47
Sutherland, Neil, 41, 137
Swift, William H, 24, 63, 93, 99, 102, 105

**T**
Taba, Hilda, 71
Talon, Jean, 19, 137
Tanner, Harold, 104
teachers, 5, 11, 37, 48, 107–8, 110
  authority to express opinion, 139, 147
  Christian service concept of citizenship, 50
  complaints about textbooks, 38
  curriculum building, 102, 104
  disagreement with values approach, 149
  extra-curricular activities, 32
  importance of order and discipline, 13–16, 89
  importance of physical games and sports, 49
  overemphasis on factual knowledge, 110
  poor academic skills, 93
  professional status, 56
  salaries and working conditions, 33, 92
  shortage, 92
  support for pro-British view, 42
  time constraints, 112
  traditional in values, 149
  training for 1981 program, 149
  under-educated and over-burdened, 12
  understanding of progressive education, 71–73
  use of community resources, 111
  use of new technology, 72
  Worth Report on, 148
Teachers' College Columbia, 60, 72
teacher's guides, 135–37
  "Teacher Helps," 36–37, 72
teaching methods, 12–13, 71, 134
  classroom discussions, 111
  "doing of history," 128
  individualized, 60

inductive teaching strategies, 60, 135
inquiry-based, 127–28, 134, 136
lecturing, 111–12
Normal Schools, 39
progressive education, 88
science of psychology, 66
stories containing strong moral messages, 25
text-driven teaching, 29, 37–38, 74–75, 134, 141
transitional approach, 136
unit method, 110
teaching methods (social studies)
research studies of, 111–12
*Teaching the Subjects in the Social Studies* (Moore), 128
Technical and Vocational Training Assistance Act, 125
technical education, 8–9, 100–101, 114. *See also* practical education
superiority of Soviet Union, 101
technological progress
equating with moral or social superiority, 140
technology, benefits of, 81, 133, 145, 152
Tennyson, Alfred
"Charge of the Light Brigade," 46
"Rule Britannia," 46
Terman, Lewis, 65
Teskey, Hugh, 15
textbooks. *See also* readers
Aboriginal groups in, 4, 18-19, 23, 46, 82, 140, 144–45, 150
after World War II, 83
on American expansionism, 146
Americanization, 42–44, 46, 146
assessments of, 38
belief in progress, 40
British content, 21–23
on Canada's role, 116, 146–47
Canadian history, 23, 42, 115, 144
chauvinism in, 140
Christianity in, 120
citizenship, 39, 44, 51
Cold War era, 115
on Communism, 117–18
cooperation, 114–17
on current global issues, 142–44
Economics, 44
emphasis on order and self-discipline, 16
enormous shift from texts of previous generation, 139
faith in government planning, 78–79

as focus of instruction, 12, 29, 37–38, 74–75, 112, 134, 141
French Canadian versions, 4, 77
French Canadians in English language textbooks, 18-19, 46-47, 81-82, 115
harmony and order, 15
history, 4, 11, 20–21, 23–24, 42, 140
inadequate coverage of course content, 111
minority groups in, 150
New Social Studies, 131
Normal Schools, 48
pessimistic view of future, 117
progress, 40
progressive education period, 74–76, 112
racial hierarchy in, 18
religion in, 120
situation ethics, 87
view of science, 118
women in, 150
world peace, 117
"Theory of Evolution, The" (Aberhart), 58
"These Make History" program, 72
Thorndike, E.L., 33–34
"The Three Bears," 16
three Rs. *See* academic skills
*Through African Eyes*, 137
Tilley, J.J., 26
tolerance, 23, 47, 83, 150
"Tom Brown's Schooldays," 22
Tomkins, George, 8, 127
"top-down" history, 142
"Torch of Life, The" (Newbolt), 49
*Toronto Globe*, 27
Toronto School board, 127
Tory, Henry M., 10
traditional virtues. *See* virtues
Trafalgar Day, 21
Treaty of Versailles, 42
Trudeau, Pierre, 124
Trudel, Marcel, 145
Tyack, David, 38
Tyler, Ralph, 71
typewriting, 69, 94

U
Union Jack, 21, 24
"unit method" of teaching, 110
United Empire Loyalists, 16
United Farmers of Alberta, 30, 40
Educational Committee, 30, 52
United Farmers of Alberta government, 32, 42–44, 55, 57
United Nations, 117, 146–47

United States, 6, 101, 140. *See also* American
  anti-Communist foreign policy, 146
  criticism of progressive education, 60
  criticism of research spending, 143
  "history wars," 2
  technical schools, 8
  in textbooks, 16–17, 76, 109, 115–16, 143, 146, 153
University of Alberta, 22, 33, 61, 94, 103, 118, 128
  Department of Secondary Education, 129–30
  Faculty of Education, 102, 104–5
  influence on high school curricula, 10
  School of Education, 85
University of Calgary, 128
University of Chicago, 33, 60, 62
University of Toronto, 61, 127
University Women's Clubs, 96
Upper Canadian rebellion (1837), 17
urbanization, 91, 123, 131
useful curriculum, 114. *See also* vocational education
  employment and, 113
  protection against Communism, 102
  strengthening of math and science, 101
  technical education, 100–101
  theme of utility, 112
"usefulness" of knowledge, 114
  marketable skills, 153 (*See also* vocational education)
  teaching of history and, 154
"utility," 120
utopians, 126

## V

*Values and Teaching* (Raths, Harmin, and Simon), 131–32
values clarification, 6, 130–34. *See also* relativism
  criticisms, 147–49
  lack of Canadian content, 148
  resources for, 137
  teachers' disagreement with, 149
  Worth Report on, 126
Van Horne (junior high school), 124
*Viewpoints in World History*, 138
virtues, 25, 85
  associated with conformity and hard work, 121
  responsibility and reliability, 113
  skills and attitudes necessary for employment, 112

traditional, 50, 57, 86
vocational education, 8–9, 30, 35, 52, 68, 114, 153
  federal funding for, 125
  "Junior-Academic Vocational Program," 125
  occupational preparation, 105, 107
Voisey, Paul, 9, 11

## W

Wallace, W. Stewart, 39, 78
Warren, Robert, 113
Watkin, J.F, 72
Watts, Morrison, 98–99, 110, 113, 130
W.C.T.U., 31
western alienation, 124
Western Canada Institute, 74
*Western Catholic Reporter*, 97
*When Grandma and Grandpa Were Kids*, 138
*Where the Buffalo Roamed* (Marsh), 23
*Whig Interpretation of History, The* (Butterfield), 18
Whiggish belief in progress, 13, 17–18
Winnipeg General Strike, 44
  omission in Canadian history, 115
Wolfe, General James, 23–24
women, 31, 46
  treatment in textbooks and curricula, 4, 150
Women's Institutes, 30, 103
world history, 23
*World of To-day* (McDougall)
  criticism and revision, 83–84
"World of Today, The" (social studies course), 70
world problems, 117, 129, 133
  overpopulation, 133, 143, 147
World War I, 28, 46
  in history textbooks, 42, 140
  repercussions, 29
World War II, 67, 83, 152
  affirmation of government intervention in economy, 78–79
  public dissatisfaction with schools, 89
  return to national focus in social studies, 77
Worth Commission, 125, 133, 145, 148
  effect on school curriculum, 126

## Y

youth culture, 31

www.ingramcontent.com/pod-product-compliance
Lightning Source LLC
Chambersburg PA
CBHW052059300426
44117CB00013B/2204